OECD Business and Finance Outlook 2018

OECD
BETTER POLICIES FOR BETTER LIVES

Please cite this publication as:
OECD (2018), *OECD Business and Finance Outlook 2018*, OECD Publishing, Paris.
https://doi.org/10.1787/9789264298828-en

ISBN 978-92-64-29881-1 (print)
ISBN 978-92-64-29882-8 (PDF)

Series: OECD Business and Finance Outlook
ISSN 2617-2569 (print)
ISSN 2617-2577 (online)

Photo credits: Cover © iStockphoto.com/OttoKrause.

Corrigenda to OECD publications may be found on line at: *www.oecd.org/about/publishing/corrigenda.htm.*

Foreword

This is the fourth edition of the *OECD Business and Finance Outlook*, an annual publication that presents unique data and analysis on the trends, both positive and negative, that are shaping tomorrow's world of business, finance and investment. Using analysis from a wide range of perspectives, this year's edition addresses connectivity, both among institutions within the global financial system and among countries. Almost a decade on from the 2008 financial crisis, the *Outlook* examines new risks to financial stability that will put financial reforms to the test, focusing in particular on the normalisation of monetary policy, debt problems and off-balance sheet activity in China. With respect to connectivity among countries, the *Outlook* examines the new phase of globalisation centred on Asia/Eurasia, using China's Belt and Road Initiative as a case study. It argues that this ambitious development plan has a number of economic issues to look out for, and that it would be best carried through with transparent "rules of the game" that will help ensure a level playing field for all.

The *OECD Business and Finance Outlook 2018* is the joint work of staff of the OECD Directorate for Financial and Enterprise Affairs. It has benefited from comments by delegates of relevant committees and other parts of the OECD Secretariat.

Table of contents

Tables

Figures

Boxes

Acronyms and abbreviations

ABOC	Agricultural Bank of China
ABS	asset-backed security
ACWI	All Country World Index
ADB	Asian Development Bank
ADBC	Agricultural Development Bank of China
AEI	American Enterprise Institute
AIIB	Asia Infrastructure Investment Bank
APs	authorised participants
ASEAN	Association of Southeast Asian Nations
BA	Bangkok Agreement
BOC	Bank of China
BRI	Belt and Road Initiative
BRIICS	Brazil, Russia, India, Indonesia, China, and South Africa
BWEI	Bloomberg World Equity Index
CBRC	China Banking Regulatory Commission
CCB	China Construction Bank
CCP	centralised clearing counter-party
CCR	capital conservation buffer
CDB	China Development Bank
CDS	credit default swap
CET	common equity tier
CFTC	US Commodity Futures Trading Commission
CIRC	China Insurance Regulatory Commission
CO_2	carbon dioxide
CNOOC	China National Offshore Oil Corporation
CNPC	China National Petroleum Corporation
COK	cost of capital
CPC	Communist Party of China
CSRC	China Securities and Regulatory Commission
CTG	China Three Gorges Corporation
DRC	Development Research Centre
DTD	distance-to-default

ECB	European Central Bank
ECO	Economic Co-operation Organisation
ECSI	European Convention on State Immunity
ECT	energy charter treaty
EECA	Eastern Europe and Central Asia
EIA	environmental impact assessments
EMIR	European Market Infrastructure Regulation
ETF	exchange traded fund
EU	European Union
ExIm	China Import-Export Bank
FDI	foreign direct investment
FED	United States Federal Reserve
FSIA	US Foreign Sovereign Immunities Act
FSB	Financial Stability Board
FTSE	Financial Times Stock Exchange
G-SIBs	globally systemic important banks
G20	Group of 20 (Argentina, Australia, Brazil, Canada, China, France, Germany, India, Indonesia, Italy, Japan, Mexico, Russia, Saudi Arabia, South Africa, Korea, Turkey, the United Kingdom, United States and the European Union)
GDP	gross domestic product
GICS	Global Industry Classification Standard
GPS	Global Positioning System
G-SIB	globally systemically important banks
HBIS	Hebei Iron and Steel Group
HLAR	higher loss absorbing requirement
IBES	Institutional Brokers' Estimate System
ICBC	Industrial and Commercial Bank of China
IFSWF	International Forum of Sovereign Wealth Funds
IMF	International Monetary Fund
IRB	internal ratings-based
IWG	International Working Group of Sovereign Wealth Funds
LR	leverage ratio
LSAP	large scale asset purchases
LTV	loan-to-value
MDB	multilateral development bank
MENA	Middle East and North Africa
MFA	Ministry of Foreign Affairs
MMIMO	Massive-Multiple-In-Multiple-Out
MMMF	money market mutual funds

MOFCOM	Ministry of Commerce (also MofCom)
MPA	macro-prudential assessment
NAFTA	North American Free Trade Agreement
NCP	National Contact Point (agencies established by adhering governments to promote and implement the OECD Guidelines for Multinational Enterprises)
NDRC	National Development and Reform Commission
NPL	non-performing loans
OECD	Organisation for Economic Co-operation and Development
OTC	over-the-counter
PBoC	Peoples Bank of China
PE	price-to-earnings and private equity
PP	private placement
PPP	public-private partnership
QE	quantitative easing
R&D	research and development
RBC	responsible business conduct
RFE	relative factor endowment variable
ROE	return on equity
RWA	risk-weighted asset
S&P 500	Standard & Poor's 500-stock index
SAARC	South Asian Association of Regional Co-operation
SDGs	Sustainable Development Goals
SEA	Strategic Environmental Assessment
SEC	Securities and Exchange Commission
SEZ	special economic zone
SIM	similarity index
SOE	state-owned enterprise
SWF	sovereign wealth fund
TALF	Term Asset-Backed Securities Loan Facility
TARP	Troubled Asset Relief Program
TBTF	too big to fail
TLAC	total loss absorbing capacity
TRNC	Turkish Republic of Northern Cyprus
UHV	ultra-high voltage
UNCTAD	United Nations Conference on Trade and Development
WGB	OECD Working Group on Bribery in International Business Transactions
WMP	wealth management products
WTO	World Trade Organization

ISO country and currency abbreviations

Country		Currency	
Australia	AUS	Australian dollar	ASD
Brazil	BRA	Brazilian real	BRL
China, People's Republic of	CHN	yuan renminbi	CNY
Chinese Taipei	TWN	Taiwan new dollar	TWD
Colombia	COL	Colombian peso	COP
Euro area	EMU	euro	EUR
India	IND	Indian rupee	INR
Indonesia	IDN	rupiah	IDR
Japan	JPN	yen	JPY
Korea	KOR	won	KRW
Russian Federation	RUS	Russian rubble	RUB
Singapore	SGP	Singapore dollar	SGD
South Africa	ZAF	rand	ZAR
United Kingdom	GBR	pound	GBP
United States	USA	dollar	USD

Editorial

The 2018 *OECD Business and Financial Outlook* comes at a time when citizens, communities and politicians are increasingly questioning the benefits of globalisation and the multilateral trading system.

Last year's *OECD Business and Finance Outlook* showed that these questions are rooted in legitimate concerns. It underlined the importance of turning the lessons of the 2008 financial crisis into sustainable reforms to the financial system, and showed how the lack of a level playing field for participants in the global economy contributes to unfair economic outcomes.

This edition builds on these themes with new analysis and practical recommendations to governments on 1) addressing the remaining vulnerabilities in the financial system and 2) how supply-side and demand-side policies can help ensure foreign infrastructure investment is high quality, sustainable and works for all, with particular reference to China's Belt and Road Initiative.

Gaps remain in global financial regulation

The global economy has been in repair mode since the 2008 financial crisis, with a series of international financial regulatory reforms. Almost a decade of unconventional monetary policy in advanced countries has brought low interest rates and plentiful liquidity – but these conditions are unlikely to last.

Gradual normalisation of monetary policy and growing levels of indebtedness, including in China, could put recent financial reforms to the test. This edition of the *OECD Business and Finance Outlook* takes stock of the remaining vulnerabilities in the financial system, especially the risks posed by levels of interconnectedness between those large banks whose business models remain largely unchanged since the 2008 financial crisis. Policy makers still need to consider whether reforms have suitably addressed the weaknesses exposed by the last crisis, and take appropriate action if they have not.

How to make infrastructure investment work for all

Last year's *Business and Finance Outlook* demonstrated the importance of a level playing field to ensure the benefits of trade and investment fall more evenly and fairly. It described how OECD standards can help set the 'rules of the game' for a level playing field, by promoting mutual market openness, fighting cross-border cartels, discouraging undue government support for internationally-active state owned enterprises (SOEs), preventing transnational bribery to win contracts, and avoiding competitive advantages based on compromised labour and environmental practices.

These are among the primary considerations as this edition turns to cross-border infrastructure investment, using China's Belt and Road Initiative as a case study. China's Belt and Road Initiative is an ambitious development plan based on infrastructure investment. It aims to increase connectivity between countries that together make up over one third of the global economy. It represents a significant contribution to meeting global and regional infrastructure needs. These needs, however, are too great to be met by any single country or investor.

There are two key issues from a supply side perspective. First, the Belt and Road Initiative will need to engage with other investing economies and institutions if it is to meet its stated aims, and if it is to maximise its contribution to filling the global infrastructure gap. All international infrastructure efforts should be mutually reinforcing, which requires transparent 'rules of the game' that will help ensure a level playing field for investment.

Second, investment projects must be viable, cost effective and appropriately selected, regardless of the source of funding. This is particularly important given that the Belt and Road Initiative's investments will be largely debt-funded, and often directed to jurisdictions with challenging business environments.

The OECD Code of Liberalisation of Capital Movements can help address both of these supply-side issues. The Codes are a long-standing instrument that builds openness to competition amongst international investors, and helps improve the policy environment in investment destinations, all while taking into account countries' differing levels of economic development.

But openness on its own is not enough. From the demand side, countries receiving investment need to focus on the project level to ensure infrastructure translates into sustainable economic growth and positive social outcomes. The *OECD Business and Finance Outlook* considers potential concerns that could accompany foreign infrastructure investment, including bribery and corruption in large scale projects, national security concerns arising from the proximity of infrastructure assets to foreign governments through SOEs, and due diligence practices in supply chains.

International organisations like the OECD play an important role in developing the 'rules of the game' that seek to avoid many of these potential pitfalls. International standards like the OECD Anti-Bribery Convention, OECD Guidelines for Fighting Bid Rigging in Public Procurement, the G20/OECD Principles of Corporate Governance and the OECD Guidelines for Multilateral Enterprises make up a toolkit for recipient countries to manage the risks and get the most out of foreign infrastructure investment. These instruments are detailed within the *OECD Business and Finance Outlook* and are available to OECD members and non-members alike.

This publication presents advice to policy makers on how to better position the financial system to serve the real economy, and how to ensure foreign infrastructure investment works for both investors and recipients. But the key to turning policy advice into positive outcomes is implementation. As always, the OECD stands ready to assist any country looking to implement these best practices, build capacity, and develop policies to make sure international trade and investment bring benefits for all.

Greg Medcraft
Director, OECD Directorate for Financial
and Enterprise Affairs

Executive summary

Connectivity, both among institutions within the global financial system and among countries, is an integral part of globalisation and a key component of how complex societies operate in their quest to become more productive. This year's *Outlook* addresses connectivity, both among institutions within the global financial system and among countries. With respect to the latter, the *Outlook* looks at the increasing weight of China in the global economy. It examines, in particular, the impact of the international development strategy known as the "Belt and Road Initiative" (BRI) on China's global trade and investment partners and the policy approaches that would help to broaden out its benefits to the whole global economy.

The outlook for the global financial system

Monetary authorities in jurisdictions that are home to globally systemic important banks (G-SIBs) have provided support for the global financial system in the form of ultra-low interest rates and large scale purchases of securities since 2008, initially to support dysfunctional markets and then to support economic recovery. As the economic backdrop has improved, the US Federal Reserve has begun to normalise its policies. Central banks in other advanced countries seem likely to follow. This has contributed to sharp movements in asset prices in 2018, particularly during the early months of the year. Managing this process will be a challenge.

As this process gets underway, the reform of the regulatory framework governing internationally-active banks, widely known as Basel III, has been finalised by the Basel Committee of Bank Supervisors. The reversal of monetary ease will test whether Basel III has achieved its goal of ensuring safety and soundness in the financial system in the face of stresses, particularly where the liquidity of products is a driver of volatility. Basel III achieved progress in the area of strengthening capital rules but leaves the G-SIBs and their business models similar to what they were before the crisis of 2008—certainly stopping short of full separation of investment banking from deposit-insured consumer banking. The vulnerabilities resulting from their interconnectedness remain an important feature of the system. One gauge of interdependence, the notional value of over-the-counter derivatives, remained at USD 532 trillion in the second half of 2017, only slightly below its pre-crisis peak of USD 586 trillion in late 2007. There has been some shifting of where these risks sit as investors have responded to the low-interest rate environment.

The financial outlook will also be shaped by China's ability to manage risks relating to high indebtedness and leverage in its banking, shadow banking and wealth management industries. While China is not directly linked to the risks in advanced economies, due to the closed nature of its financial system, any problems there could see Chinese authorities shedding holdings of US securities. This would increase liquidity pressures in advanced economies. The extent of non-performing loan problems in China is obscured by the lack of information about which assets are sitting in off-balance sheet vehicles. But it is clear that these vast off-balance sheet exposures have increased leverage risk and could lead to destabilising credit events. They have the potential to disrupt growth beyond China if further changes to the structure of financial markets and institutions are not considered in major advanced and emerging economies.

The BRI in the global trade, investment and finance landscape

China's BRI is an ambitious development strategy to build connectivity and co-operation across the six main economic corridors shown in Figure 2.3. The Asian Development Bank estimates that Asia needs USD 26 trillion in infrastructure investment to 2030, and China can certainly help to achieve some of this. The BRI, which prioritises the funding of infrastructure, is also a strategy to achieve a number of longer-term objectives: connectivity; energy and food security; balanced regional development and better capacity utilisation; freer trade; sustainability goals; and cultural and scientific exchanges.

China is investing in technology transfer to move toward higher value activities and, in the longer term, aims to follow what other major countries have done in technology standards, innovation and trading value chains. Connectivity is an important element of the strategy, particularly regarding energy, given the numerous and varied sources along the BRI corridors. More generally, empirical analysis in this *Outlook* suggests that connectivity among both advanced and emerging markets enhances the benefits of trade and investment. However, the infrastructure funding needs of developing Asia are large and China's own financial issues at home point to limits on what China alone can do. This means significant contributions from OECD countries will be needed if the BRI is to succeed. This will require an increasing role for markets in resource allocation decisions. Property rights, competition, level playing fields and sound governance will need to be strengthened to make this possible.

Towards levelling the playing field for sustainable growth

The BRI is a phase of globalisation that is long term in nature that, as with similar issues in the world economy, needs a transparent foundation of sound principles conducive to cost-effective solutions and fairness to all stakeholders.

Five broad areas that could benefit from greater alignment with international standards stand out:

- The growing role of state-owned enterprises (SOEs) in the global economy calls for ways to ensure a level playing field that discourage subsidies and non-transparent processes and allow recipient countries to benefit from investments based on widely accepted practices of corporate governance. Recipient economies must address national security concerns, especially those involving strategically sensitive technology and gaps in the legal accountability of SOEs.
- Open and transparent arrangements for procurement, especially for large infrastructure investments, are needed.
- The heavy costs that bribery and corruption can impose must be avoided, both in the case of large infrastructure projects and elsewhere. Social and environmental costs need to be taken into account by ensuring responsible business conduct that minimises disruption to local communities.

- Complementing what is expected of companies in respecting the environment, governments need to conduct environmental impact assessments prior to implementing proposed projects for facilities and infrastructure.
- Open and transparent regimes for cross-border investment are needed to reduce costs and increase options regarding technology. These will work to encourage the connectivity and economies of scale that the infrastructure strategies are intended to build.

In all five areas, OECD and other international standards provide essential guidance for both infrastructure-recipient economies and supplying economies.

Chapter 1. The financial system outlook

Three major risks are set to shape the financial outlook:

1. *Monetary policy normalisation: with the unwinding of ultra-low interest rates and the large-scale holdings of sovereign and private sector securities on central bank balance sheets, the transition may be volatile.*
2. *Financial sector vulnerabilities and the extent to which the recent finalisation of G20 reforms, including Basel III, has achieved the goal of a safe and sound financial system in the face of future stresses.*
3. *High indebtedness and leverage, especially related to China's bank, shadow bank and wealth management businesses, and how well the Chinese authorities will be able to manage related risk.*

All these risks have the potential to disrupt sustainable growth in the global economy. This chapter examines these three topics, concluding that financial system risk will be elevated in the period ahead.

The statistical data for Israel are supplied by and under the responsibility of the relevant Israeli authorities. The use of such data by the OECD is without prejudice to the status of the Golan Heights, East Jerusalem and Israeli settlements in the West Bank under the terms of international law.

1.1. Introduction

Since the global financial crisis of 2008, monetary policy has been focused on supporting both the financial system (in the early stages) and real economic activity in line with price stability objectives (in the later stages) with ultra-low interest rates and massive buying of debt securities by central banks, mainly in jurisdictions where global systemically important banks (G-SIBs) are located. Fawley and Neely (2013) states: "*Initially, the Fed, BOE, BOJ, and ECB policies focused on restoring function to dysfunctional financial markets, but concern soon shifted to stimulating real growth and preventing undesirable disinflation*".[1]

Over two years ago, the US Federal Reserve (Fed) decided to begin the reversal of its accommodative policy stance via interest rates, given that the economy is operating closer to its capacity, which is when inflation pressures are more likely to arise. More recently, it has announced the reversal of quantitative easing. Inflation pressure has not yet emerged in the euro area and Japan, though the *OECD Economic Outlook* foresees a moderate pick up in the euro area over the next two years. While there have been signs of more inflation pressure in the United Kingdom, it has not yet begun the reversal of quantitative easing, since this is likely due to past depreciation of sterling.

The timing and scaling of reversals can also be linked to the recovery of the safety and soundness of the institutions that were at the centre of the crisis, and to any changes in the structure of markets that may warrant higher longer-term holdings on central bank balance sheets as a share of GDP compared to that which prevailed prior to the crisis. Banks in the United States have already reached that point which, coinciding with the sound shape of the economy, has supported the case for the Fed to announce a schedule for the gradual unwinding of large holdings of central bank assets. This shift to normalisation has already led to extreme movements in asset prices in the early part of 2018. This may be a foretaste of things to come, underlining the delicate balancing act required of central banks.

The beginning of monetary policy tightening in the United States in the fourth quarter of 2015 preceded the finalisation of the Basel III rules at the beginning of December 2017. The period of monetary support for the banking system would have been a good opportunity to fundamentally change the business models and governance of banks (to not mix commercial banking and investment banking, recommended by the OECD since the crisis). This opportunity was used only partially: capital requirements were raised but G-SIBs' business models remained more or less the same as they were before the crisis. These banks have strongly defended their business models (limiting separation policies which lie outside the scope of the Basel process) but G20 reforms, including to over-the-counter (OTC) derivatives markets and liquidity requirements, offer mitigants to high degrees of interconnectedness.

The notional value of OTC derivatives, an indicator of the interdependence of G-SIBs,[2] stood at USD 532 trillion in the second half of 2017, compared to USD 586 trillion in the second half of 2007, just prior to the crisis. This has fallen as a share of the recovered global economy over that period (by roughly one third). Credit default swaps– the most significant derivative type for interconnectedness – has fallen as a share of the total OTC derivatives market from 10.5% at its 2007 peak to 1.8% at end of 2017. In terms of OTC derivative counterparties, reporting dealers make up 15%, other financial institutions 80%, and non-financial customers 5%.

Clearing and margin rule improvements under Dodd-Frank and European Market Infrastructure Regulation (EMIR) have helped to reduce systemic risk for broker dealers, either by netting through Central Counterparty (CCP) clearers, or through margin requirements for un-cleared derivatives. CCPs cleared 60% of OTC derivatives by the end of 2017.

CCPs represent larger 'nodes' of interconnectedness, but initial design and subsequent implementation of work to strengthen CCP recovery and resolvability have helped address concerns on whether CCPs are sufficiently resilient. Nonetheless, default resolution and recovery will still depend on how members cooperate and the extent of panic in a future crisis.[3]

Thus the unwinding of central bank support for the interbank system is set to occur in an environment where interdependence risk has softened but remains. Other factors affecting conditions include:

- European banks have been reducing their non-performing loan (NPL) ratios but they are still too high.
- Markets have become used to easy policy, causing bonds and to some extent equities to become overvalued by end-2017.[4]
- Low yields have pushed some institutional investors into less-liquid, higher yielding securities.
- The US government has cut taxes which will increase its budget deficit, so that the private sector will need to absorb even more bonds in addition to the unwinding of central bank holdings accumulated during a period of quantitative easing.

Debt levels in the global economy have increased in a number of jurisdictions, and there is an interesting discussion of these issues in the latest *OECD Economic Outlook* (OECD, 2018). In last year's *Business and Finance Outlook* (OECD, 2017a), there was some discussion about how bank regulation is shifting the structure of finance towards the non-bank financial system, both in OECD countries and in China. This year's Outlook looks at this again in more detail with respect to China and at what the authorities there are doing about this issue. Off-balance sheet activities in China have expanded, causing debt levels and risk exposures to become dangerously high. In 2009, China expanded credit sharply to counter perceived potential effects of the crisis. Even though bank credit growth has since eased, responding to tighter policy, attempts to reduce a broader measure of credit growth have proved more difficult. This is because monetary policy tools such as interest rate ceilings, reserve requirement changes and quantitative credit controls can be avoided through off-balance sheet activity and market-based financing channels. Monetary policy tools may need to become more market oriented, given the ambitious policies authorities are pursuing to maintain solid growth and to reduce inequality in poorer regions, while also raising the 'quality' of GDP. This has resulted in greater use of macro-prudential tools and a number of other important reforms in Chinese monetary and regulatory policies.

The following sections cover:

- Section 1.2 – the prospects for interest rate normalisation and the unwinding of central bank securities in advanced economies, including the debate concerning how large central bank balance sheets should remain in the longer run.
- Section 1.3 – the finalisation of Basel III.

- Section 1.4 – developments in the Chinese financial system, including the high levels of debt, off-balance sheet activity and what Chinese policy is doing about the situation.
- Section 1.5 – general conclusions on the financial system outlook.

1.2. Prospects for the unwinding of ultra-low interest rates and central bank assets

Figure 1.1. Evolution of short-term interest rates, 1999-2018

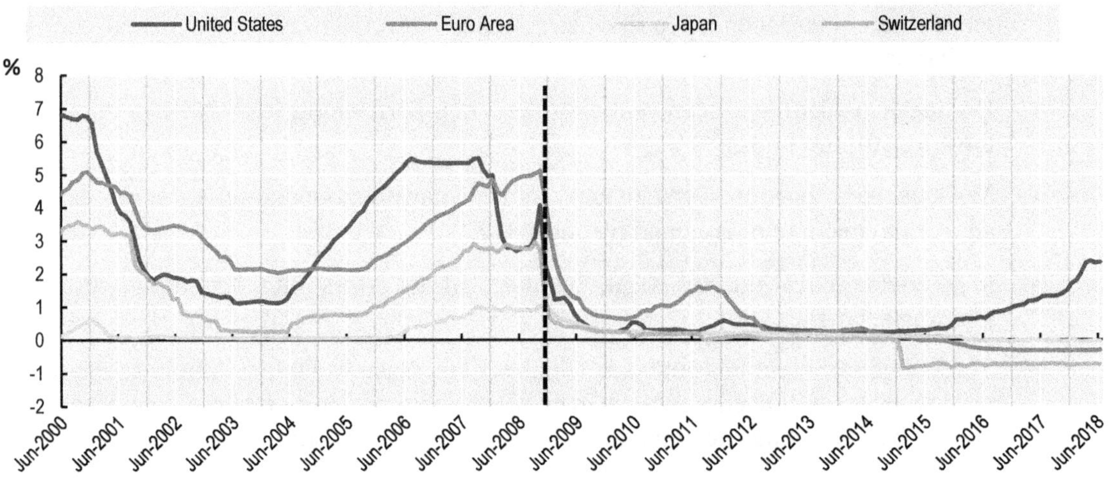

Note: 2018 data are to end-June.
Source: Thomson Reuters, OECD calculations.

StatLink http://dx.doi.org/10.1787/888933786097

Figure 1.2. Central bank holdings of assets, 2007-2018

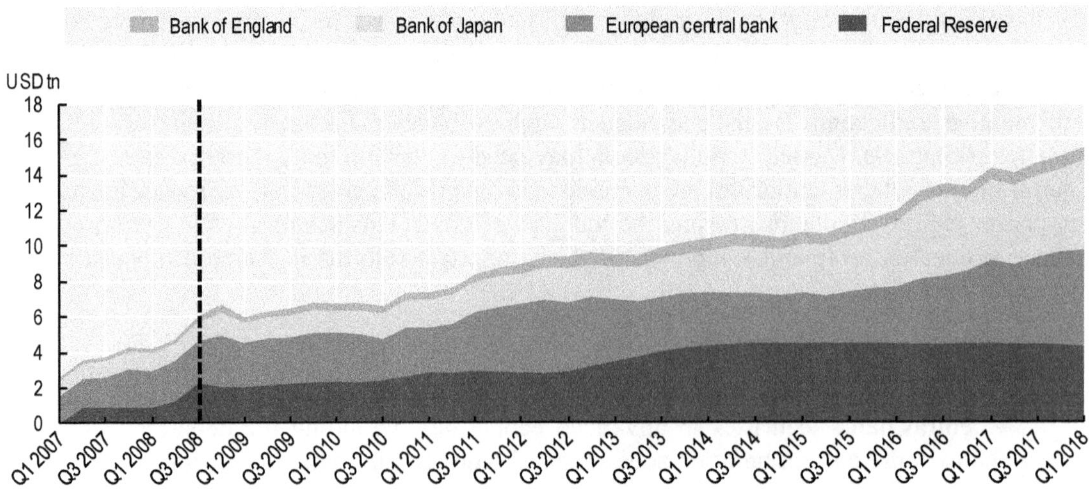

Note: Q1 = first quarter 2018.
Source: Thomson Reuters, OECD calculations.

StatLink http://dx.doi.org/10.1787/888933786116

The level of short (3-month) interest rates for selected countries where G-SIBs are headquartered is shown in Figure 1.1. The cut in rates to ultra-low levels from 2008 is unprecedented – particularly where negative rates apply. Only in the United States have interest rates begun to normalise. How fast the Fed will increase policy rates will depend on the outlook for growth and inflation, the strength of US bank balance sheets and the development of the US dollar exchange rate (since other central banks have not moved to raise interest rates in line). Only in the United States – where many of the securitised mortgages with Fannie Mae and Freddie Mac are held in conservatorship – is the economy strong enough, the banking system sufficiently profitable and the rebuilding of capital advanced enough to begin the normalisation of policy.

The size of central bank balance sheets for the United States, the euro area, the United Kingdom and Japan is shown in Figure 1.2. From around USD 3.2 trillion in total in January 2007, the central banks of the countries hosting G-SIBs increased this to some USD 15.0 trillion by the start of 2018. In fact, in order to deal with the crisis and exert targeted control over financing conditions for the broader economy (via the yield curve), central banks took USD 11 trillion of assets onto their balance sheets. Combined with low interest rates, investors have benefited from the liquidity-driven recovery in asset prices. Central banks, too, have benefited from an increase in the value of their holdings as a result of falling rates and tightening credit spreads for the large quantity of assets that they hold.

The raising of short-term interest rates toward more historically normal levels will have implications for bond markets, given the expectations theory of the yield curve.[5] A return to historically normal interest rates will imply sustained lower bond returns from this point (see the bond simulation below in Figure 1.5). It would be reasonable to expect this adjustment to be accompanied by periods of volatility, as occurred in 1994 but for different reasons this time.[6] With respect to central bank balance sheets, private portfolios will have to absorb the increased supply of assets into the financial system. The cash is obviously there to cover this mechanically and the economy is strengthening, but potential liquidity effects could prove to be significant.[7] It remains to be seen:

a) whether banks and other financial institutions are ready to get along comfortably without the large liquidity cushions that have been the counterpart of central bank quantitative easing; and

b) how the post-crisis regulatory liquidity rules will affect behaviour in the face of central banks' actions.

The bond market adjustment can have spill-over effects on equity markets though these on the whole do not appear to be excessively overvalued by historical standards. Figure 1.3 shows price-to-earnings (PE) ratios for the United States, the euro area and the United Kingdom in mid-2018.[8] At end-2017, the US stock market was ripe for a correction, which duly followed in February 2018.[9]

The average price to expected earnings (PE) ratio is around 15 for most major equity markets, and is considered to be a 'normal' metric in the United States as it has mean-reverted to this level since 1881. Possibly reflecting the problems about banks' assets in these markets and the implications for economic growth, PE ratios have become stuck at, or below, the level of 15 in the United Kingdom and Europe.

While equity markets have been a favoured asset class as interest rates declined over time, equity risk premiums are (surprisingly) not especially low. They have been able to maintain levels even somewhat higher than historical averages — seemingly making some allowance for excessively low bond rates when discounting future cash flows. The main risk to equities will be from an interruption to earnings growth from any significant slowing of the economy.

Figure 1.3. Price-to-earnings expansions, 1989-2018

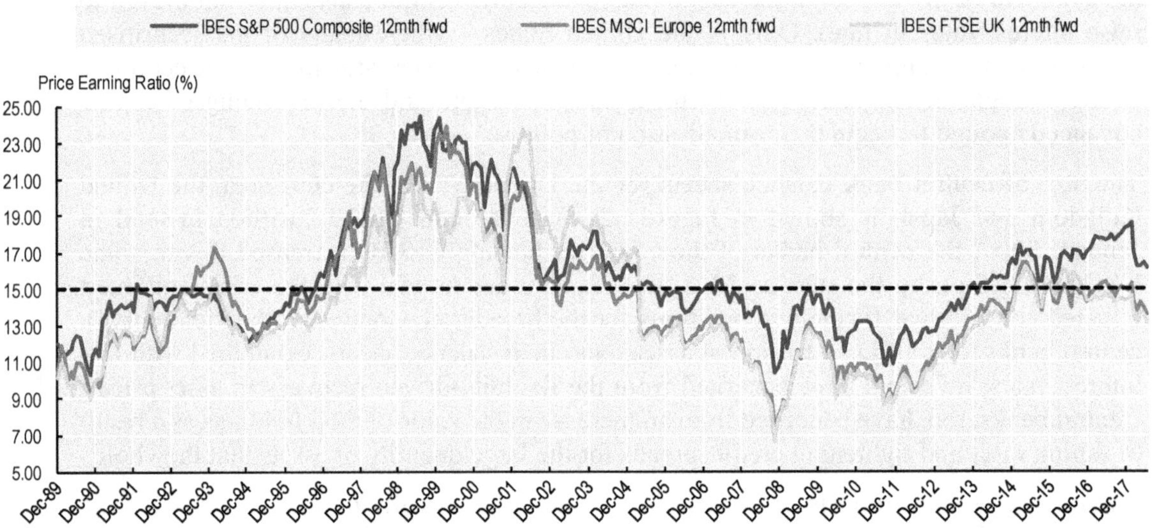

Note: 2018 data are to end-June.
Source: Thomson Reuters, OECD calculations.

StatLink http://dx.doi.org/10.1787/888933786135

In the United States, where bank return-on-equity (ROE) measures are showing a healthy recovery across all large banks, economic growth is strong and tax cuts have been added to the mix. PE ratios expanded more than in other regions during the course of 2017. The Standard & Poor's 500-stock index (S&P 500) average PE ratio for December 2017 was 18.5, not as high as the monthly peak of 24 at the height of the tech bubble at the end of the 1990s. A further correction of around 8% from the March level (based on forward earnings) would be required to return it to the normal PE ratio level of 15. These adjustments do not come about in a straight line. Bouts of volatility in both directions are usually present when markets are trying to find direction in a changing return environment. Derivative-based notes, algorithmic trading and index fund redemptions operate to increase the amplitude of volatility, particularly if views of investors and policy makers on the speed of policy normalisation and other economic issues are not in line. Some mechanisms, whereby index funds might play a role in increased volatility, are set out in Box 1.1.

The reversal of central bank policy cannot happen overnight. The impact on the bond market in expectation of this regime change has already been significant. This is why central banks will proceed in a gradual and well telegraphed way. Nevertheless, as discussed below, a number of disruptive mechanisms may come into play in the future.

Box 1.1. The potential of exchange trade funds (ETFs) to drive the US market

By the end of 2016, ETFs constituted 10% of US market capitalisation, 30% of daily trading volume and 20% of aggregate short interest (Ben-David et al., 2017). In the 6 May 2010 'flash crash' 42% of US equity trading was in ETFs and this transmitted to underlying stocks and liquidity dried up (Borkevic et al., 2010). On 20 June 2013 ETF prices fell sharply due to the absence of arbitrageurs and authorised participants (Ben-David et al., 2017 and references therein). On 24 August 2015, ETFs experienced a run on prices causing them to move to steep discounts to their net asset value and to account for 83% of the trading halts (SEC, 2015). In February 2018, there was another significant test of the market. On this occasion, even with heavy trading, there were minimum net outflows from ETFs, with tight bid-ask spreads and apparently adequate liquidity.

Figure 1.4. ETF passive funds in redemption sell-off

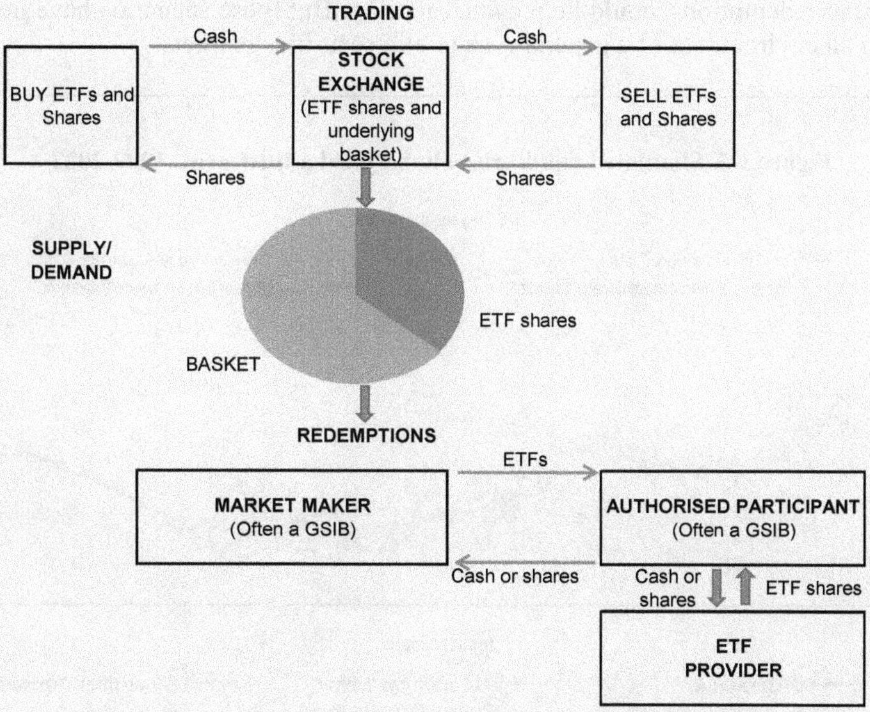

Authorised participants (APs) and high frequency traders arbitrage ETFs vis their underlying stocks. For example, APs short sell ETFs and buy the basket when the former trades at a premium to the underlying. At the end of the day, the short sales are covered by delivering the basket to the ETF in exchange for ETF shares. The reverse process happens when ETFs trade at a discount to the underlying. The case of ETF selling can be seen by following the arrows in Figure 1.4.

There is a large amount of academic research on ETFs. Ben-David et al. (2014) find that stocks with higher ETF ownership display significantly higher volatility. The Pan and Zeng (2017) study of corporate bond ETFs over the periods 2004-2016 suggests that liquidity mismatch can lead to mispricing, consistent with the idea that authorised participant arbitrageurs may stay on the sidelines during periods of market stress, due to concerns that mispricing will widen. This then becomes self-fulfilling due to the absence of arbitrageurs. Agarwal et al. analyse the consequences of having an extra layer of trading in ETFs on top of the trading that occurs anyway in the underlying stocks. They use the 2015 episode which includes periods of trading halts to ETFs affected by extreme price swings, allowing them to look at situations with and without the extra layer of trading. Controlling for index and mutual fund activity, they find a commonality factor in liquidity between ETFs and the constituent underlying stocks driven by the above market arbitrage activity. The commonality was not present during trading halts. They conclude that the ETF market reduces the ability of investors to diversify liquidity shocks due to the increase in the commonality in liquidity of stocks included in ETF portfolios. This and other research suggest there are significant policy issues that justify further analysis to improve understanding about risks that could be associated with ETFs.

Market mitigants are already in place should a more substantial stress conditions occur, through the structure and design of ETFs and funds more broadly. The ability for ETFs to pay in kind, or in the worst case, to use other tools such as gates, fees, side pockets or freeze fund redemptions, could help calm volatility. But these scenarios have not been tested in an environment of a general rush to exit securities markets.

Figure 1.5. Simulated equilibrium bond yield adjustment, 1999-2022

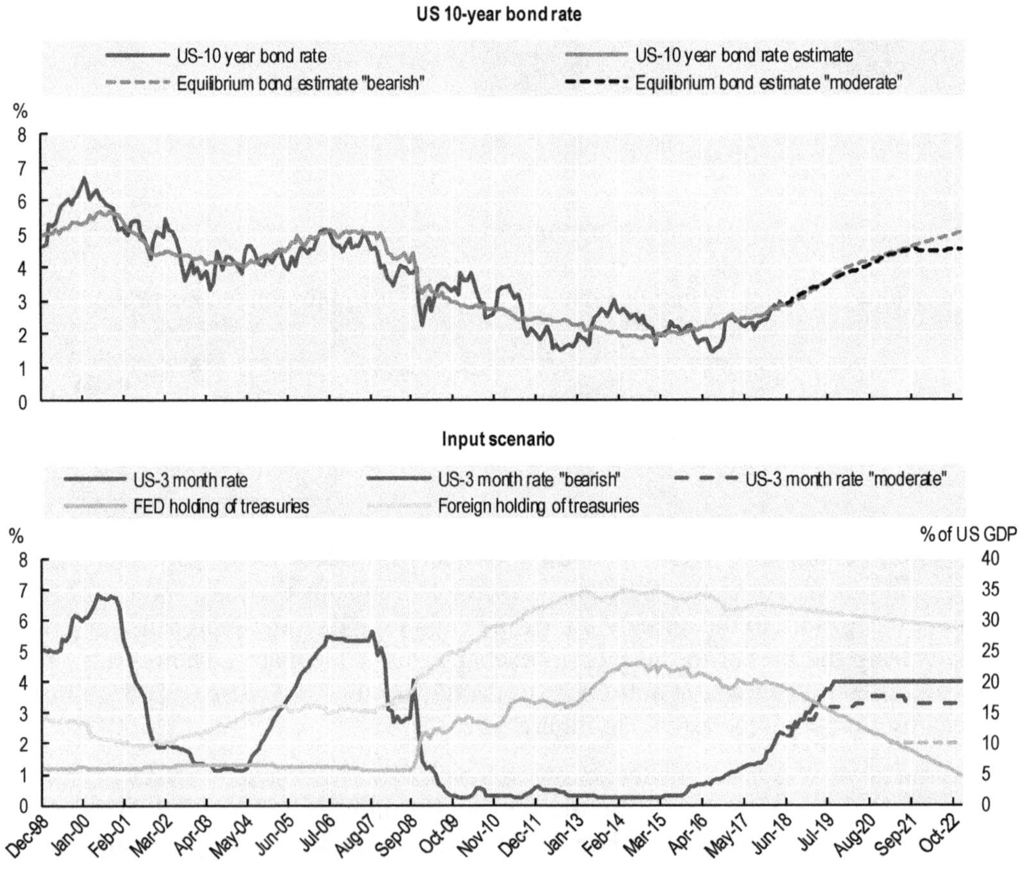

Source: Thomson Reuters, OECD calculations.

StatLink http://dx.doi.org/10.1787/888933786154

Potential impacts on bond valuations

The Fed has given a good indication of how it intends to proceed in reducing its holdings of securities as interest rises. It intends to do this by gradually decreasing its reinvestment in maturing securities – it will reinvest only amounts that exceed pre-set caps. These caps then are an estimate of the extent of the decline of its holdings (Federal Reserve, 2017). Assuming the Fed does not offset any of these maturity-driven declines with other active policy actions, the declines are scheduled to be:

- Treasury securities: USD 6 billion initially, and increasing every three months in steps of USD 6 billion over 12 months until the decline reaches USD 30 billion per month (in the last quarter of 2018).
- For payments of principal from its agency securities and mortgage-backed securities, reinvestment caps start at USD 4 billion and increase every three months in steps of USD 4 billion until they reach USD 20 billion per month.[10]
- The USD 30 billion and USD 20 billion caps will then be held in place until the balance sheet arrives at the level necessary to implement monetary policy efficiently and effectively.

An OECD bond yield model is used to simulate some possible impacts of this scenario in order to quantify the overall extent of price adjustment that may become necessary in the bond market. The main inputs and outcomes are shown in Figure 1.5. The dotted lines are estimates of the equilibrium bond rate tendency based on the factors included in the model – these are not forecasts as such, as there is uncertainty about future Fed policy and no account can be taken of market liquidity and trading influences.[11] The scenarios are intended to give a broad idea of the sort of adjustment that may lie in front of the bond market in the period ahead.

The uncertainty about Fed policy arises in terms of the ultimate size of the balance sheet best suited to running monetary policy 'efficiently and effectively'. The argument at one extreme is to keep the balance sheet at current levels on the basis of three arguments:[12]

- That there is strong demand for safe short-term securities in the financial system and this should not be left up to the private sector to provide (implying there is no need to restore the interbank market to its pre-crisis mode of operation).
- The Fed's balance sheet is too large to control the Fed Funds Rate by varying the quantity of reserves, but interest rates can anyway be set by fixing the rate paid on excess reserves.
- Banks will be more willing to borrow in a liquidity crisis without 'stigma' if the Fed balance sheet remains large.

The announcement of the Fed caps profile suggests this view is not the most likely scenario. There were significant effects on spreads between mortgage-backed security yields and Treasuries in 2008 and the interbank market stopped functioning due to the serious liquidity crisis at the time. The quantitative easing policy was designed at first to address illiquidity in markets (dysfunction) and later to stimulate demand with interest rates at the lower bound. In the United States, this situation has now been satisfactorily reversed—it therefore makes sense to reduce Fed holdings that were associated with these earlier periods. Moreover, the bond model estimated at the OECD has important portfolio channels. If more securities are held on the Fed balance sheet then this gives rise to a reduced risk premium on holding such securities in the private sector. In looking at this process the Fed states: *"The primary channel through which LSAPs appear to work is the risk premium on the asset being purchased. By purchasing a particular asset, the Federal Reserve reduces the amount of the security that the private sector holds, displacing some investors and reducing the holdings of others, while simultaneously increasing the amount of short-term, risk-free bank reserves held by the private sector. In order for investors to be willing to make those adjustments, the expected return on the purchased security has to fall. Put differently, the purchases bid up the price of the asset and hence lower its yield. This pattern was described by Tobin (1958) and is commonly known as the 'portfolio balance effect'."*[13] The OECD model used is in this spirit.

One of the contributing factors of the 2008 crisis was a general underpricing of risk, a situation that policy makers might wish to avoid in the future. Keeping risk premia artificially low will encourage markets to take on more risk than they should and perhaps also to believe that a rescue package similar to that following the crisis might always be forthcoming should it be needed in the future. For these reasons reducing the holdings of securities on the Fed's balance sheet in the manner suggested by the caps approach would see risk premiums rise gradually to more appropriate levels which, for this reason, seems to be a sensible way to proceed.

The bottom panel of Figure 1.5 shows the scenario for Fed securities holdings consistent with its caps to reinvestment as a share of GDP (GDP being assumed to grow at trend). Two scenarios are shown for 3-month interest rates and the holdings by the Federal Reserve of Treasury securities:

1. Moderate scenario: shown with dotted lines in the period ahead is a moderate scenario where the short rates follow a path implied by Federal Open Market Committee views as set out in the minutes for the March 2018 meeting. With respect to Fed holdings, these are assumed to follow the pattern implied by the above caps until they reach 10% of GDP in early 2021. The Fed, therefore, is assumed not to return to the lower levels that prevailed prior to the crisis.[14]
2. Bearish scenario: shown with the solid line for the period ahead is a bearish scenario for bonds (that would require a faster period of growth and inflation risk ahead than currently implicit in official views). The Fed funds rate moves to 4%, and short rates sit slightly higher. On this view, and for illustrative purposes only, it is assumed that the caps profile is followed until holdings fall to around the 5% level that prevailed prior to the crisis. Short rates are assumed to rise gradually to a maximum of 4%.

In both of the above cases foreign holdings are assumed to stay constant in nominal terms and decline gradually as a share of GDP.

- Under the moderate scenario, which is shown with the grey dotted line in the top panel of Figure 1.5, the equilibrium 10-year bond rate rises to 3.8%.
- Under the bearish scenario the bond rate rises to 4.3%.

Other scenarios may also be considered, but these quite different views give some idea of the 'digestion' issues that may lie ahead for the bond market. These rate scenarios imply a significant amount of price adjustment in the more liquid Treasury bond markets, but it is worth stressing that the implied price volatility could be much greater for other illiquid bond markets in the adjustment process.[15]

Possible disruptive effects

A number of effects that could make the path of adjustment more turbulent:

- *Mortgage-backed securities prices move more than Treasury Securities in a rising interest rate environment:* This is because borrowers of fixed-rate mortgages are less likely to prepay loans in order to refinance at a lower rate, which extends the average maturity of the bonds, making them more volatile. This is sometimes referred to as convexity and it produces more volatility in Treasury and swap markets (see Box 1.2).
- *Volatility and derivatives:* When volatility increases, the potential for losses by investors, speculators and bank broker dealers in the derivatives market also rises. Hedging is imprecise in these vast markets and problems always arise. It might be recalled, for example, that even three years after the financial crisis had broken out, the Morgan Stanley joint venture with Mitsubishi UFJ Securities – despite Morgan Stanley's expertise – incurred a USD 1.76 billion loss.[16] This resulted from imperfectly hedged derivative portfolios exposed to a small movement of the term structure of interest rates.
- *Large block trades in illiquid securities:* Large pension schemes, insurance companies, mutual funds and hedge funds may need to deal in volume and respond to possibilities of withdrawals in the event of a sell-off affecting fixed interest portfolios. Low interest rates incentivise buying of higher-yielding illiquid securities and structured products. While funds have flexibility to manage redemptions, including liquidity management plans, large-scale attempts to unwind less-than-investment-grade illiquid holdings could cause extreme volatility. Some of the issues are summarised in Box 1.1.
- *Higher regulatory costs for market making:* The regulatory changes under Basel III, changes in derivative margin and collateral rules, the Dodd-Frank capital requirements and the Volcker rule process (see Box 1.4) increase the cost of broker-dealer market-making activities. This has caused some pull-back of participation in collateralised agreement markets, reducing liquidity. The increased cost of renting space on a broker-dealer balance sheet increases the cost of all the ancillary trading linked to broker-dealers.[17]
- *Inflation:* there are still weak signs of a pickup in inflation at the start of 2018. While forward-looking indicators, such as current consensus expectations for core US inflation, suggest the rate moving close to the Fed's 2% target in the second quarter of 2018 and recent historical data for average hourly earnings in the United States rose slightly in the twelve months to February 2018 (to 2.6%), and modest productivity growth running at around 1.1% should keep unit labour costs at an under 2% pace. The US core Personal Consumption Expenditure Deflator as a fundamental guide remains weak thus far. Of course, this could change. Any sign of inflation in the United States would cause a more serious rout in the bond market, because it would be seen as steepening the tightening curve. UK inflation in 2017 was related to exchange rate effects and this contribution should drop out in the absence of further depreciation.
- *Brexit and other trade issues:* the uncertainty about the outcome of Brexit negotiations and the impact it will have on the future of the City continues to hang over financial markets at a time when monetary normalisation is taking place. The

UK and Europe are strong trading partners and London is the largest agglomeration for trade in financial services. Other potential trade disruptions also need to be avoided to help smooth the transition.

Figure 1.6. Federal Reserve and foreign holdings of US Treasuries, USD billion, end-May 2018

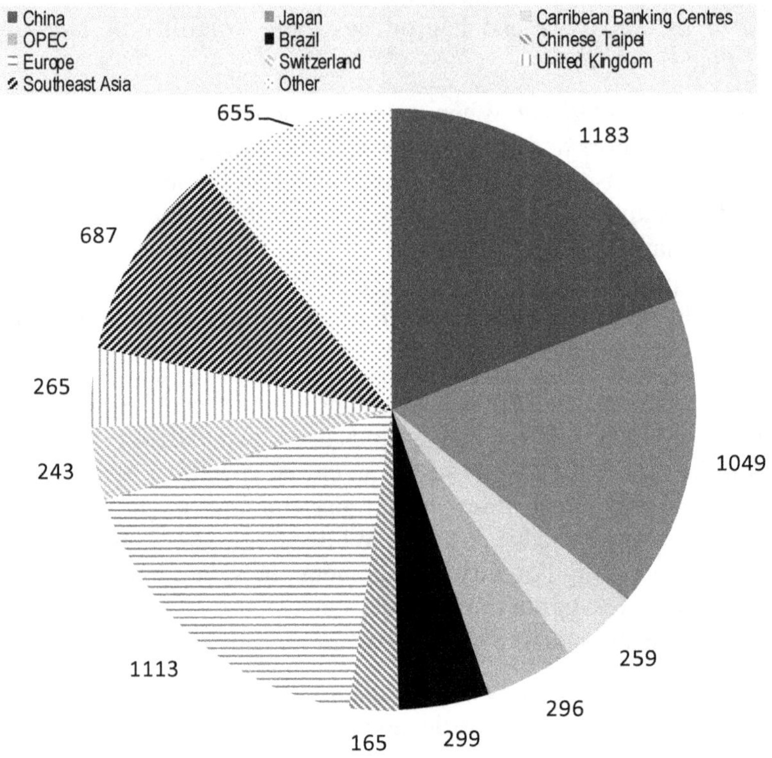

Source: Thomson Reuters, OECD calculations.

StatLink http://dx.doi.org/10.1787/888933786173

- *US Treasury holdings by China:* The three biggest holders of US Treasury securities, other than the Federal Reserve, are China, Europe and Japan, as shown in Figure 1.6. The major presence of China in the US Treasury market is potentially problematic for the above bond rate scenario. China itself has a number of financial problems to deal with related to high levels of debt, much of which is linked to property developers and off-balance sheet shadow banking (see Section 1.4). Local authorities are heavily involved and state-owned banks are the ultimate providers of funds. While it is difficult to develop scenarios, financial stress at home could bring about changes in the way China manages its foreign reserves portfolio. China could withdraw funds by selling Treasuries to deal with business defaults in China, loss of foreign reserves due to proposed capital account opening or, as some market strategists suggest, for geopolitical reasons.[18] This would most likely require some adjustment in the above reinvestment caps proposed by the Fed or in the path of future interest rates. Otherwise pressures on interest rates would become greater than envisaged in the above scenario.

Overall, the outlook for bonds and equities in 2018 and beyond is for much greater volatility and security price corrections. This began in early 2018, particularly in the United States, where valuation distortions for bonds and equities had become more extreme at the end of 2017. In part, the strong equity market in 2017 has been due to a better approach to dealing with the crisis that resulted in a stronger US economy and cutting the corporate tax rate, which caused increased enthusiasm in markets. Two roughly 1 000 point falls in the Dow Jones index in a single week during early February 2018 is indicative of two-way risks now being factored in.[19] However, concerns remain about the longer-run resilience of the financial system following the re-regulation process (see Section 1.3).

Box 1.2. Mortgage bond convexity and fixed income volatility

The unhedged mortgage-backed securities (MBS), which the Fed will gradually push back onto the market, are very well known for their convexity. In other words, when interest rates fall, MBS prices rise less than Treasuries and, when interest rates rise, MBS prices fall by more than Treasuries. This happens because prepayments of mortgages rise in a falling interest rate environment (because of a lack of breakage costs for fixed-rate mortgages by borrowers), whereas extensions occur with rising rates (no-one wants to lock into higher interest rates so 30-year mortgages will be paid off much later than usual). The price of MBS moves less because it tends to shorter duration (i.e. expected maturity) in falling rates and by more because it tends to longer duration in rising rates.

The risk to portfolio values and structures is therefore very high in a rising rate environment and this leads fund managers to hedge their portfolios to keep duration at their required level. Duration hedging in a rising rate environment is achieved either by selling Treasury bonds, which directly exacerbates the effect of rising rates on Treasuries (makes the sell-off worse), or by dealing in the interest rate swaps market. In the swap market, this hedging can be achieved by paying fixed against floating – thus, when rates rise the fixed payer is protected from rising rates and the value of the contract rises with rates. Swap contract pricing therefore reflects the market's expectation about future interest rates and is a useful tool for (speculative) investors. The floating rate payer faces a lot of risk in a tightening cycle and so the swap rate (i.e. the interest rate demanded by the floating rate payer) will rise if the outlook for tightening by a central bank like the Federal Reserve becomes more bearish. The spread between the swap rate and Treasuries reflects: (a) the (varying) credit spreads between banks and the safe sovereign bond (which widens in a crisis); (b) the supply and demand for swaps; and (c) swap market liquidity. There is an arbitrage to Treasury securities if the demand to be a fixed payer rises in a tightening situation.

In short, the duration hedging of MBS as short rates rise and the need to absorb more MBS in the market will exacerbate the rise in longer-term Treasuries and cause more volatility in the swap market. The impact may be softened in part by the limits on banks' investment activities through the Volcker Rule, and stronger capital requirements, which will weigh on wider demand for MBS as they return to the market. Central banks are broadly aware of this set of issues, but interest rates have been falling for a very long time and the test of how volatile this will prove to be lies ahead (e.g. Maltz et al., 2014).

The need for liquidity in securities markets

There is considerable difference between the size and foreign holding composition of global fixed income markets. For example:

- In Q3 2017 the US fixed income market, according to the BIS, was USD 38.9 trillion with foreigners owning 26% of it; while for the Treasury market the equivalent numbers were USD 17.2 trillion with foreigners owning 36%.
- For Japan total debt was USD 12.6 trillion with government bonds at USD 9.4 trillion. Foreigners owned 11% and 6.1%, respectively.
- For China total debt was USD 11.2 trillion and sovereign debt was at USD 4.1 trillion. Foreigners owned 1.1% and 1.2% of these respectively.

The next largest markets for total debt are the United Kingdom (USD 5.8 trillion), France (USD 4.5 trillion), Germany (USD 3.6 trillion), Italy USD 3.3 trillion, Netherlands (USD 2.2 trillion) and Spain and Australia (both on USD 2 trillion). All of these latter markets are fairly open.

Central banks and sovereign wealth and pension funds would benefit from a wider choice of liquid investment grade-bonds around the world. The liquidity of a security is the ease with which it can be transacted without affecting its price, which requires market depth; i.e. that larger-sized orders do not move the market by very much. Even large bond markets can be relatively less liquid if the bulk of securities are tightly held and the free trading part of the market is small; or if capital controls are pervasive and only small amounts of bonds markets are tradeable by foreigners.

In the volatile environment expected in 2018 and beyond, as policy is normalised, liquidity considerations of very large pension and sovereign wealth funds may favour increasingly bonds denominated in the US dollar, euro and sterling, as well as large cap equities. This trend is likely to emerge in a significant part of the investor universe because large funds find it difficult to deal and manage to benchmarks in assets other than those that are very liquid. Norges Bank, which runs the largest sovereign wealth fund in the world, was recently asked by the Norwegian Ministry of Finance to examine all of its investment benchmarks with many of the above risks in mind. One of their key conclusions was stated as follows:

"Thus we find that the risk reduction that a long-term investor achieves by diversifying investments across countries and currencies differs between equities and bonds. In the long term, the gains from broad international diversification are considerable for equities but moderate for bonds. For an investor with 70% of his investments in an internationally diversified equity portfolio, there is little reduction in risk to be obtained by also diversifying his bond investments across a large number of currencies.

The benchmark index for bonds currently consists of 23 currencies. Our recommendation is that the number of currencies in the bond index is reduced. This will have little impact on risk in the overall benchmark index. We propose that the Ministry goes back to a specific list of currencies for the bond index rather than leaving this decision to the index supplier. The currencies on the list must be liquid and investable for the fund. The most liquid market for bonds is currently that for US Treasuries, followed by those for bonds issued by countries in the euro area and the United Kingdom. The Japanese bond market is large but far less liquid than those for the other currencies that currently have a substantial weight in the index. An index consisting of bonds issued in dollars, euros and pounds alone will be sufficiently liquid and investable for the fund" (Norwegian Ministry of Finance, 2017).

Deepening and opening securities markets in Asia

The openness and depth of Asian bond markets in both local currency and dollar-denominated securities needs to be increased in economies that have reached an appropriate level of development, including by reducing restrictions on capital inflows and outflows that prevent building more liquidity in these markets—a view echoed by the former Peoples Bank of China governor Zhou at the 19th Party Conference (see section 1.4).

Interest rate rises and the growth of corporate cash flow

Figure 1.7. Corporate cash flow and capital expenditure, 2003-2017

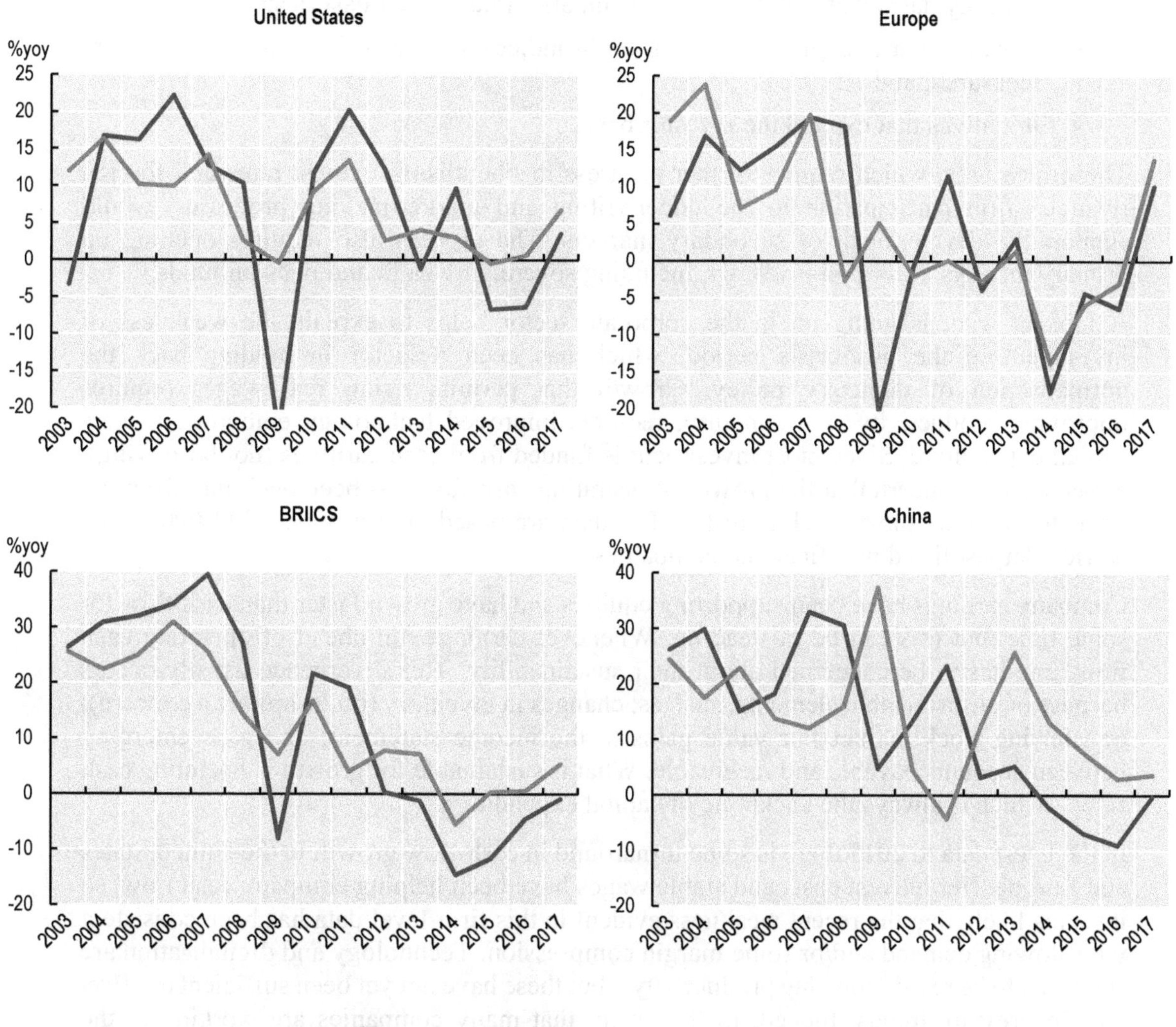

Note: The acronym "BRIICS" stands for the following group of countries: Brazil, Russia, India, Indonesia, China, Peoples Republic of, and South Africa. "Europe" refers to the euro area (including 19 member states). YOY = year on year.
Source: Bloomberg, OECD calculations.

StatLink http://dx.doi.org/10.1787/888933786192

Global policies and good practice offer measures to assist developing liquidity in Asian markets by focussing on market structures and specific investor and issuer activities.

For market structures such measures could include:

- increasing pre- and post-trade transparency to improve price discovery;
- derivatives markets to allow hedging of risk, and
- developing new electronic trading platforms.

Investor and issuer-focussed measures could include:

- standardisation of documentation and reporting;
- maturity dates that match liquid benchmark indices like treasuries;
- issuance that is eligible for inclusion in indices against which fund managers are measured; and
- initiatives that expand the investor base.

These measures, which require further progress in liberalising interest rates and foreign financial firm participation in the underwriting and market-making processes, would support the development of secondary markets. The process also requires opening up primary markets to foreign investors, including sovereign wealth and pension funds.

A look at what is going on in the corporate sector helps to explain the weakness of investment in the post-crisis period, which has been a factor in holding back the normalisation of monetary policy. Growth that permits rising real wages requires improving productivity. This, in turn, requires improved technology embodied in new capital expenditure. Since most investment is funded from cash earnings (not borrowing), it has been of concern that the growth of operating cash flow has been declining from the crisis to 2016, as shown in Figure 1.7. The data are based on a sample of 11 000 of the world's largest listed non-financial companies.

Company earnings have been supporting equities and have grown faster than cash flow for some time, but this can be misleading. Whenever earnings run ahead of operating cash flow, one has to be concerned about their sustainability. This divergence usually occurs because of unsustainable elements, such as: changes in inventory (build-ups are a concern); transferring stock market fair value gains to the income statement; and gaps emerging between accounts payable and receivable. What is sustainable for growth is operating cash flow – which is always the backbone of capital expenditure.

In the latest data to 2017 there is some turnaround in cash-flow growth in the United States and Europe. Net interest costs and stable wages have been helping company cash flow, so it seems likely that the recent weakness evident in this firm-level data has been consistent with slowing demand and/or some margin compression. Technology and digitalisation are supposed to be revolutionising productivity – but these have not yet been sufficient to offset margin pressure trends. Indeed, to the extent that many companies are working in the digitalisation space (hardware, components, software, robotics, cloud computing, etc.), unit prices may be falling as these items are commoditised while the diffusion of the use of technology often takes many years (and sometimes decades) to lead to substantial productivity gains.

The signs of a cash-flow pick-up in 2017, if sustained, could lead either to more investment or allow firms to engage in increased share buybacks, though some estimates from private analysts using a different sample of companies show a more muted picture in 2017-18.[20] It is of interest to note that cash flow is not yet accelerating in China where excess capacity in certain sectors has been centred. Increased pricing power in the US and Europe would support the case for more investment and a gradual normalisation of monetary policy. But much will depend on the progress being made in eliminating excess capacity in the global economy more generally, given the interconnected nature of supply chains.

Figure 1.8. Non-performing loans by bank size and region, 2008-2018

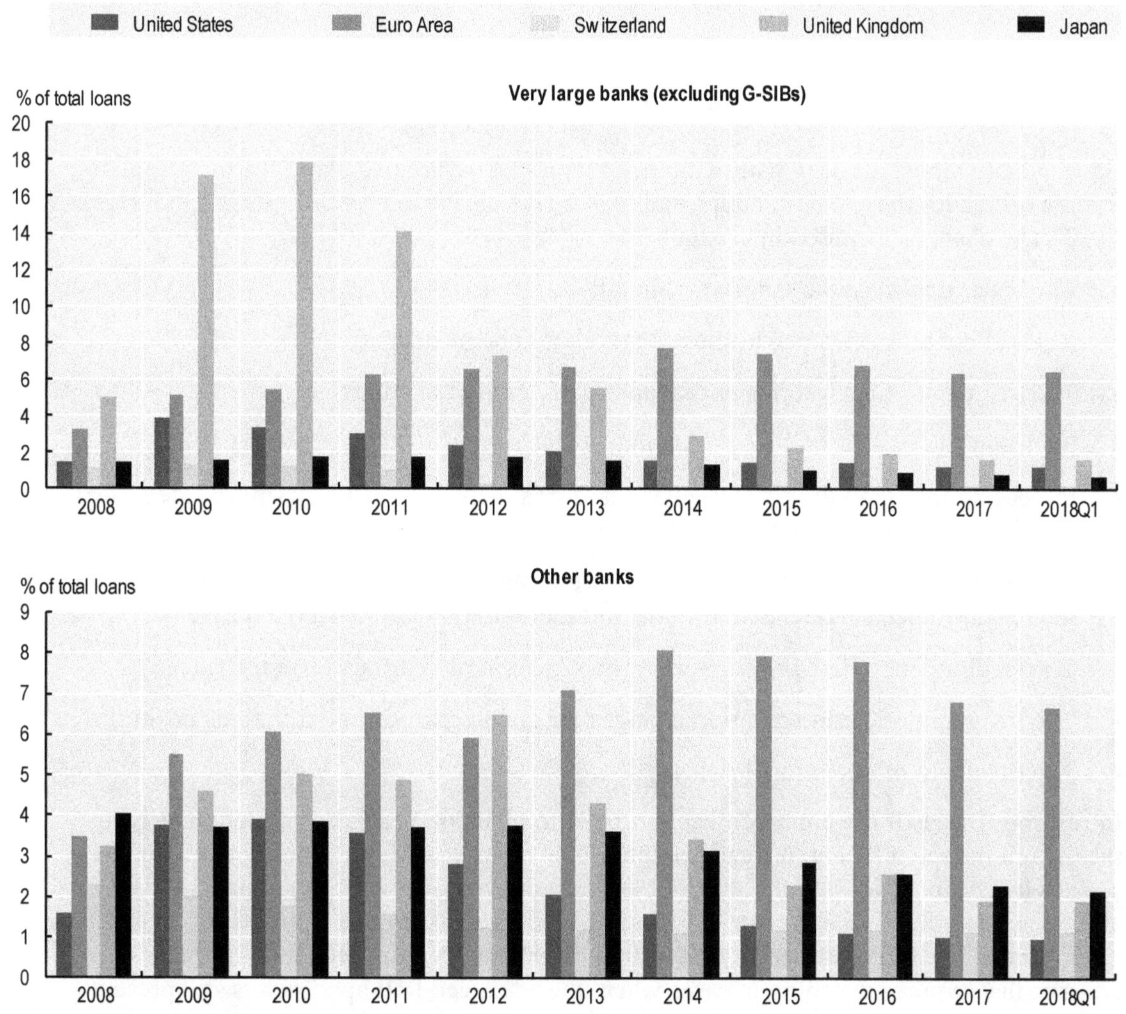

Note: Q1 = first quarter 2018
A bank is considered very large if its total assets are above USD°50 billion. G-SIBs are excluded from this group.
Source: S&P Global Market Intelligence, OECD calculations.

StatLink http://dx.doi.org/10.1787/888933786211

1.3. Dealing with risks in the banking system through reforms

Jurisdictions differ in terms of the importance of capital market versus banking finance– the euro area and Japan are more bank-dominated and in the United States and the United Kingdom financing is more market-based, giving capital markets a greater role in financing the economy. Related to this, not all regions adopted the accepted wisdom for dealing with financial crises to the same extent. This requires the following four steps:

1. provide liquidity to the system;
2. guarantee deposits;
3. deal with the bad assets (get the bulk of them off balance sheets); and
4. recapitalise the bad-assets-cleansed banks.

Box 1.3. Risk-weighted assets: From Basel II to Basel III

Basel III attempted to deal with a number of issues related to flaws in the Basel II framework, and these were supported by work in the Financial Stability Board (FSB).The changes included inter alia:[1]

- The better quality and quantity of capital.
- Rules about how off-balance sheet items should be measured.
- The treatment of market risk and counterparty credit risk charges.
- Increasing so-called 'bail-in' bonds for resolvability (FSB TLAC work).
- Increasing the 'granularity' in the standard treatment of credit risk (more categories) and the risk sensitivity required in various models.
- The imposition of output floors (versus the standard approaches) which can help reducing problems associated with the internal ratings-based (IRB) approach.
- The singling out of G-SIBs for special treatment in the various leverage rules.[2]
- The treatment of credit valuation changes for counterparties in derivatives positions.
- The treatment of operational risk.

In revising Basel II, the approach has not been to abandon the basic model underlying the Basel framework, but instead to introduce more granularity and greater model sensitivity. Assumptions of the original Basel framework such as portfolio invariance and a single global risk factor have remained in the revised framework.[3] Some constraints have been imposed to deal with the subjectivity of inputs, though this is still an issue that requires watching in cases where the advanced IRB approach is still present and where internal assessments are made.

1. Full details on these developments are on the BIS website: www.bis.org/bcbs/publ/d424.htm.
2. The RWA must be calculated as the higher of: (a) the approach that banks are approved to use (external ratings, standardised or IRB); or, (b) 72.5% of the RWA calculated by the standardised approach. This will apply to most aspects of Basel III: credit risk, counterparty credit risk, the credit valuation adjustment charge, market risk, and operational risk.
3. Portfolio invariance means that idiosyncratic risks can be identified, separated out, modelled and risk weighted (with different models depending on the levels of sophistication for obligors) to calculate capital charges for each that can be added up to derive total capital requirements. Because the Basel method applies to all global banks, this mathematical model also assumes a single global risk factor common to all banks (presumably the global macro cycle) – and has nothing to do with local jurisdiction risk issues.

Most jurisdictions achieved the first two steps, but the failure to take the third step in some jurisdictions has meant that central bank involvement in buying assets as liquidity policy has had to be larger and for longer to ensure that the interbank market continues to function (with large quantities of assets of uncertain quality remaining within the system).[21] The euro area was partly constrained in dealing with bad assets by its state-aid rules.[22] But the real issue has been its dependence on banking to finance the economy in the face of a significant quantity of bad assets. Thus, while banks' non-performing loans (NPLs) have declined in most regions, they remain too high in some European economies and also in a number of emerging economies.

NPLs for large and small banks, distinguished by using a USD 50 billion asset base as a threshold, are shown in Figure 1.8. The size of the problem in parts of the euro area is larger than for other advanced economies, for both large and smaller banks. Since euro area growth has underperformed, and because the NPL problem there is significant, banks and policy makers have argued for a lower leverage ratio (LR) in order for their economy not to be disadvantaged compared with jurisdictions that have a larger role for capital markets.[23] The United States, which followed the sequence of reform steps more rigorously, has had a stronger economy and has pushed through greater regulations onto its banks – particularly with respect to the LR via the Dodd-Frank Act.

While risk weighting has a role (see Box 1.3), it is at best a rough estimate of the sorts of losses that might apply in a crisis. The list of risks is large and has become even larger in recent years. These could include all manner of credit risks from traditional bank lending functions, but they also could include a vast array of risks from investment banking functions. Most of these risks arise from investment banking activities: they are interconnected in ways that differ in crisis periods compared to normal times and cannot be easily separated out and parameterised with portfolio invariance assumptions. These activities are not a significant part of traditional deposit banking in national and smaller regional banks.

The Basel III risk-weighting framework is not aimed at new risks that have been growing in recent years: misconduct risks and fraud, legal penalties for money laundering; operational risk, disruptive new technologies in the areas of blockchain and digital currencies and cyber risk.[24] According to conduct costs data released by the CCP Research Foundation (2017), G-SIBs have paid USD 308 billion in fines between 2012 and 2016, and such issues have continued through 2017 and 2018. Global efforts to strengthen corporate governance and conduct are multiplying, including through the:

- OECD guidance on responsible business conduct for institutional investors (OECD, 2017b);
- FSB toolkit to strengthen governance frameworks to mitigate misconduct risk (FSB, 2018); and
- Growing adoption and expansion of individual responsibility and accountability and regimes, like those developed in the United Kingdom and Hong Kong, China.

Such efforts should help to improve conduct and compliance, and reduce losses and fines in the future, though it is still early days.

These risks add on to and interact with credit and interconnectedness risks and, like these latter risks, they cannot be predicted, risk-weighted and allowed for with any confidence. The Basel III approach to operational risk is illustrative. Operational risk is idiosyncratic and depends on trust, corporate governance, bank culture and due diligence. The size of bank income categories, multiplied by a history-of-past-loss parameters (the essence of the Basel III treatment), has little to do with these causes of operational and non-market losses.

The leverage ratio

It is for these reasons that the OECD Secretariat has, on the basis of empirical research, argued that the simple leverage ratio should be given a more prominent role (see Blundell-Wignall and Atkinson, 2010). Banks prefer a RWA capital rule because it leaves them a degree of control over how much capital they need to hold.[25] For the RWA ratios, the tougher Common Equity Tier 1 (CET-1) definition of capital is used, but the exposure measure in the denominator can be influenced by banks, thereby weakening its role as a binding constraint.

The LR is binding and can be used to ensure sufficient capital is held no matter where the origin of unpredictable losses. The LR limit in Basel III is, according to the analysis referred to above, too small; it uses Tier 1 capital in the numerator (not CET-1) and is less binding than it should be due to the nature of the deductions in the exposure measure. For the finalised Basel III, the LR is left at 3% for non-G-SIB banks, and introduces a LR buffer for G-SIBs set at 50% of their risk-weighted Higher Loss Absorbing Requirement (HLAR) versus RWA (see BIS, 2017).[26] For G-SIBs, the required capital conservation buffer and the HLAR (along with the other requirements) is not onerous compared to the risks they run. The most risky G-SIB would have to hold only 10.5% of RWA as CET-1 capital and 4.75% of Tier-1 capital versus the LR exposure measure. The safest Basel-ranked G-SIB would face a LR of only 3.5%. Despite the greatest levels of support for banks in history, the 2008 crisis saw G-SIB losses well in excess of this range.

Separation of investment banking from deposit taking businesses

OECD empirical evidence suggests by far the biggest issue for G-SIBs is the business model that mixes investment banking activities and extensive use of derivatives for creating complex investment products, and for regulatory and tax arbitrage purposes (Blundell-Wignall, Atkinson and Roulet, 2013). This creates leverage and contributes to financial risk. These uses of derivatives are not helping to fund the real economy (such as through simple hedging on behalf of clients). These activities should not be mixed with traditional deposit banking that cross-subsidises such risk-taking activities and causes a general under-pricing of risks.

Hoenig (2016) points out that US bank losses and Troubled Asset Relief Program (TARP) support amounted to 6% of their balance sheets in the crisis – notwithstanding the biggest monetary injections in history; the official large-scale buying of private sector assets; direct capital injections into banks; placing Fannie Mae and Freddie Mac assets into conservatorship and guaranteeing all of their assets; and the paying out of all AIG's CDS liabilities to banks. Without these measures, the global financial system losses could have been larger.

OECD Secretariat research shows that the LR has a greater mitigating effect on G-SIB risk than the Basel RWA concepts, though this may change as Basel III comes into full effect.[27]

The United States and the United Kingdom have done a lot with respect to bank business models.[28] The US Treasury has recommended further sensible alterations to the Volcker Rule following a review in 2017.

The EU countries, having dropped the Liikanen proposals (Liikanen, 2012), and Switzerland, having rejected separation from the outset, believe that a resolution regime is sufficient to deal with too big to fail (TBTF). In the United States, the Orderly Liquidation Framework for emergency circumstances and the requirement for living wills under the Dodd-Frank Act also goes in this direction. However, Duffie (2016) is sceptical of this approach at its current level of advancement because to have any chance of working, there are three basic requirements:

a) that the firm has enough bail-in securities;[29]
b) that the process of resolution should not lead to an early termination of contracts that the firm and its counterparties rely on for their financial stability across multiple jurisdictions; and
c) that policy makers act in a predictable and decisive manner.[30]

Some of these issues are being dealt with, but at the time of writing none have been settled in a satisfactory way. This is mainly because the amounts involved are large in a financial crisis:

- Deposits, covered bonds and other securities ineligible for bail-in are a large component of liabilities.
- The interconnectedness between G-SIBs is extensive across jurisdictions with different regulatory structures – and rules pertaining to the previous points differ.

More generally, the resolution approach to TBTF does not deal with reducing the subsidy to risk-taking for derivative activity in an ex ante sense. Indeed, the resolution of a bank through the bail in of unsecured bond holders makes it *ex ante* clear that counterparty positions of banks will be settled (even with any stay of early termination) at the expense of creditors first and the taxpayer second in cases where the seizing of collateral would be insufficient.

Box 1.4. The Volcker Rule and The Treasury Review

Section 619 of the Dodd-Frank Act, commonly referred to as the "Volcker Rule", prohibits depository institutions from engaging in proprietary trading and from investing in covered funds (such as hedge funds and private equity) beyond small limits (Dodd-Frank, 2010). There are three tests for the blanket trading restriction:

1. instruments covered by the market risk capital rules cannot be traded for proprietary gain;
2. if the transaction would normally require the entity to be registered with the U.S. Commodity Futures Trading Commission (CFTC) or the Securities and Exchange Commission (SEC) as a dealer then it cannot be done (status test); and
3. the trade cannot be made for the purpose of short-term resale, benefiting from short-term price movements, realising arbitrage profits, and hedging any of the foregoing.

Treasury Review (2017), in response to an executive order, recommends removing this latter element because it is subjective and leads to conservatism and costly documentation.

The Volcker Rule 'tests' raised issues for market-making and, in the end, it was agreed that banks could continue this latter role provided that they did not build inventory beyond reasonable forecasts for serving expected client demand (which would cause excess inventory to arise).[1] The Treasury review argues that this asks traders to forecast the impossible – particularly for illiquid OTC derivatives – and documentation is costly to firms. The review argues that such forecasts should not be required if the firm stands ready to buy and sell the instruments and if that appropriate hedging and compensation arrangements are in place.[2]

With respect to the ban on investing and sponsoring covered funds, the review suggests that it is too extensive and may not limit itself to hedge funds and private equity which are not defined clearly enough under the Volcker Rule. They argue that this might exclude the seeding of venture capital and other useful tools to support economic growth. It suggests longer seeding periods (from the current 1 year to 3 years).

The Treasury review recommends that all small institutions (less than USD 10 billion in assets) and even larger firms if they have less than USD 1 billion in trading assets (or the latter is less than 10% of its balance sheet) should be exempt from Volcker. The review goes as far as to suggest that any bank with an unweighted LR of 10% or more should be 'off-ramp' for the Dodd-Frank Act.[3]

The potential recommended changes follow on from the changes to section 716, which prohibit the granting of any US federal assistance to entities that are registered with the CFTC or SEC as swap dealers or major swap participants. In its original form, this rule would have limited a US insured depository institution's exposure to the risks from engaging in such derivatives activities. Such activities were to be 'pushed out' into separate execution facilities. The provision was amended by being tacked on to a spending bill to ensure it passed both houses.[4] Banks can now hold many important swaps on their balance sheet.[5]

The Treasury review rightly criticises market making restrictions. This is because the activity is about immediacy for clients (see Duffie, 2011). It is unreasonable to restrict quantities of inventories to levels forecast by some past rule of thumb about client needs. It is clear, too, that compliance costs are high, demonstrating 'intent of a trade' is difficult, and small uninvolved financial institutions (such as community banks) should be exempt.

1. Duffie (2016) points out that market making and proprietary trading are essentially the same thing.
2. This is consistent with Duffie's (2012) views.
3. Consistent with the proposed Financial Choice Act 2017.
4. https://dealbook.nytimes.com/2014/12/12/citigroup-becomes-the-fall-guy-in-the-spending-bill-battle/
5. An exception is structured finance swaps, such as ABS swaps (see Warren, 2015).

It is worth noting that the idea of using Central Bank Digital Currency (CBDC) to manage systemic risk has gained traction in some jurisdictions, for example with Sweden's eKrona project. CBDC could be made available to banks on a wholesale basis, or could take the form of electronic money made available directly to the general population, effectively providing retail deposit-taking accounts with a central bank. The constitutional referendum in Switzerland on the Vollgeld or *'sovereign money'* proposal, which was held and failed to pass on 10 June 2018, might have achieved a similar outcome.

While such a transformation of monetary systems is unlikely in the immediate future, it is a longer-term possibility given the level of institutional interest. Retail CBDCs could call into question the nature and purpose of traditional deposit-taking institutions, particularly those that fail to separate deposits from exposure to risker business activities.

Conclusions on banking reform

The RWA approach to controlling leverage is improved under Basel III but still allows G-SIBs to alleviate standard capital rules via their internal risk and pricing models. This has the potential to corrupt the risk management process by linking internal bank processes to regulatory capital charges. Banks may be obliged to minimise important risk weights to improve the return on equity for shareholders. The imposition of finalised Basel III output floors are a big improvement, but still not as binding on leverage as they might be. Under the final Basel III, G-SIBs can still achieve a 27.5% cut in RWA by using their models compared to the standard approach for all categories.[31] The standard approach for banks is similar to Basel II for external ratings for banks and companies. For mortgages, risk weightings based on loan-to-value (LTV) ratios are an important improvement because they introduce more risk sensitivity, though these need to reach nearly 90% before the old 35% risk weight is surpassed.

Financial crises cannot be predicted, and to ensure that central bank and taxpayer support in a crisis like that of 2008 will not recur in the future, an important part of the overall reform process was the introduction of Total Loss Absorbing Capacity (TLAC) of 16% of RWA by January 2019 and 18% by 2022 (and to be 6% and 6.75% of the leverage ratio denominator by those dates). Total regulatory capital may be applied to TLAC (but not the regulatory buffers) and other instruments issued by the entity are then added to this. These instruments must be: 'paid in'; unsecured; non-callable; not redeemable; not subject to netting; at least one year to maturity; and exclude exposures to other entities in the G-SIB group. [32] TLAC facilitates single point of entry resolution. These instruments may be 'bailed in' in the event of resolution issues (requiring an implementation trigger, such as a credit default swap (CDS) spread and other supervisory metrics and judgements). TLAC makes resolution a more credible outcome, and therefore helps to reduce the TBTF problem.

OECD research has found that implicit guarantees ultimately financed by taxpayers matter and they distort financial incentives. Making bank failure resolution more efficient and foreseeing the bail-in of bank creditors is a promising initiative, even if it might take time to see market expectations adapt to the new frameworks (see, for example, Schich and Toader, 2017).

Financial regulation has been improved, but has not been crisis-tested, and it remains to be seen to which extent it has made the financial system resilient to absorb shocks like those of 2007/2008. In this sense it may be too early to conclude that the regulatory reform process is finished.

1.4. Risks building in the Chinese banking system

A more immediate concern may be risks in the Chinese financial system, especially in the banking sector.

The Chinese banking system consists of:

- The big four commercial banks: the Bank of China (BOC); the Industrial and Commercial Bank of China (ICBC); the China Construction Bank (CCB), and the Agricultural Bank of China (ABOC).
- Three large policy banks: the China Development Bank (CDB) which focuses on funding infrastructure, housing policy and industrial SOEs; the Agricultural Development Bank of China (ADBC); and the China Export-Import Bank (ExIm Bank) for international trade. The CDB and the ExIm Bank are also heavily

involved in funding the vast Belt and Road Initiative (BRI) projects, which has picked up since 2013.

- A large number of smaller state-owned commercial banks.
- A small sector of joint stock banks.

Figure 1.9 shows the structure of banking in billions of US dollars in the top panel and as a share of GDP in the bottom.

Figure 1.9. Structure of Chinese banks, 2007-2017

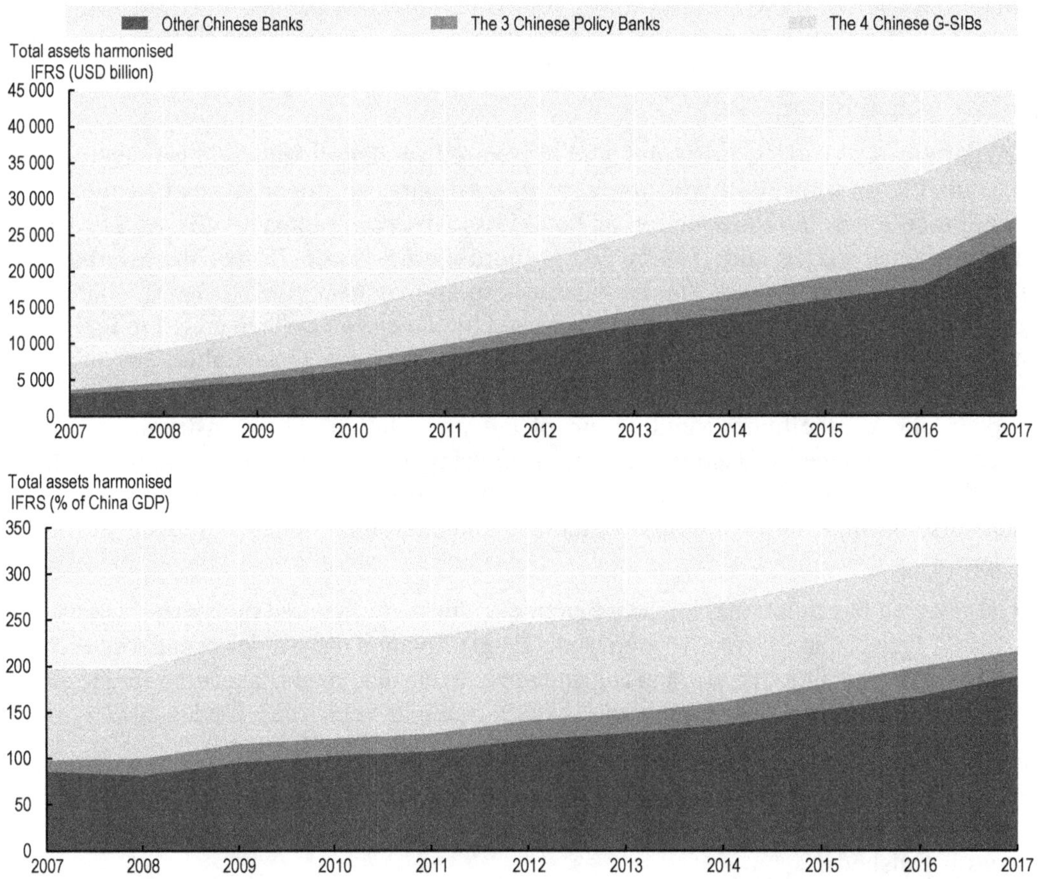

Note: China aggregate total banking assets are from China Banking Regulatory Commissions (CBRC) annual reports and released supervisory statistics. The three Chinese policy banks are the following: Export-Import Bank of China, Agricultural Development Bank of China and China Development Bank. The four Chinese G-SIBs are the following: Agricultural Bank of China, Bank of China, China Construction Bank and Industrial and Commercial Bank of China.

Source: China Banking Regulatory Commissions (CBRC), S&P Global Market Intelligence, OECD calculations.

StatLink http://dx.doi.org/10.1787/888933786230

In 2009, China expanded credit to state-owned firms to support investment spending in order to avoid the impact of the 2008 global crisis on the Chinese economy. This spending was supported in part by the big four banks, whose joint balance sheets expanded from 98% of GDP in 2007 to 109% by 2010. However, the bulk of the credit expansion came from the smaller state-owned banks that fund activity in regional planning zones. These banks expanded their balance sheets from around 82% in 2008 to 103% of GDP by 2010, an increase of some 21% of GDP. By 2017, the balance sheet assets of the Chinese banking system had reached USD 39.3 trillion, or around 310% of GDP. This does not include the off-balance sheet exposures of banks. Shadow banking (i.e. entrusted loans, trust company loans and un-discounted bank acceptances), plus wealth management products (WMPs), add another 63% of GDP in exposures. This is not all, since these numbers do not include the Dai Cha market – a parallel repo market for banks, brokerages and wealth managers.

Since interest rates in China are subject to guidance and are not fully market determined, there is a potential for a financial repression scenario. Financial repression refers to a policy framework that keeps the return on saving below the rate of inflation, reducing the real debt burden and allowing banks to lend cheaply to companies (McKinnon, 1973). In China, this is usually accompanied by a monetary policy based around window guidance, credit ceilings, and changes in reserve requirements as some of its main instruments.[33] After the expansion of 2009, China tried to rein in credit expansion at a time when financial demands on the economy were becoming greater and more complex. This has led to the boom in off-balance exposures in shadow banking and WMPs as shown in Figure 1.10.

At the end of 2017, bank balance sheets added to 310% of GDP and have increased only modestly since 2010. But off-balance sheet activity has taken the total to 387% of GDP. This comes about because there is a fundamental inconsistency between Chinese development, which is reaching a more diversified and complex stage, and the quantitatively-constrained banking system. Banks are able to bypass restraints with a variety of off-balance sheet mechanisms (an issue raised by Governor Zhou, see below).

Figure 1.10. Chinese bank assets, on- and off-balance sheet, 2008-2017

In per cent of GDP

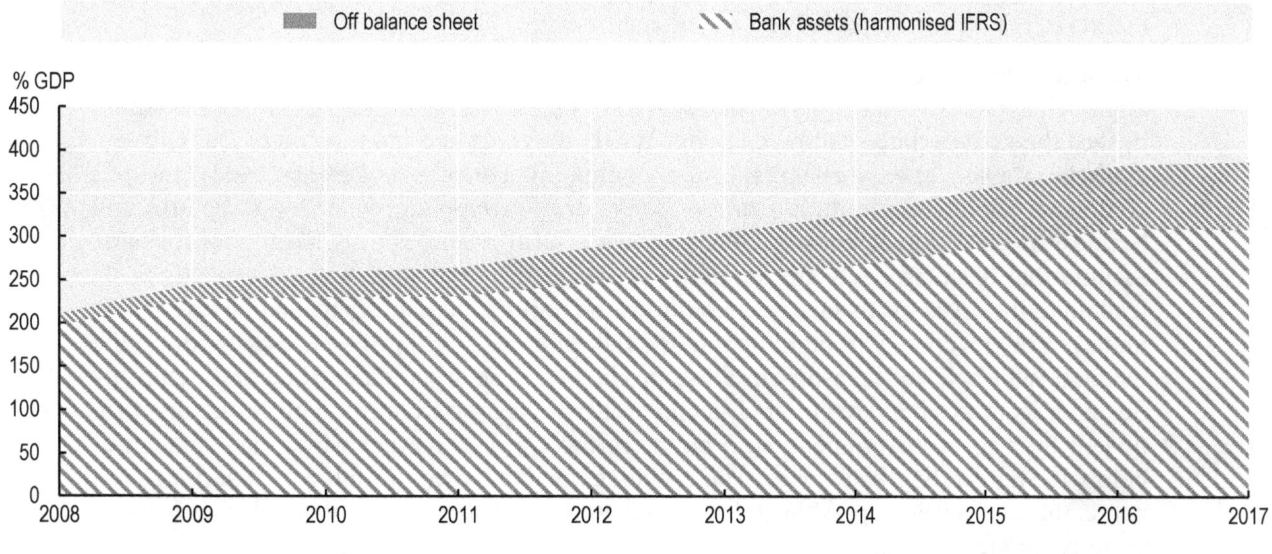

Note: Off-balance sheet includes notional amount of entrusted loans, trust loans, undiscounted bank acceptances and wealth management products.

Source: China Banking Regulatory Commissions (CBRC), Bloomberg Intelligence, OECD calculations.

StatLink http://dx.doi.org/10.1787/888933786249

Companies are able to lend to each other through three mechanisms that involve banks as intermediaries only, and to which reserve requirements and ceilings on interest rates and bank credit do not apply.

1. With bank acceptances, companies can issue a bill that instructs the bank to pay XYZ amount to company ABC, provides the money for the payment and the bank acts as a guarantor (the acceptance liability replacing the money paid to the third party). This remains off the balance sheet of the bank unless the bill is discounted.
2. The company can also lend XYZ amount to company ABC directly, with the bank again acting as intermediary only.
3. Banks also administer trust funds on behalf of individuals and entities and may lend funds.

In all cases, the off-balance sheet activity of banks is motivated by these lenders achieving higher returns than are available via controlled deposit rates.

The Chinese interbank market includes both bank and non-bank participants (such as wealth managers and brokerages) and is a pledged market. This has the benefit of avoiding re-hypothecation which is a key feature of advanced-economies repos – where the latter require the transfer of ownership of the securities sold. With a pledged market, the ownership does not change hands and the bonds cannot be lent or used in other transactions. But this demand for a 're-hypothecation mechanism' finds an outlet in the 'Dai Chi' market: a large informal repo market. Dai Chi is not based on legally-enforceable contracts – a bond is sold for cash, but not on an exchange, and there is an informal agreement to buy it back at a later date and at an agreed price. The risk is that if prices fall below the agreed price, the seller may walk away from the agreement because it is not legally enforceable. Nevertheless, some rough estimates suggest that Dai Chi could be as much as double the size of the formal interbank market (CNY 12 trillion in 2015; Kendall and Lees, 2017).

The interconnectedness of all of these markets does not sit well with a financial repression approach to policy, as attempts to control credit of banks via quantitative restrictions simply pushes the activity into shadow banking, WMP activities and interbank and Dai Chi repo markets. Banks, asset managers (often owned by banks), brokerages, and industrial companies all interact in these markets. There are overlapping ownership structures and, because of the involvement of SOE banks with WMP vehicles, it is likely that investors assume that these products are implicitly guaranteed by the state. Like the events in the lead up to the crisis in advanced economies, such implicit guarantees mean that risk will be underpriced, leverage will build up and the risk of a crisis will grow. The assumption that the state will bail out investors in these products has been validated time and again: the Sealand Securities bond default in December 2016 is a good example. This brokerage firm, owned by a local government, sold bonds in the Dai Chi market which had fallen well below the agreed buy-back price. The brokerage walked away from the deal and, to avoid panic, the supervisor stepped in and arranged anonymous repos, sharing the losses between various counterparties.

The size of the off-balance sheet activity in China is materially larger as a share of the economy than the securitisation that played such a large role in the 2008 financial crisis. China is using its macro-prudential assessment (MPA) framework to try to deal with these off-balance sheet processes – mainly through window guidance – but it is proving difficult to control.

Comparison of advanced-economy G-SIBs and Chinese G-SIBs

Figure 1.11. Total balance sheet of advanced-economy G-SIBs versus Chinese G-SIBs and policy banks, 2007-2017

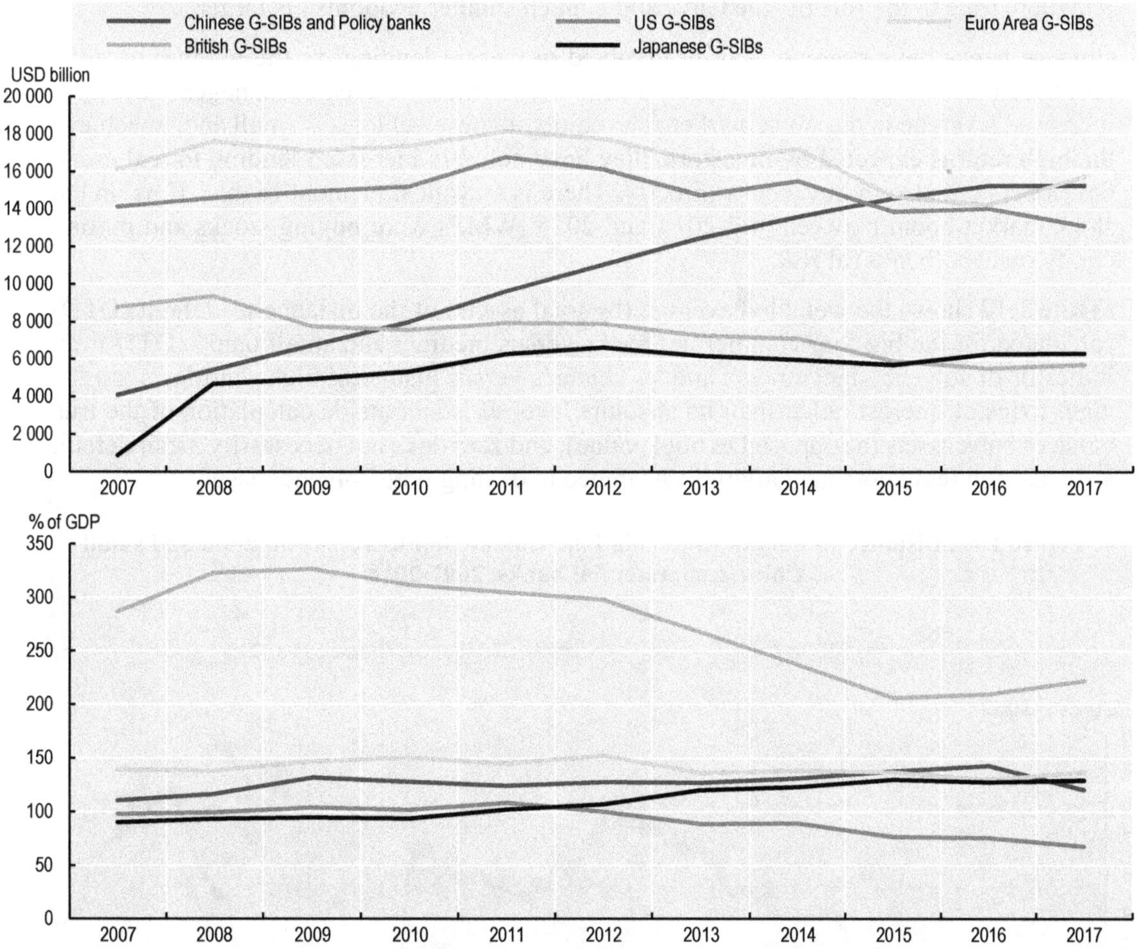

Note: The banks considered as G-SIBs are those listed in the "2017 list of global systemically important banks (G-SIBs)" released by the Bank for International Settlements (November, 2017). The three Chinese policy banks are: Export-Import Bank of China, Agricultural Development Bank of China and China Development Bank.
Source: China Banking Regulatory Commissions (CBRC), S&P Global Market Intelligence, OECD calculations.

StatLink http://dx.doi.org/10.1787/888933786268

Figure 1.11 compares G-SIB assets in advanced economies with those of the big four Chinese state-owned commercial banks, plus the three policy banks. The top panel shows the balance sheet assets of the United States, the United Kingdom, the euro area and Japan compared to those of the large Chinese banks, from just before the crisis to the present. UK G-SIB assets peaked in 2008 and have declined since then, both in dollar terms and as a share of GDP. The euro area G-SIB assets peaked around 2011 and have declined since the euro crisis. Over this same period, Japanese G-SIB assets have been rising moderately as a share of GDP. China, with a more quickly growing economy, has seen the absolute size of its large systemic bank assets grow very rapidly versus those of advanced economies.

In 2007, the seven Chinese banks had balance sheet assets of around USD 4.1 trillion and 110% of GDP. By 2017, this had risen to USD 15.3 trillion and 120% of GDP, larger in nominal terms than any other jurisdiction. Large Chinese bank assets constituted 189% of GDP in 2017, some 103% of GDP higher than in 2007 – with most of this gain occurring with the expansionary policy push in 2009. As a share of the economy, only the United Kingdom (due to the role of 'the City' and a much smaller economy) is larger.

Chinese banks have become heavily involved in margin lending, as the number of retail investors borrowing funds to invest in stocks has multiplied. Wealth managers have also increased leverage in the stock market. The equity in these vehicles is small and, to achieve the high returns expected by investors, they have not only increased lending to real estate developers but also to buy stocks directly. There is a cyclical element to this. Thus, in the stock market boom between mid-2014 and 2015, WMPs were buying stocks and putting equity owners (banks) at risk.

Figure 1.12 shows the weighted average (by total assets) of the distance-to-default (DTD) calculated for the big four commercial banks versus medium and small banks. DTD is an indicator of solvency movements and its changes versus historical highs and lows are the main focus of interest rather than its absolute level. It is an outside calculation of the true value of bank assets (as opposed to book value), and zero does not necessarily mean default as banks and regulators may allow forbearance in dealing with solvency issues.[34]

Figure 1.12. Distance-to-default of the big four Chinese banks versus medium and small Chinese commercial banks, 2007-2018

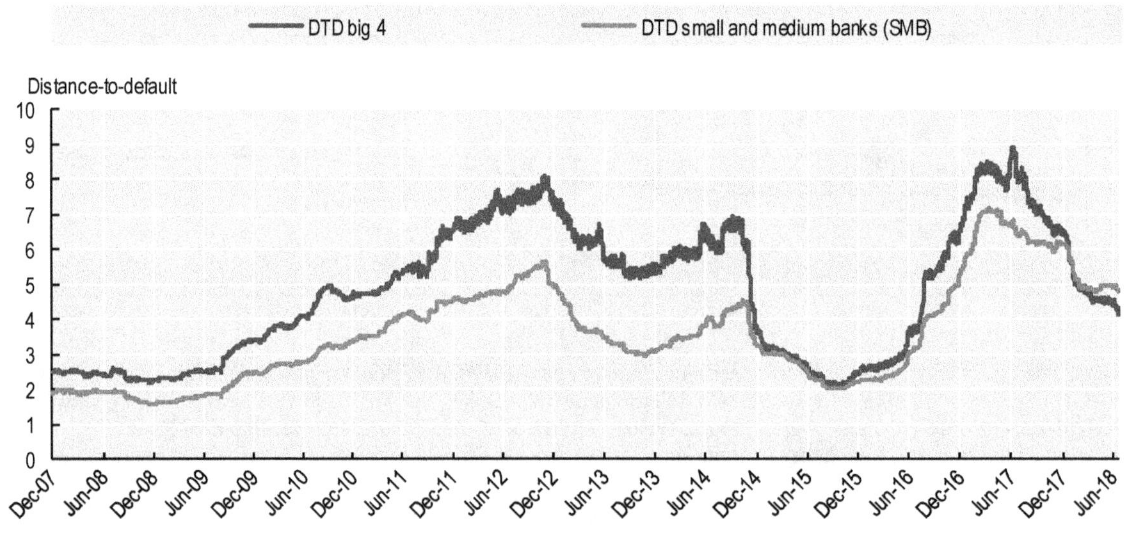

Note: This figure shows the weighted average DTD of 20 publicly traded Chinese banks. 17 banks are publicly traded in China and 4 banks are publicly traded in Hong-Kong, China only. The banks considered as G-SIBs are the ones listed in the "2017 list of global systemically important banks (G-SIBs)" released by the Bank for International Settlements (November, 2017). The four Chinese G-SIBs are the following: Agricultural Bank of China, Bank of China, China Construction Bank and Industrial and Commercial Bank of China.
Source: Thomson Reuters, OECD calculations.

StatLink http://dx.doi.org/10.1787/888933786287

The overall stock market peaked in May 2015, but bank DTD calculations began to fall from late 2014, anticipating the growing risk in the banking system.

As the economy slowed and the stock market crashed, authorities stepped in with a range of policy measures to limit trading and stop the collapse, possibly reflecting their concerns about possible systemic risk to banks:

- In mid-June, many company shares were suspended from trading.
- At end-June, interest rates in the interbank market were cut, and in August the yuan was devalued.
- In early July, big holders of stocks, including WMPs, were banned from selling shares, margin rules were relaxed, and IPOs were suspended.

By August 2015, the big four commercial banks were close to the DTD default point similar to their position in the 2008 financial crisis. The stock market intervention, devaluation and fiscal expansion measures to avoid adverse effects on the Chinese economy eventually turned the situation around. But, without these, the 2015 crisis might have required large recapitalisations from the state. In other words, the Chinese financial system, with its vast off-balance-sheet vehicles, is extremely risky. In 2017, the DTD has begun to decline again from high levels, and it is vulnerable to economic slowdowns and default accidents in the shadow banking and WMP sectors.

Chinese policy views and responses at the 19th Party Conference

It is very encouraging that then Governor Zhou Xiaochuan of the Peoples Bank of China (PBoC) spoke to many of the problems discussed above (see Zhou, 2017). He focused on the problems of structural imbalances in the real economy, excessive corporate debt, rising credit defaults in the bond market, inadequate corporate governance, lack of openness of the Chinese economy, and credit growth through innovative channels leading to the risk of financial bubbles and financial instability. In addition, he mentioned:

- Off-balance sheet financial activity was a contribution to the 2015 stock market volatility, and real estate price bubbles in some cities is related to excessive mortgage credit.
- Financial internet companies that are adopting strategies and products tantamount to Ponzi schemes (and without sufficient protection for consumers).
- Local government enthusiasm for growth is adding to financial leverage.
- Financial regulation is behind international standards, with a lack of clarity in responsibilities between different authorities.
- The financial system is not sufficiently market-oriented, and the lack of openness to the outside world leads to wasteful arbitrage profit trading and misallocation of resources.

This has been widely seen as heralding in important reforms many of which are already under way or implemented. While full implementation may take some time, some of the elements include:

- The China Banking Regulatory Commission (CBRC) and the China Insurance Regulatory Commission (CIRC), in order to better coordinate micro/institutional-level financial supervision functions, have been merged.

- Centralisation of macro-level financial regulatory functions in PBoC which will take a leading role in gauging systematic risks and financial regulatory reforms.
- To further strengthen China's Macro Prudential Assessment (MPA) framework to include more financial products, in order to crack down on shadow banking activities and to provide safeguards against systemic risks. These have been already used to control leverage and off-balance sheet activities in 2017.
- Reflecting President Xi'' desire to elevate risk prevention as a top priority, The State Council is to oversee financial stability and development, with a new Financial Stability and Development Committee playing a key role.[35]

In the longer run, Zhou suggests the need: to expand direct financing through better development of the capital markets (the more general need for which was suggested earlier in this chapter); to reduce intervention in the equity market; and to pursue capital account convertibility and the internationalisation of the yuan.

New Governor Yi Gang confirmed this orientation in a major speech in April 2018, announcing that China will encourage foreign investors to enter its trust, financial leasing, auto finance, money brokerage and consumer finance sectors. He also stressed that the opening-up should proceed apace with the reform in exchange rate formation mechanism, the advancement of capital account convertibility, and the reinforcement of financial regulation.

It would also be helpful to introduce greater transparency on China's NPL issues. There has been some concern in the private sector that banks may shift weaker assets to WMPs with which they are connected so that official balance sheet NPLs may be understated. Clarifying and dealing with these issues, should they be found to be present would help to reduce financial stability risks.

1.5. Conclusions

There are parallels between China and advanced economies with respect to the interconnectedness of banks, wealth managers, the equity market and leverage, which spells a high level of risk for markets and institutions in the period ahead – though via mechanisms that reflect quite different levels of economic development. In advanced economies, interconnectedness is high because of the huge role of derivatives beyond that needed for hedging that helps fund the real economy, and because the transfer of securities in repo transactions allows re-hypothecation. Complex structured notes have been issued to clients seeking to beat the low-return environment. The risk in markets for large financial institutions and/or for investors is high. As experience of the crisis fades in the collective memory, bank separation proposals have been shelved, and the finalisation of Basel III has not given the leverage ratio the prominent role it successfully plays in the US regulation. Non-performing loan levels in Europe remain high, and their extent in China is obscured by the lack of transparency about which assets are sitting in off-balance sheet vehicles.

Against an improving economic backdrop, the US Federal Reserve is reversing low interest rate policies and is beginning to reduce their extensive holdings of securities. At some point other central banks will follow. To get back to 2007 levels, the central banks of the United States, Japan, the euro area and the United Kingdom would need to shed some USD 10 trillion in assets. It may be decided to hold more assets than prior to the crisis in the longer run, but even so the task of normalisation is likely to be on-going for years to come (especially since some central banks have not started yet). This process will, however, force shifts in asset allocations that will be associated with greater security price volatility in the period ahead. While China is not directly linked to these risks in advanced economies, due to the closed nature of its financial system, any problems there could see authorities shedding holdings of US securities which would increase liquidity pressures in advanced economies. Problems in China, should they arise, could be caused by credit events in the vast off-balance sheet exposures that have increased leverage risk.

The imbalances in global fixed-income market liquidity are problematic. Asian banks have a large presence in the United States and Europe, but in their own, often regulation-bound shallow markets, they are not playing an equivalent role in providing market liquidity to advanced economy investors. Liquidity events, volatility and complex market interactions via derivatives-based structured products (involving increased shadow banking firms) in advanced economies, together with the sizeable use of off-balance sheet vehicles in Asia, may combine to make for a more testing time in the period ahead.

Notes

1 See Fawley and Neely (2013). It should be recalled that in the early phases the aims were to reduce market stress After Lehman Brothers failed there was a run against money market mutual funds (MMMFs) as the buck was broken (values fell below a $1 invested). The Asset-backed Commercial Paper Money Market Mutual Fund Liquidity Facility was launched, providing loans to depository institutions to buy high quality asset-backed commercial paper from MMMFs that needed cash to meet redemptions. Loans to SPVs followed and, on 25 November, the Term Asset-Backed Securities Loan Facility was launched: collateralised loans to eligible investors to buy asset-backed securities. In Europe, the ECB president made the early motivation clear: “the idea is to revive the market, which has been very heavily affected, and all that goes with this revival, including the spreads, the depth and the liquidity of the market. We are not at all embarking on quantitative easing” (www.ecb.europa.eu/press/pressconf/2009/html/is090507.en.html). Finally, the Bank of England states: “the Bank’s operations since 2009 under its Asset Purchase Facility, designed to improve the functioning of the commercial paper and corporate bond markets……. are sometimes characterised as the central bank acting as market-maker of last resort, but can be viewed essentially as just one of a gamut of actions a central bank may need to contemplate to address strains on the financial system” (Bank of England, 2012).

2 Note that other indicators are available. For example, the indicator-based measurement approach developed by the Basel Committee on Banking Supervision considers intra-financial system assets, intra-financial system liabilities, and securities outstanding at the firm level to assess the interconnectedness of banks.

3 CCPs concentrate interconnectedness of capital and liquidity. In the event of member defaults, matched books have to be re-established without suspension of activity which can be difficult in a panic event. The CCP operates as a waterfall: the defaulting member’s initial margin and default fund contributions are absorbed first, followed by CCP capital, and then non-defaulting member contributions. This is where the interconnectedness bites. Many actions are possible including tearing up contracts with defaulting members, auctioning contracts, forced loss allocation by the regulator, etc. There are extra-territoriality issues too, as jurisdictions have different views. In all cases co-operation between members and regulators will be essential.

4 This is perfectly consistent with the comment later in this chapter that equity risk premiums (ERPs) are not especially low. The cost of equity in a simplified model is $e/p+g=r+ERP$, where e is earnings (dividends), p is the level of the stock price, g is trend earnings growth and r is the risk free rate. When the risk free rate is very low the stock price may be very high, the cost of equity low, the ERP high and stock overvalued compared to normalised risk free interest rates.

[5] Under the expectations theory of the term structure, for example, the long rate is the sum of expected future short rates plus a risk premium and equilibrium in this sense needs to be maintained. From a trading point of view, if short rates were expected to rise due to inflation expectation increasing, then longer duration selling would lead to a 'bear steepening'.

[6] The 1994 bond market sell off was caused by complacency on the part of investors about the likelihood of a tightening scenario. While this is less likely in cash markets this time, due to a more careful focus on Fed communication, the composition of investment is very different. There has been a heavy substitution into lower grade and illiquid fixed income markets. This presents new forms of bond risk for the normalisation of rates.

[7] Because interest rates are very low in safe assets (cash and government bonds), fund managers and pension funds have moved into illiquid longer-term assets, including emerging market debt—as documented in previous Business and Finance Outlooks. These markets are easy to get into, but would require large price discounts in a bear market scenario. This has been a major concern at the Financial Stability Board (contingency plans for how to deal with a redemption scenario).

[8] Price-to-earnings (PE) ratios are proxied by using the IBES S&P 500 Composite 12-month forward for the United States, the IBES MSCI Europe 12-month forward for the euro area and the IBES FTSE UK 12-month forward for the United Kingdom.

[9] PE ratios can become higher than sustainable when interest rates are very low and earnings are in the process of returning to normal growth. See note 4. This point coincides with the value of market capitalisation rising versus GDP, the longer-run 'Buffet' valuation metric.

[10] The caps are not binding until maximum caps are reached.

[11] Specifically, it is the co-integrating equation estimated in Blundell-Wignall and Roulet (2014) using up-dated data until end-2017. This equation is found to be co-integrated with error correction tests. A risk premium shift crisis dummy variable is included from 2008.

[12] See Bernanke (2017), and the paper and views reference therein.

[13] See Gagnon et al. (2011), p. 3. The LSAP acronym is Large Scale Asset Purchases.

[14] See Gagnon et.al (2011) for a discussion of why and how QE was implemented, and Bernanke (2017) for a discussion of the case for a larger than historical balance sheet.

[15] A 10-year on-the-run Treasury with a coupon of 2.7% could expect to lose 9% of its value on the more moderate scenario and 13-14% of its value on the more bearish scenario. Mortgage securities and junk bonds could expect to lose more than this.

[16] See Wall Street Journal: www.wsj.com/articles/SB10001424052748704071704576276350338480020. Many other cases may be cited, including the case of Societe Generale for even larger amounts.

[17] Duffie (2016) makes this argument with respect to the US supplementary leverage ratio.

[18] Zhou (2017) refers to significant corporate leverage (above international benchmarks for 'problems' and defaults). He also presents the unusually strong view to open the capital account. His views are set out in section 1.4.

[19] The correction in the US stock market triggered an increase in volatility -- as measured, for example, by the Chicago Board Options Exchange (CBOE) Volatility Index, VIX. Algorithmic traders were able to switch positions to the short side very quickly, exacerbating the sell-off and the spike in the VIX. This hurt investors in exchange traded products that had been betting on low volatility of that index continuing. Investment banks, having spotted business opportunities, had created products to give investors better returns in the low-interest-rate environment. They were betting that the VIX would stay low because it had stayed low for such a long time. These structured notes allow the investor to buy the future at a discount to a future date (normal backwardation), and take advantage of the roll at maturity every month or quarter. But when volatility spiked (in what

was probably the largest 1-day spike in history of the VIX from 17 to 37, a 116% rise, on 5 February 2018), there was a rush to get out causing covering buy-trades and 'whipsaw' effects in futures.

[20] Societe Generale's top-rated analyst is reported (in early 2018) to be focusing on declining growth in operating cash flow in the United States as a negative signal for equity markets and earnings, see for example: www.marketwatch.com/story/why-a-slowdown-in-cash-flow-growth-is-bad-news-for-stocks-2018-01-22.

[21] Bernanke (2016) sets out quite neatly the obvious reason for all of the bond buying following the crisis in terms of the lender-of-last-resort function. In a liquidity crisis banks would have to dump assets at any price (fire sales), exacerbating their losses. There was a need to lend cash against assets such as treasuries and guaranteed mortgage bonds. Very clearly this has nothing to do with inflation and the usual channels for monetary policy. A debate has emerged about the extent to which this can or should be removed.

[22] OECD (2016) provides an excellent discussion of options to deal with NPLs and the circumstances when state aid rules might be adjusted due to 'serious economic disturbance' considerations.

[23] There are numerous examples of this in European bank submissions in the Basel III consultation process. Policy makers usually support their national champions without making it too explicit. But for Europe, Dombrovskis (2016) clearly stated the competitiveness objectives versus other regions, like the United States, as the main reason for objecting to output floors: "We want a solution that works for Europe and does not put our banks at a disadvantage compared to our global competitors."

[24] Blockchain and digital currencies are difficult to factor into a financial outlook for the year ahead. There may be surprises, but the effects are expected to occur of a longer run horizon. Banks are experimenting with the new technologies, including central banks. But the share of transactions via these channels is still very small. In next year's *Business and Finance Outlook* these issues for the longer run will be taken up in more detail.

[25] This is evident in bank submissions during the consultation processes undertaken in the Basel III process. See Bank for International Settlements (2009). The most common theme is support for risk weighting and criticism of simple leverage ratio definitions. In previous publications the OECD has drawn attention to letters to clients of major banks pointing to the ability to reduce risk weighted assets as targets linked to return on equity.

[26] For the finalised Basel III, the LR is Tier 1 Capital divided by an exposure measure. The final version of Basel III leaves the permitted ratio at 3% for non-G-SIB banks, and introduces a LR buffer for G-SIBs set at 50% of their risk-weighted Higher Loss Absorbing Requirement (HLAR). For the HLAR, G-SIBs are divided into 5 buckets (5 is worst, through to 1 the best). By 2019, banks must hold a base 4.5% CET-1 ratio versus RWA plus a capital conservation buffer (CCR) of 2.5%, for a total on average over the cycle of 7%. The HLAR for G-SIBs consists of: 3.5% additional CET-1 capital for the level-5-assessed G-SIB bucket, then 2.5%, 2.0%, 1.5% and 1% (for the level-1 bucket). The most risky G-SIB would have to hold only 10.5% of RWA as CET-1 capital. For the leverage ratio base of 3%, (the less demanding Tier 1 versus the exposure measure), this translates to 4.75% only for the riskiest G-SIB, and then 4.25%, 4%, 3.75% and 3.5% (for the level 1 'safest' G-SIB). Dividend distribution constraints apply to banks below any of these requirements.

[27] See Blundell-Wignall, Atkinson and Roulet (2012) and Haldane (2012). The 2017 update of this work shows that these results have remained stable for G-SIBs. This evidence is also consistent with the idea that G-SIB risk can be reduced by separating certain investment banking functions for those G-SIBS with high interconnectedness risk, as in Blundell-Wignall and Roulet (2013).

[28] Only a few European countries have implemented aspects of the initial Liikanen separation proposal, and the United States has reduced the impact of the 'swaps push-out' aspect of the Volcker Rule—only a limited number of swaps are subject to the rule (https://dealbook.nytimes.com/2013/05/23/banks-lobbyists-help-in-drafting-financial-bills/). The United Kingdom has introduced a ring-fencing policy (the so-called Vickers reform), see UK Government (2011) and is closest to early OECD proposals, which were referenced in the interim

consultation process. It aims to ring-fence the domestic retail business from international financial shocks and to limit taxpayer costs for losses given default and applies to all banks with more that GBP 25 billion of core retail deposits. The rules come into full effect in 2019.

[29] In the case of the EU/UK a statutory bail-in power applies to a broad range of liabilities subject to certain exclusions.

[30] The Bank of Portugal case, with respect to the resolution of Banco Espirito Santo into a bad bank and a new 'good bank' Novo Banco, is illustrative of how EU law works in practice. Specifically chosen international investor's bonds (not European) were bailed in from the new bank to the bad bank, causing them to collapse in value (because they were not backed by good assets). Litigation on a range of issues, including EU competition law, is currently under way. The summarised history of this saga can be found in: https://ftalphaville.ft.com/2018/01/19/2197893/the-novo-banco-debacle-and-the-rule-of-law-in-europe/.

[31] Which is only a little less than compared with Basel II regulatory relief from the IRB approach. This compares to the 2004 quantitative impact study for Basel II which showed a regulatory benefit for risk weights achieved by using the IRB approach (compared to the standard approach) of -21.9% for banks and financial firms; -61% for residential mortgages; -6.5% to -74.3% for retail; and -21.9% to -41.4% for corporates and commercial real estate (Blundell-Wignall and Atkinson, 2008).

[32] Deposits, derivative liabilities, debt with derivative links (like structured notes), tax liabilities, encumbered securities, and securities where bail-in can be legally challenged are all excluded.

[33] China, though it is experimenting with an interest rate corridor approach in the interbank market.

[34] The distance to default (DTD) is an important measure for monitoring banks because while the book value of liabilities can be observed the true value of bank assets cannot. In principle if the value of assets falls below liabilities the banks is in a default position, but only the reported book value of assets is reported not their saleable value. The formula to calculate the distance-to-default is derived from the option pricing model of Black and Scholes (1973) and is set out as follows:

$$\mathrm{DTD_t} = \frac{\log\left(\frac{V_t}{D_t}\right) + \left(r_f - \frac{\sigma_t^2}{2}\right).T}{\sigma_t\sqrt{T}}$$

Where: V_t is the Market value of bank's assets at time t; r_f , is the risk-free interest rate; D_t , is the book value of the debt at time t; σ_t, is the volatility of the bank's assets at time t; and T, is the maturity of the debt. However, the market-value of assets (Vt) and its volatility (σ_t) have to be estimated. Equity-holders have the residual claim on a firm's assets and have limited liability. Equity can be modelled as a call option on the underlying assets of the bank, with a strike price equal to the total book value of the bank's debt. Thus, option-pricing theory can be used to derive the market value and volatility of bank's underlying assets from equity's market value (VE) and volatility (σ_E), by solving some further equations (see Blundell-Wignall and Roulet, 2013). Obviously it follows that an actual default and the DTD at zero are not the same thing because banks and regulators may allow forbearance in dealing with solvency issues. Hence the DTD is an indicator of solvency issues and its changes versus highs and lows historically is of some interest for analysts monitoring banks without inside information.

[35] www.bloomberg.com/news/articles/2017-11-08/china-s-vice-premier-ma-kai-leads-financial-stability-committee.

References

Agarwal, V., P. Hanouna, R, Moussawi C. Stahel (2017), "Do ETFs Increase the Commonality in Liquidity of Underlying Stocks?", https://fisher.osu.edu/sites/default/files/etf_paper_osu_mar15.pdf.

Bank of England (2012), Review of the Bank of England's Provision of Emergency Liquidity Assistance in 2008-09, as presented to the Court of the Bank of England, October.

Bank for International Settlements (2009), Comments Received on the Consultative Documents "Strengthening the Resilience of the Banking Sector" and "International Framework for Liquidity Risk Measurement, Standards and Monitoring", www.bis.org/publ/bcbs165/cacomments.htm.

Bank for International Settlements (2017), "2017 list of global systemically important banks (G-SIBs)". www.fsb.org/2017/11/2017-list-of-global-systemically-important-banks-g-sibs/

Ben-David, I., F.A. Franzoni and R. Moussawi (2018), "Do ETFs Increase Volatility", Journal of Finance, forthcoming.

Ben-David, I., F.A. Franzoni and R. Moussawi (2017), "Exchange Traded Funds", Annual Review of Financial Economics, https://0.annualreviews.org/doi/pdf/10.1146/annurev-financial-110716-032538.

Bernanke, B. (2016), "Should the Fed Keep its Balance Sheet Large", Brookings Institution, Washington DC, September, www.brookings.edu/blog/ben-bernanke/2016/09/02/should-the-fed-keep-its-balance-sheet-large/.

Blundell-Wignall, A. and P. Atkinson (2010), "Thinking beyond Basel III: Necessary Solutions for Capital and Liquidity", *OECD Journal: Financial Market Trends*, vol. 2010/1, https://doi.org/10.1787/fmt-2010-5km7k9tpcjmn.

Blundell-Wignall, A. and Atkinson, P.E. (2008), "The Subprime Crisis: Causal Distortions and Regulatory Reform", in Lessons from the Financial Turmoil of 2007 and 2008, Kent and Bloxham (eds.), Reserve Bank of Australia. www.rba.gov.au/PublicationsAndResearch/Conferences/2008/Blundell-Wignall_Atkinson.pdf.

Blundell-Wignall, A. and C. Roulet (2014), "Problems in the international financial system", *OECD Journal: Financial Market Trends*, vol. 2014/1, https://doi.org/10.1787/fmt-2014-5jxzmkg91s0t

Blundell-Wignall, A. and C. Roulet (2013), "Business models of banks, leverage and the distance-to-default", *OECD Journal: Financial Market Trends*, vol. 2012/2, https://doi.org/10.1787/fmt-2012-5k4bxlxbd646.

Blundell-Wignall, A., P. Atkinson and C. Roulet (2014), "Bank business models and the separation issue", *OECD Journal: Financial Market Trends*, vol. 2013/2, https://doi.org/10.1787/fmt-2013-5jzb2rhk9b6j.

Blundell-Wignall, A., Atkinson, P.E. and Roulet, C., (2012), "The Business Models of Large Interconnected Banks and the Lessons of the Financial Crisis", National Institute Economic Review, No. 221.

Boissel, C. F. Derrien, E. Örs and D. Thesmar (2016), "Systemic risk in clearing houses: Evidence from the European repo market, European Systemic Risk Board, Working Paper No. 10, May.

Borkevec, M., I. Domowitz, V. Serbin and H. Yegerman (2010), "Liquidity and Price Discovery in Exchange-Traded Funds: One of Several Possible Lessons from the Flash Crash", The Journal of Index Investing, Fall, vol.1 issue 2.

CBO (2018), "Bi-partisan Budget Act of 2018", US Congressional Budget Office, www.cbo.gov/publication/53556.

CCP Research Foundation (2017), "Conduct Costs Project Report 2017", London. http://foreigners.textovirtual.com/ccp-research-conduct-costs/274/221515/conduct-costs-project-report-2017-updated.pdf.

Dodd-Frank, (2010), Wall Street Reform and Consumer Protection Act, www.govtrack.us/congress/bills/111/hr4173/text

Duffie, D. (2016), "Financial Regulatory reform after the Crisis: an Assessment", ECB Forum on Central Banking, 27-29 June 2016. www.darrellduffie.com/uploads/policy/DuffieSintraJune2016.pdf.

Dombrovskis, V.P. (2016), "Embracing Disruption", speech to the European Banking Federation, 29 September.

Federal Reserve (2017), "FOMC issues addendum to the Policy Normalization Principles and Plans", press release, 14 June, www.federalreserve.gov/newsevents/pressreleases/monetary20170614c.htm.

FSB (2018), Strengthening Governance Frameworks to Mitigate Misconduct Risk: A Toolkit for Firms and Supervisors, Financial Stability Board, www.fsb.org/2018/04/strengthening-governance-frameworks-to-mitigate-misconduct-risk-a-toolkit-for-firms-and-supervisors/.

Fawley, B.W. and C.J. Neely (2013), "Four Stories of Quantitative Easing", Federal Reserve Bank of St Louis Review, vol 95, issue 1, January/February.

Gagnon, J., M. Raskin, J. Remache, and B. Sack (2011), "Large Scale Asset Purchases by the Federal Reserve : Did They Work ?", FRBNY Review, May.

Haldane, A. (2012), "The Dog and the Frisbee", speech given at the Federal Reserve Bank of Kansas City's 36th economic policy symposium, "The Changing Policy Landscape", Jackson Hole, Wyoming.

Kendall, R. and J. Lees (2017), "The Chinese Interbank Repo Market", Reserve Bank of Australia Bulletin, June.

Liikanen, E. (2012), High-Level Expert Group on Reforming the Structure of the EU Banking Sector: Final Report; Brussels, October, http://ec.europa.eu/internal_market/bank/docs/high-level_expert_group/report_en.pdf.

Maltz, A.M., E. Schaumberg, R. Shiminov, and A. Strzodka (2014), "Convexity Event Risk in a Rising Interest Rate Environment", Federal Reserve Bank of New York, March, http://libertystreeteconomics.newyorkfed.org/2014/03/convexity-event-risks-in-a-rising-interest-rate-environment.html.

McKinnon, R. I. (1973), Money and Capital in Economic Development, Brookings Institution, Washington, DC.

Medcraft, G. (2015) "IOSCO and FSB's Work on Asset Management and Liquidity", speech delivered at Investment Company Institute Global Asia Pacific Chapter Meeting, (Sydney, Australia), November. http://download.asic.gov.au/media/3450488/speech-to-ici-global-4-november-2015.pdf.

Norwegian Ministry of Finance (2017), "Bonds in the Government Pension Fund Global", memorandum, 1 September 2011.

OECD (2018), *OECD Economic Outlook*, Volume 2018 Issue 1, OECD Publishing, Paris, https://doi.org/10.1787/eco_outlook-v2018-1-en.

OECD (2017), *OECD Business and Finance Outlook 2017*, OECD Publishing, Paris. https://doi.org/10.1787/9789264274891-en.

OECD (2017b), *Responsible Business Conduct for Institutional Investors*, Key considerations for due diligence under the OECD Guidelines for Multinational Enterprises, http://mneguidelines.oecd.org/rbc-financial-sector.htm.

Pan, K. and Y. Zeng (2017), "ETF arbitrage under liquidity mismatch", European Systemic Risk Board, Working Paper No. 59, December.

Schich, S. and O. Toader (2017), "To be or not to be a G-SIB: Does It Matter? Journal of Financial Management, Markets and Institutions, Vol. 5, No. 2, pp. 169-192, www.jfmi.mulino.it/doi/10.12831/88826.

SEC (2015), "Equity Market Volatility on August 24, 2015", Research Note, December, www.sec.gov/marketstructure/research/equity_market_volatility.pdf.

Treasury Review (2017), (Mnuchin, S.T. and C.S. Phillips), A Financial System that Creates Economic Opportunities: Banks and Credit Unions, Report to President Donald J. Trump, Executive Order 13772 on Core Principles for Regulating the United States Financial System, US Department of the Treasury.

UK Government (2011), Independent Commission on Banking: Final Report Recommendations, (Vickers Report), London, September, http://webarchive.nationalarchives.gov.uk/20131003105424/https:/hmt-sanctions.s3.amazonaws.com/icb%20final%20report/icb%2520final%2520report%5B1%5D.pdf.

Zhou, X. (2017), Report to the Nineteenth Party Conference, November, www.pbc.gov.cn/goutongjiaoliu/113456/113469/3410388/index.html.

Annex 1.A. Company data and sample description

Company data are based on the Bloomberg World Equity Index (BWEI). The sample includes all companies which have been listed in the BWEI over the period 2002-2017. 10 098 listed companies in 76 economies were selected (i.e. 6 506 in advanced economies and 4 592 in emerging economies according to IMF country group classifications) operating in 9 GICS industry sectors. Annual consolidated financial statements are collected on an annual basis, at the firm level and in current USD.[1] The current primary source of this information is Bloomberg and some data are extracted from Thomson Reuters. All variables are winsorised at the 1st and 99th percentile levels to reduce the effect of outliers. Annex Table 1.A.1 presents the number of companies by country and sector.

To examine the financial characteristics of firms that succeed, the following financial variables are considered and are defined as follows:

- **Capital expenditure:** Amount the company spent on purchases of tangible fixed assets. It may include intangible assets when not disclosed separately.
- **Operating cashflow:** Amount of cash generated or used by a company in a given period solely related to core operations. It is calculated as the sum of net income, non-cash expenses (usually depreciation expense) and the changes in working capital.
- **Return on equity (ROE):** Ratio of net income to common equity. Net income is the profit after all expenses have been deducted. It includes the effects of all one-time, non-recurring, and extraordinary gains, losses, or charges. Common equity is the amount that all common shareholders have invested in a company.
- **Cost of capital (COK):** Weighted average (by the share of equity and debt in total assets, respectively) cost of equity and cost of debt.

Note

[1] The items on the balance sheet represent stock variables, and elements from the income statement as well as the cash flow statements represent a flow. Bloomberg provides the option to collect the information in current USD values. Bloomberg, for example, reports items on the balance sheet using the exchange rate set on the date of publishing; income statements and statements of cash flow items are reported using the average exchange rate for the period. Thomson Reuters on the other hand uses the WMR Spot Rate set on the date of publishing for items on the balance sheet, income statement and statement of cash flows.

Annex Table 1.A.1. Distribution of companies by economy and sector

Distribution by economy			
Advanced economies	Number of companies	Emerging economies	Number of companies
Australia	457	Argentina	17
Austria	25	Bahrain	2
Belgium	38	Bosnia-Herzegovina	14
Canada	808	Brazil	144
Cyprus (1)	22	Bulgaria	25
Czech Republic	6	Chile	43
Denmark	43	China	1407
Estonia	4	Colombia	14
Finland	48	Croatia	51
France	205	Egypt	35
Germany	208	Gabon	1
Greece	79	Hungary	9
Hong Kong, China	129	India	971
Ireland	30	Indonesia	114
Israel (2)	46	Jordan	9
Italy	91	Kenya	3
Japan	1099	Korea	515
Latvia	7	Kuwait	20
Lithuania	9	Macedonia	4
Luxembourg	6	Malaysia	226
Malta	5	Mexico	55
Netherlands	58	Montenegro	1
New Zealand	18	Morocco	8
Norway	37	Oman	5
Portugal	19	Pakistan	21
Singapore	57	Peru	17
Slovakia	8	Philippines	29
Slovenia	13	Poland	190
Spain	65	Qatar	9
Sweden	149	Romania	138
Switzerland	81	Russia	120
Chinese Taipei	192	Saudi Arabia	53
United Kingdom	365	Senegal	1
United States	2079	Serbia	39
		South Africa	81
		Sudan	1
		Thailand	50
		Turkey	98
		Ukraine	21
		United Arab Emirates	15
		Venezuela	2
		Vietnam	14
TOTAL	6 506		4 592

Distribution by economy			
Advanced economies	Number of companies	Emerging economies	Number of companies
Distribution by sector			
Sector		Advanced economies	Emerging economies
Energy		607	220
Materials		838	870
Industrials		1 412	1 045
Consumer discretionary		1268	918
Consumer staples		402	447
Healthcare		653	308
Information technology		988	468
Telecommunication services		110	93
Utilities		228	223

1. Note by Turkey. The information in this document with reference to "Cyprus" relates to the southern part of the Island. There is no single authority representing both Turkish and Greek Cypriot people on the Island. Turkey recognises the Turkish Republic of Northern Cyprus (TRNC). Until a lasting and equitable solution is found within the context of the United Nations, Turkey shall preserve its position concerning the "Cyprus issue".

Note by all the European Union Member States of the OECD and the European Union. The Republic of Cyprus is recognised by all members of the United Nations with the exception of Turkey. The information in this document relates to the area under the effective control of the Government of the Republic of Cyprus.

Source: OECD compilation.

StatLink http://dx.doi.org/10.1787/888933786306

Annex 1.B. List of economies by group

Two groups of economies are defined considering the IMF country group classification: advanced economies and emerging and developing economies.

Advanced economies

Australia, Austria, Belgium, Canada, Cyprus, Czech Republic, Denmark, Estonia, Finland, France, Germany, Greece, Hong Kong (China), Iceland, Ireland, Israel, Italy, Japan, Korea, Latvia, Lithuania, Luxembourg, Macau, China, Malta, Netherlands, New Zealand, Norway, Portugal, Puerto Rico, San Marino, Singapore, Slovak Republic, Slovenia, Spain, Sweden, Switzerland, Chinese Taipei.

Emerging and developing economies

Afghanistan, Albania, Algeria, Angola, Antigua and Barbuda, Argentina, Armenia, Azerbaijan, Bahamas , Bahrain, Bangladesh, Barbados, Belarus, Belize, Benin, Bhutan, Plurinational State of Bolivia, Bosnia and Herzegovina, Botswana, Brazil, Brunei Darussalam, Bulgaria, Burkina Faso, Burundi, Cabo Verde, Cambodia, Cameroon, Central African Republic, Chad, Chile, People's Republic of China, Colombia, Comoros, Democratic Republic of the Congo, Republic of the Congo , Costa Rica, Côte d'Ivoire, Croatia, Djibouti, Dominica, Dominican Republic, Ecuador, Egypt, El Salvador, Equatorial Guinea, Eritrea, Ethiopia, Fiji, Gabon, Gambia, Georgia, Ghana, Grenada, Guatemala, Guinea, Guinea-Bissau, Guyana, Haiti, Honduras, Hungary, India, Indonesia, Islamic Republic of Iran, Iraq, Jamaica, Jordan, Kazakhstan, Kenya, Kiribati, Kosovo, Kuwait, Kyrgyzstan, Lao People's Democratic Republic, Lebanon, Lesotho, Liberia, Libya, Former Yugoslav Republic of Macedonia, Madagascar, Malawi, Malaysia, Maldives, Mali, Marshall Islands, Mauritania, Mauritius, Mexico, Federated States of Micronesia, Republic of Moldova, Mongolia, Montenegro, Morocco, Mozambique, Myanmar, Namibia, Nauru, Nepal, Nicaragua, Niger, Nigeria, Oman, Pakistan, Palau, Panama, Papua New Guinea, Paraguay, Peru, Philippines, Poland, Qatar, Romania, Russian Federation, Rwanda, Samoa, Sao Tome and Principe, Saudi Arabia, Senegal, Serbia, Seychelles, Sierra Leone, Solomon Islands, Somalia, South Africa, South Sudan, Sri Lanka, Saint Kitts and Nevis, Saint Lucia, Saint Vincent and the Grenadines, Sudan, Suriname, Swaziland, Syrian Arab Republic, Tajikistan, United Republic of Tanzania, Thailand, Timor-Leste, Togo, Tonga, Trinidad and Tobago, Tunisia, Turkey, Turkmenistan, Tuvalu, Uganda, Ukraine, United Arab Emirates, Uruguay, Uzbekistan, Vanuatu, Bolivarian Republic of Venezuela, Viet Nam, Yemen.

Chapter 2. The Belt and Road Initiative in the global trade, investment and finance landscape

The Belt and Road Initiative (BRI) development strategy aims to build connectivity and co-operation across six main economic corridors encompassing China and: Mongolia and Russia; Eurasian countries; Central and West Asia; Pakistan; other countries of the Indian sub-continent; and Indochina. Asia needs USD 26 trillion in infrastructure investment to 2030 (Asian Development Bank, 2017), and China can certainly help to provide some of this. Its investments, by building infrastructure, have positive impacts on countries involved. Mutual benefit is a feature of the BRI which will also help to develop markets for China's products in the long term and to alleviate industrial excess capacity in the short term. The BRI prioritises hardware (infrastructure) and funding first. This chapter explores and quantifies parts of the BRI strategy, the impact on other BRI-participating economies and some of the implications for OECD countries. China faces internal financial constraints (see Chapter 1), which means that other countries and multilateral institutions (such as the World Bank) will need to be involved to meet the huge funding requirements.

The statistical data for Israel are supplied by and under the responsibility of the relevant Israeli authorities. The use of such data by the OECD is without prejudice to the status of the Golan Heights, East Jerusalem and Israeli settlements in the West Bank under the terms of international law.

2.1. Introduction

The world has a large infrastructure gap constraining trade, openness and future prosperity. Multilateral development banks (MDBs) are working hard to help close this gap. Most recently China has commenced a major global effort to bolster this trend, a plan known as the Belt and Road Initiative (BRI). China and economies that have signed co-operation agreements with China on the BRI (henceforth BRI-participating economies[1]) have been rising as a share of the world economy. The BRI is overseen by the "Leading Group" for promoting its work hosted by the National Development and Reform Commission (NDRC) which oversees and coordinates all BRI projects (including inter alia with the Ministry of Commerce (MOFCOM), the Ministry of Foreign Affairs (MFA), and the Development Research Centre of the State Council (DRC)).[2]

BRI investment projects are estimated to add over USD 1 trillion of outward funding for foreign infrastructure over the 10-year period from 2017.[3] While new vehicles have been formed to help with the financing, such as the Silk Road Fund, most of the Chinese funding for these projects will actually come from state-directed development and commercial banks. China is also supporting a multilateral approach to investment including MDBs and private-public partnerships (see Xi, J., 2017a, page 5).

Because the Belt and Road is a Chinese initiative, it is important to give weight to how the authorities there state and characterise its objectives, as would be the case for policy statements for any country. Countries may or may not carry out and/or achieve all of their goals but, as a first step, it is important to document the stated aims and not to second-guess what these might be. This chapter adopts that approach using statements of the most senior policy makers in China. It then provides data on various aspects of the initiative and considers areas that may pose problems in the future with a view to help in the implementation of the BRI. How to deal with these latter issues is the subject taken up in Chapter 3.

The BRI is best summarised by President Xi: "*China will actively promote international co-operation through the Belt and Road Initiative. In doing so, we hope to achieve policy, infrastructure, trade, financial, and people-to-people connectivity and thus build a new platform for international co-operation to create new drivers of shared development*" (Xi, J., 2017b, page 61).

While the Belt and Road may also have some geopolitical goals associated in the linking of its neighbours economically more closely to China, this chapter focuses only on the economic aspects of the initiative. It discusses the BRI within the context of broader global infrastructure needs and China's longer-term economic strategy for itself and other participating economies, both those in the Asian region and beyond (Africa, Europe, Australasia and Latin America have all been mentioned). Considerations of ways in which OECD instruments and codes can best help China and BRI-participating economies to gain better integration within the world economy, and thereby benefit more from the BRI process, are taken up in Chapter 3.

President Xi emphasises "*policy, infrastructure, trade, financial, and people-to-people connectivity*". The latter involves education, cultural and scientific exchanges to help other countries learn from China's development experience and the President has launched the *Centre for International Knowledge on Development*[4] and *China's National Plan on Implementation of the 2030 Agenda for Sustainable Development* along with other related initiatives.[5]

Section 2.2 sets out the huge infrastructure requirements of the global economy and particular needs in Asia that the BRI is playing some role in alleviating. Section 2.3 presents the essence of the BRI as a global strategy from the viewpoint of how China explains what it is doing. The motivations for this important initiative, which cover both connectivity and more sustainable growth for China are set out in section 2.4. China's global infrastructure investment strategy, focusing on connectivity for the BRI, is discussed in section 2.5. Debt in China as a major policy issue was discussed in Chapter 1. While that chapter focused on bank and shadow bank debt at the macro level, Chapter 2 looks at the more micro issues linked to the BRI. One concern discussed in section 2.5 relates to the extent of investments in economies that are below-investment-grade or, in some cases, not rated at all. Debt associated with these economies could prove to be more problematic for lenders in the future, regardless of whether the loans are to Chinese companies or to foreign governments. Potential problems to watch out for on the debt funding of construction investment therefore are considered in section 2.6. Section 2.7 focuses on China's high- technology corporate investment, often acquired from abroad and used in its strategy to move up in the value-added chain while also supporting its role in development, both nationally (e.g. the Western provinces) and in BRI-participating economies. The amount and location of the sums invested and the issues that have arisen with troubled assets are presented. Debt issues from the viewpoint of developing borrower countries are taken up later in Chapter 3.[6] The BRI as a platform for expanding global trade is assessed in section 2.8. Concluding remarks are made in section 2.9.

2.2. Global infrastructure needs

Table 2.1. Comparison of estimates of global infrastructure investment needs

Source	Sectoral scope	Actual / expected annual investment (USD trillion) 1	Investment need (USD trillion)		
			Time frame	Total	Per annum
Bhattacharya et al. (2016)	Including power generation, transmission and distribution, primary energy supply, energy demand and efficiency, transport, water and sanitation and telecommunication	3.4 (2015)	2015 - 2030	75–86	5–6
NCE (2014)		-	2015 - 2030	96	6.4
OECD (2017a)		3.4–4.4 (2017)	2016 - 2030	95	6.3 (or 6.9 under a 2°C scenario)
GI Hub (2017)	Including roads, railways, airports, electricity generation, transmission and distribution, water and telecommunication	2.3 (2015) growing to 3.8 (2040)	2015 - 2040	94	2.9 (2015)–4.6 (2040)
McKinsey (2016)	Including transport (roads, railways, airports, and ports), water, power and telecommunication	2.5	2016 - 2030	49	3.3

1. The approaches to estimating actual investment needs and expected investment trends vary widely among studies. See also OECD (2017b).

StatLink http://dx.doi.org/10.1787/888933786515

Figure 2.1. Infrastructure investment needs in Asia by sector, 2017

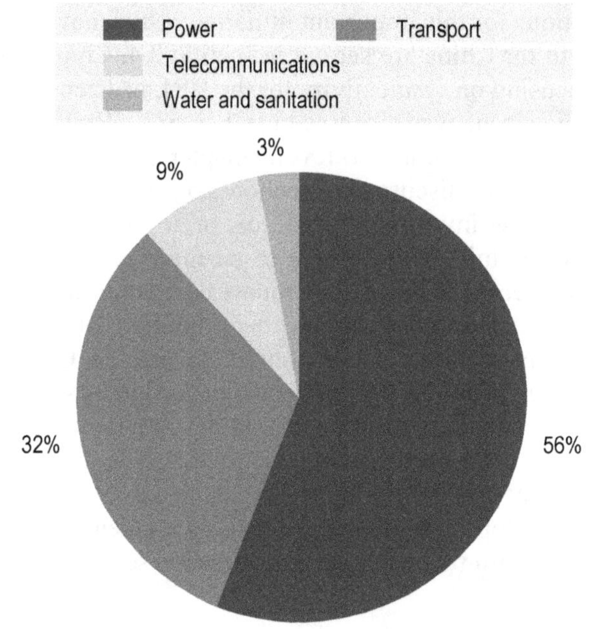

Source: ADB, 2017.

StatLink http://dx.doi.org/10.1787/888933786325

A stocktaking of global infrastructure needs reveals varying numbers and methods, yet all sources point to a growing global infrastructure investment deficit. Much of the global investment deficit covers key connectivity sectors important to the BRI, such as transportation, energy, water and telecommunications. Table 2.1 presents a selection of reviewed global estimates, covering different time frames as well as different sectoral scopes.

Based on these sources, annual investment needs range between USD 2.9 trillion and USD 6.3 trillion. At current investment trends, this is expected to translate into a cumulative investment gap of between USD 5.2 trillion until 2030 (McKinsey, 2016), or as high as USD 14.9 trillion until 2040 when the achievement of the sustainable development goals (SDGs) is taken into account (GI Hub, 2017). On an annual basis, this means that global infrastructure investments are, on average, falling short by USD 0.35 - 0.37 trillion per year (GI Hub, 2017 and McKinsey, 2016).

Globally, by sector, the largest investment needs lie in transport and energy infrastructure. In particular, road transport and energy supply infrastructure are expected to comprise around 60% of global investment needs (GI Hub, 2017; OECD, 2017a and McKinsey, 2016). They are followed by rail transport, telecommunications and water infrastructure. The highest rates of underinvestment are expected in the road and energy infrastructure sectors. GI Hub (2017), for instance, expects global investments in road infrastructure in the coming decades to fall short by almost USD 0.4 trillion annually, along with an annual investment deficit in energy infrastructure of around USD 0.15 trillion. Looking in particular at transport connectivity, around USD 0.44 trillion of expected annual investment needs will not be met (see Miyamoto, K. and Y. Wu, forthcoming, 2018).

For Asia alone, estimates by the Asian Development Bank (ADB, 2017) point to investment needs of around USD 26 trillion until 2030 (including climate-related needs). This is supported by GI Hub (2017) and McKinsey (2016) who see around 50% of their respective investment need estimates related to the Asian region.[7] Spending under the BRI strongly contributes to financing Asia's infrastructure needs. Nonetheless, a cumulative gap of about USD 4.6 trillion, or over four times USD 1 trillion estimated for BRI foreshadowed projects, is expected to emerge by 2040 (GI Hub, 2017). In particular, investments in sustainable and quality infrastructure in the region are needed to allow Asia to maintain its growth momentum, adequately address climate change and bring down high levels of persistent poverty.

The highest investment needs, in percent of GDP, within the region are seen in the Pacific (9.1%) as well as in South (8.8%) and Central Asia (7.8%) (ADB, 2017). This compares to around 5.7% in Southeast Asia and 5.2% of GDP in East Asian economies.[8] With current investment trends not expected to meet these needs, Asia's annual infrastructure investment gap will widen to USD 459 billion until 2020, equal to 2.4% of the region's projected GDP (ADB, 2017).[9] In particular, lower-income economies in South Asia are faced with higher gaps (on average 5.7% of projected GDP) compared to more developed nations in Southeast Asia (on average 4.1 % of GDP). Distinctively setting itself apart from most of its Asian neighbours, China's domestic infrastructure gap is estimated at only around 1.2 % of its projected GDP until 2020 (ADB, 2017).

On a sectoral level, around USD 14.7 trillion, or over half of Asia's infrastructure needs until 2030, lie in the energy and power sector, as 400 million people still lack access to electricity (Figure 2.1). Transport infrastructure needs rank second at USD 8 trillion, amounting to just under one-third of the investment needs in Asia's infrastructure landscape. These are followed by investment needs in telecommunications infrastructure of around USD 2.3 trillion, or 9% of the total. With 300 million Asians also lacking access to safe drinking water and about 1.5 billion people lacking access to basic sanitation, such investment needs are expected to account for 3%, or USD 800 billion, of Asia's total infrastructure needs until 2030.[10]

Asia's infrastructure financing needs widely exceed current and planned investments under the BRI. Addressing these needs will therefore remain an essential priority on the international development agenda. In particular, regions not lying within the current six BRI corridors will also require increased investment in infrastructure to support economic development and avoid the widening of geographical divides. There is some risk that investment in other critical sectors, such as water and sanitation, could be under addressed in these countries. It is also critical that investments in low-carbon, sustainable and high-quality infrastructure, which are a focus of the BRI, are given adequate support elsewhere, along with the maintenance, rehabilitation and upgrading of existing infrastructure. This is going to require the involvement of multiple investors, including China, other government groupings and multilateral development banks, an issue that is returned to at the end of this chapter. But there can be little doubt that the BRI is, by far, the most significant contribution to these needs.

Figure 2.2. Size comparison of selected regions and those identified in the BRI, 1980-2017

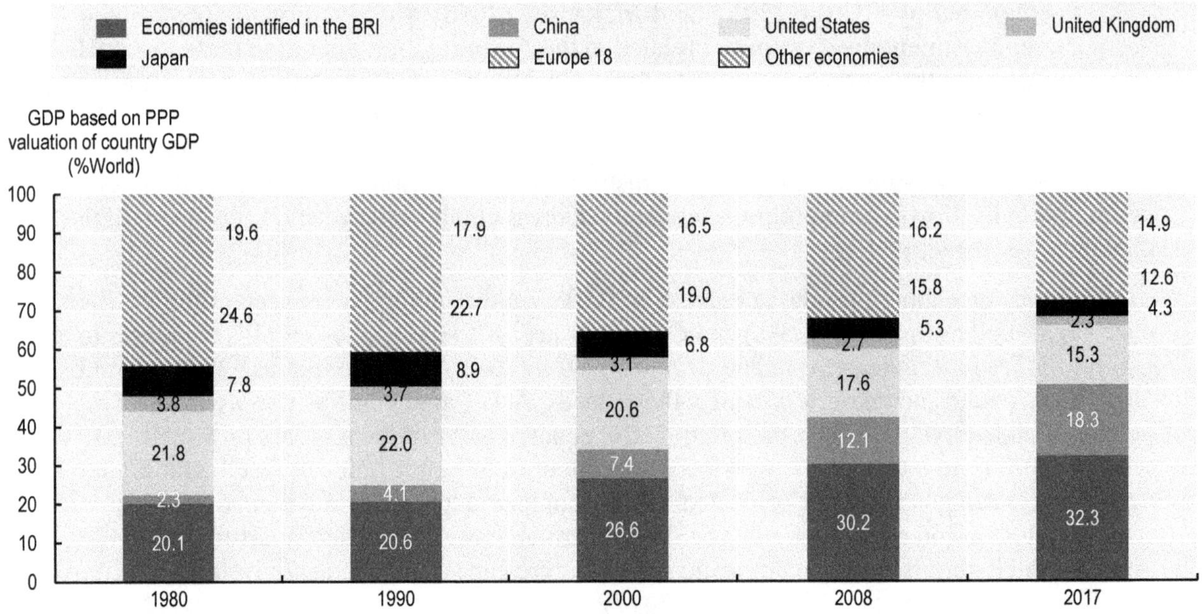

Notes: The "Europe 18" includes: Austria, Belgium, Cyprus, Denmark, Finland, France, Germany, Greece, Ireland, Italy, Luxembourg, Malta, Netherlands, Norway, Portugal, Spain, Sweden and Switzerland. "BRI-participating" includes 66 of the 72 BRI-participating economies. No data are available for Kenya, Morocco, Palestinian Authority or West Bank and Gaza Strip, Panama and Timor-Leste. See Box 2.1 for the full list of BRI-participating economies. "Other" includes 99 economies, namely: Algeria, Angola, Antigua and Barbuda, Argentina, Bahamas, Barbados, Belize, Benin, Plurinational State of Bolivia, Botswana, Brazil, Burkina Faso, Burundi, Cabo Verde, Cameroon, Central African Republic, Chad, People's Republic of China, Colombia, Comoros, Democratic Republic of the Congo, Republic of the Congo, Costa Rica, Côte d'Ivoire, Djibouti, Dominica, Dominican Republic, Ecuador, El Salvador, Equatorial Guinea, Eritrea, Fiji, Gabon, Gambia, Ghana, Grenada, Guatemala, Guinea, Guinea-Bissau, Guyana, Haiti, Honduras, Hong Kong (China), Jamaica, Kenya, Kiribati, Kosovo, Lesotho, Liberia, Libya, Macau, Madagascar, Malawi, Mali, Marshall Islands, Mauritania, Mauritius, Federated States of Micronesia, Morocco, Mozambique, Namibia, Nauru, Nicaragua, Niger, Nigeria, Palau, Panama, Papua New Guinea, Paraguay, Peru, Puerto Rico, Rwanda, Samoa, San Marino, Sao Tome and Principe, Senegal, Seychelles, Sierra Leone, Solomon Islands, South Sudan, Saint Kitts and Nevis, Saint Lucia, Saint Vincent and the Grenadines, Sudan, Suriname, Swaziland, Chinese Taipei, United Republic of Tanzania, Timor-Leste, Togo, Tonga, Trinidad and Tobago, Tunisia, Tuvalu, Uganda, Uruguay, Vanuatu, Bolivarian Republic of Venezuela, Zambia and Zimbabwe.

* Note by Turkey: The information in this document with reference to "Cyprus" relates to the southern part of the Island. There is no single authority representing both Turkish and Greek Cypriot people on the Island. Turkey recognises the Turkish Republic of Northern Cyprus (TRNC). Until a lasting and equitable solution is found within the context of the United Nations, Turkey shall preserve its position concerning the "Cyprus issue".

* Note by all the European Union Member States of the OECD and the European Union: The Republic of Cyprus is recognised by all members of the United Nations with the exception of Turkey. The information in this document relates to the area under the effective control of the Government of the Republic of Cyprus.

GDP = Gross Domestic Product. PPP = Purchasing Power Parity.

Source: IMF World Economic Outlook Database. 2017 estimates.

StatLink http://dx.doi.org/10.1787/888933786344

2.3. The Belt and Road Initiative as a strategy to promote and sustain growth

In March 2015, China issued an action plan which described the main objectives of the BRI (see Box 2.1 which states the broad objective and lists the economies included for the purposes of this study).[11] The BRI-participating economies represent more than one-third of global GDP, and over half of the world's population (Figure 2.2). While infrastructure investment is a key aspect of the BRI, China states that it is much broader in its objectives, encompassing all aspects of the sustainable growth for itself and including more balanced regional growth, the upgrading of its industry and greener economic growth at home. Problems of excess capacity in some products have led to the WTO and the OECD, amongst others, to highlight the issues to watch out for at a global level. China will need to ensure that the BRI does not simply shift excess capacity and less environmentally-friendly energy sources to other countries with little net gain from a global perspective. In this way the BRI could make a strong contribution to 2030 sustainable development goals.

Box 2.1. Which economies are related to the Belt and Road Initiative?

The Belt and Road Initiative is a large project aiming at improving regional co-operation through better connectivity among countries lying on the ancient Silk Road and beyond. It includes the Silk Road Economic Belt for the land part and the 21st Century Maritime Silk Road for the naval part. At the start, it involved 64 economies but its scope has since broadened over 100 in some form. Table 2.2 shows the list of economies that have co-operation agreements with China.

Table 2.2. List of the 72 BRI-participating economies included in this study

Region	Economy
East Asia	People's Republic of China, Mongolia
Southeast Asia	Brunei, Cambodia, Indonesia, Lao People's Democratic Republic, Malaysia, Myanmar, Philippines, Singapore, Thailand, Timor-Leste, Viet Nam
South Asia	Afghanistan, Bangladesh, Bhutan, India, Maldives, Nepal, Pakistan, Sri Lanka
Central Asia	Kazakhstan, Kyrgyzstan, Tajikistan, Turkmenistan, Uzbekistan
Middle East and North Africa	Bahrain, Egypt, Iran, Iraq, Israel, Jordan, Kuwait, Lebanon, Oman, Qatar, Saudi Arabia, Palestinian Authority, Syria, United Arab Emirates, Yemen
Europe and Central Asia	Albania, Armenia, Azerbaijan, Belarus, Bosnia and Herzegovina, Bulgaria, Croatia, Czech Republic, Estonia, Georgia, Hungary, Latvia, Lithuania, Former Yugoslav Republic of Macedonia, Moldova, Montenegro, Poland, Romania, Russian Federation, Serbia, Slovakia, Slovenia, Turkey, Ukraine
21st Century Maritime Silk Road	Ethiopia[1], Kenya[1], Morocco[1], New Zealand[1], Panama[1], Korea[1], South Africa[1]

1. Economies not listed in the 2015 Official Action Plan.
Economies are grouped based on the World Bank Group's classification by region.
Source: China International Trade Institute.

Specific objectives for the BRI: growth through connectivity

As stated by China, the focus on connectivity within the BRI is both about facilitating trade and investment, and thereby development of neighbouring countries, as well as strategically shoring up its own security of energy, resources and food by taking a regional leadership role with its most important neighbours.[12] It has a very broad scope encompassing economic, strategic and cultural connectivity. The objectives have been stated in the speeches referenced earlier; they are also set out clearly in Chapter 51 and other parts of the 13th Five-Year Plan (see People's Republic of China, 2016).

- To increase trade and investment in the BRI: *"We will improve the bilateral and multilateral co-operation mechanisms of the Belt and Road Initiative focusing on policy communication, infrastructure connectivity, trade facilitation, capital flow, and people-to-people exchanges."*
- Free trade zones along the Silk Road: *"We will speed up efforts to implement the free trade area strategy, gradually establishing a network of high-standard free trade areas. We will actively engage in negotiations with countries and regions along the routes of the Belt and Road Initiative on the building of free trade areas."*[13]
- To enhance financial co-operation in the region to fund infrastructure: *"We will strengthen co-operation with international organizations including international financial organizations and institutions, work actively to promote the development of the Asian Infrastructure Investment Bank and the New Development Bank, put the Silk Road Fund to effective use, and attract international capital for the creation of a financial co-operation platform that is open, pluralistic, and mutually beneficial."*
- To gain access to natural resources: *"We will strengthen international co-operation on energy and resources and production chains, and increase local processing and conversion."*
- To strengthen transport infrastructure in the BRI corridors: *"We will advance the development of multi-modal transportation that integrates expressways, railways, waterways, and airways, build international logistics thoroughfares, and strengthen infrastructure development along major routes and at major ports of entry. We will work to develop Xinjiang as the core region for the Silk Road Economic Belt and Fujian as the core region for the 21st Century Maritime Silk Road."*
- To deepen cultural exchanges in the region: *"We will conduct extensive international co-operation in the areas of education, science, technology, culture, sports, tourism, environmental protection, health care, and traditional Chinese medicine."*

The "high-standard free trade areas" noted above presumably refer to dealing with illicit activities in free trade zones. There are some 1 843 global free trade areas, with 802 in Asia. These zones are correlated with fake and pirated goods exports (see OECD, 2018). Eliminating this in the BRI would enhance the environment for cooperative outcomes in the global economy that are discussed in Chapter 3.

The six economic corridors of the BRI

Thinking about development in terms of economic corridors has been an important aspect of China's development model. Infrastructure investment along the Belt and Road is concerned with six economic corridors covering a large energy- and resource-rich part of the world:

1. *New Eurasia Land Bridge*: involving rail to Europe via Kazakhstan, Russia, Belarus, and Poland.
2. *China, Mongolia, Russia Economic Corridor*: including rail links and the steppe road—this will link with the land bridge.
3. *China, Central Asia, West Asia Economic Corridor*: linking to Kazakhstan, Kyrgyztan, Tajikistan, Uzbekistan, Turkmenistan, Iran, and Turkey.
4. *China Indochina Peninsula Economic Corridor*: Viet Nam, Thailand, Lao People's Democratic Republic, Cambodia, Myanmar, and Malaysia.
5. *China, Pakistan Economic Corridor*: Xinjiang Province will be most affected. This important project links Kashgar city (free economic zone) in landlocked Xinjiang with the Pakistan port of Gwadar, a deep water port used for commercial and military purposes.
6. *China, Bangladesh, India, Myanmar Economic Corridor*: This is likely to move more slowly due to mistrust over security issues between India and China.[14]

Figure 2.3. One (land) belt one (maritime) road

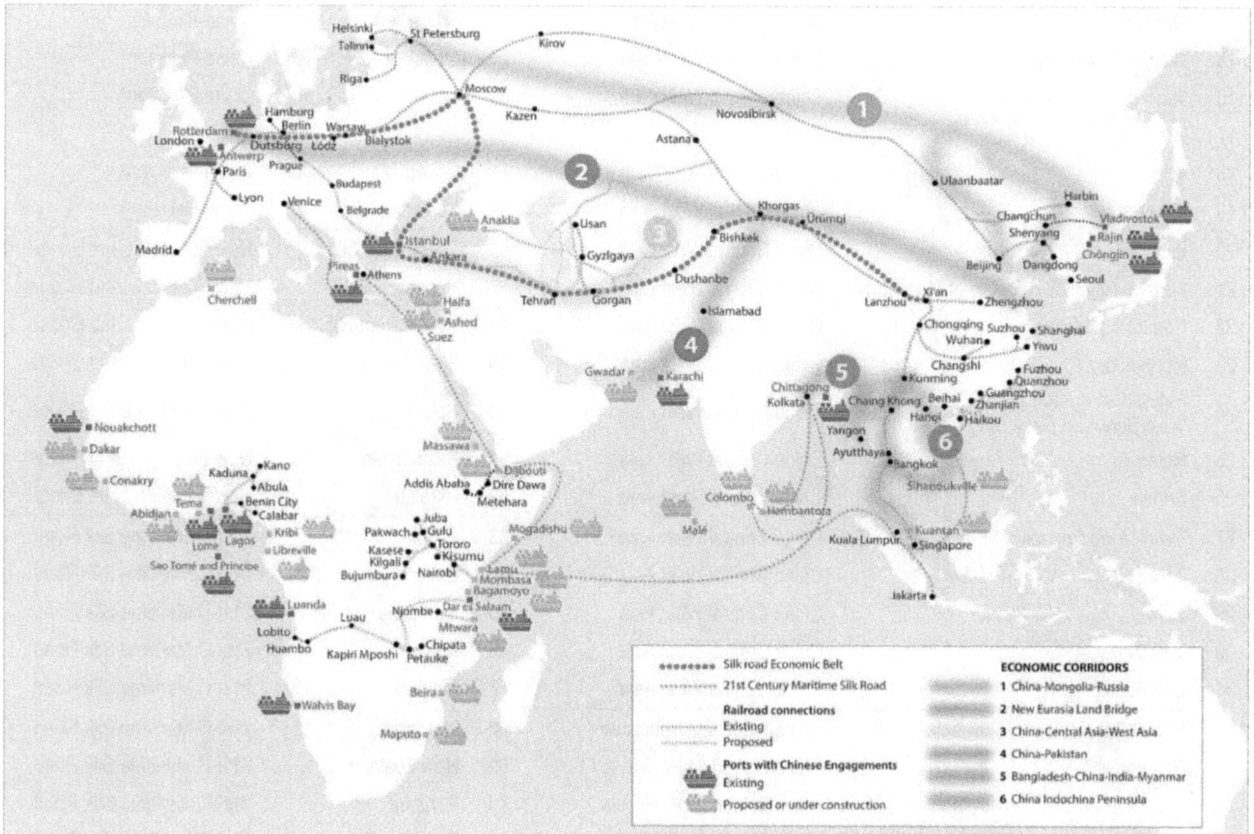

Source: OECD research from multiple sources, including: HKTDC, MERICS, Belt and Road Center, Foreign Policy, The Diplomat, Silk Routes, State Council Information Office of the People's Republic of China, WWF Hong Kong (China).

Linking up road and rail connections with global ports is essential for the functioning of the maritime road aspects of the BRI. Figure 2.3 shows the broad pattern of these connections.

Table 2.3. BRI-participating economies and economic corridors

	Economy	Economic Corridor		Economy	Economic Corridor
1	People's Republic of China	-	37	Singapore	China-Indochina Peninsula
2	Bangladesh	Bangladesh-China-India-Myanmar	38	Thailand	China-Indochina Peninsula
3	Bhutan	Bangladesh-China-India-Myanmar	39	Timor-Leste	China-Indochina Peninsula
4	India	Bangladesh-China-India-Myanmar	40	Viet Nam	China-Indochina Peninsula
5	Myanmar	Bangladesh-China-India-Myanmar	41	Belarus	China-Mongolia-Russian Federation
6	Nepal	Bangladesh-China-India-Myanmar	42	Estonia	China-Mongolia-Russian Federation
7	Sri Lanka	Bangladesh-China-India-Myanmar	43	Latvia	China-Mongolia-Russian Federation
8	Albania	China-Central West Asia	44	Lithuania	China-Mongolia-Russian Federation
9	Armenia	China-Central West Asia	45	Mongolia	China-Mongolia-Russian Federation
10	Azerbaijan	China-Central West Asia	46	Russian Federation	China-Mongolia-Russian Federation
11	Bosnia and Herzegovina	China-Central West Asia	47	Afghanistan	China-Pakistan
12	Bulgaria	China-Central West Asia	48	Pakistan	China-Pakistan
13	Croatia	China-Central West Asia	49	Bahrain	China-Pakistan[1]
14	Georgia	China-Central West Asia	50	Kuwait	China-Pakistan[1]
15	Islamic Republic of Iran	China-Central West Asia	51	Oman	China-Pakistan[1]
16	Iraq	China-Central West Asia	52	Qatar	China-Pakistan[1]
17	Israel	China-Central West Asia	53	Saudi Arabia	China-Pakistan[1]
18	Jordan	China-Central West Asia	54	United Arab Emirates	China-Pakistan[1]
19	Kyrgyzstan	China-Central West Asia	55	Yemen	China-Pakistan[1]
20	Lebanon	China-Central West Asia	56	Czech Republic	New Eurasian Land Bridge
21	Former Yugoslav Republic of Macedonia	China-Central West Asia	57	Hungary	New Eurasian Land Bridge
22	Republic of Moldova	China-Central West Asia	58	Slovak Republic	New Eurasian Land Bridge
23	Montenegro	China-Central West Asia	59	Slovenia	New Eurasian Land Bridge
24	Palestinian Authority or West Bank and Gaza Strip	China-Central West Asia	60	Poland	New Eurasian Land Bridge
25	Romania	China-Central West Asia	61	Kazakhstan	New Eurasian Land Bridge[1]
26	Serbia	China-Central West Asia	62	Ukraine	New Eurasian Land Bridge[1]
27	Syrian Arab Republic	China-Central West Asia	63	Egypt	21st-C Maritime Silk Road
28	Tajikistan	China-Central West Asia	64	Ethiopia	21st-C Maritime Silk Road
29	Turkey	China-Central West Asia	65	Indonesia	21st-C Maritime Silk Road
30	Turkmenistan	China-Central West Asia	66	Kenya	21st-C Maritime Silk Road
31	Uzbekistan	China-Central West Asia	67	Maldives	21st-C Maritime Silk Road
32	Brunei Darussalam	China-Indochina Peninsula	68	Morocco	21st-C Maritime Silk Road
33	Cambodia	China-Indochina Peninsula	69	New Zealand	21st-C Maritime Silk Road
34	Lao People's Democratic Republic	China-Indochina Peninsula	70	Panama	21st-C Maritime Silk Road
35	Malaysia	China-Indochina Peninsula	71	Korea	21st-C Maritime Silk Road
36	Philippines	China-Indochina Peninsula	72	South Africa	21st-C Maritime Silk Road

Note: This list contains the 65 economies listed in China's Official Action Plan for the BRI launched in March 2015 and seven economies that have been associated with the initiative more recently.

1. May also be counted as part of the China-Central West Asia Economic Corridor

Source: OECD research from multiple sources, including: HKTDC, MERICS, Belt and Road Center, Foreign Policy, The Diplomat, Silk Routes, State Council Information Office of the People's Republic of China, WWF Hong Kong (China).

2.4. Motivations for the Belt and Road Initiative

Connectivity

This is clear in the 13th Five Year Plan and has been emphasised by the highest ranking leaders and key ministries: "*We should deepen industrial co-operation so that industrial development plans of different countries will complement and reinforce each other.... create new models of investment and financing, encourage greater co-operation between government and private capital and build a diversified financing system and a multi-tiered capital market.... Infrastructure connectivity is the foundation of development through co-operation. We should promote land, maritime, air and cyberspace connectivity, concentrate our efforts on key passageways, cities and projects and connect networks of highways, railways and sea ports. The goal of building six major economic corridors under the Belt and Road Initiative has been set, and we should endeavour to meet it"* (Xi, J., 2017a).

How best to achieve these goals while levelling the playing field to maximise the benefits of global trade and investment is taken up fully in Chapter 3.

Openness

"*We should embrace the outside world with an open mind, uphold the multilateral trading regime, advance the building of free trade areas and promote liberalization and facilitation of trade and investment. Of course, we should also focus on resolving issues such as imbalances in development, difficulties in governance, digital divide and income disparity and make economic globalization open, inclusive, balanced and beneficial to all.*" (Xi, J., 2017a)

Innovation

"*We should pursue innovation-driven development and intensify co-operation in frontier areas such as digital economy, artificial intelligence, nanotechnology and quantum computing, and advance the development of big data, cloud computing and smart cities so as to turn them into a digital silk road of the 21st century."* (Xi, J., 2017a)

Sustainable development motivations

China is proposing a holistic implementation of the BRI, covering a number of broad aspects that will be important for achieving the 2030 sustainable development goals. Aspects of this much broader approach include:

- Peace: *"All countries should respect each other's sovereignty, dignity and territorial integrity, each other's development paths and social systems, and each other's core interests and major concerns."* (Xi, J., 2017a)
- Ecology and environment: *"We need to seize opportunities presented by the new round of change in energy mix and the revolution in energy technologies to develop global energy interconnection and achieve green and low-carbon development. We should improve trans-regional logistics network and promote connectivity of policies, rules and standards so as to provide institutional safeguards for enhancing connectivity"* (Xi, J., 2017a). This issue is taken up by the relevant ministry: *"China will improve green and low-carbon operation, management and maintenance of infrastructure by clarifying environmental protection requirements in infrastructure construction standards and enforcing environmental standards*

and practices in such sectors as green transportation, green building and green energy. ...and ..."China will jointly create eco-industrial parks with focus on enterprise agglomerations, eco-industrial chains and service platforms. Environmental protection facilities will be constructed, centralized sewage treatment and recycling and corresponding demonstration be promoted, and public service platforms on eco-environmental information, technology and business put in place in industrial parks" (Ministry of Ecology and Environment, 2017). Table 2.7 documents some of the clean energy projects China is investing in across the Belt and Road, though against this must be balanced reports that China is also building a large number of coal-fired power stations along with a number of other countries.[15]

- Water Conservation: *"The Chinese government proactively promotes policy coordination, technology sharing and engineering co-operation with neighbouring countries in the protection and development of cross-border rivers. It has launched joint studies with the countries concerned on the protection and use of water resources of cross-border rivers, in order to better protect these resources. China encourages the sharing of hydrological data during the flood season, and has established a Sino Russian mechanism for co-operation in flood prevention and control."* (Office of the Leading Group, 2017)
- Civil Society: *"We should establish a multi-tiered mechanism for cultural and people-to-people exchanges, build more co-operation platforms and open more co-operation channels. Educational co-operation should be boosted, more exchange students should be encouraged and the performance of cooperatively run schools should be enhanced. ... efforts should be made to establish think tank networks and partnerships...(and co-operation in) cultural, sports and health sectors... Historical and cultural heritage should be fully tapped to jointly develop tourist products and protect heritage .... We should strengthen exchanges between parliaments, political parties and non-governmental organizations... women, youths and people with disabilities... We should also strengthen international counter-corruption co-operation so that the Belt and Road will be a road with high ethical standards."* (Xi, J., 2017a)

Energy and food security motivations

The 13th Five Year Plan also focuses on food and energy security, expressed most clearly in chapters other than that dedicated to the Belt and Road. Thus, in Chapter 30: "*We will build a modern energy system that is clean, low-carbon, safe, and efficient, and will safeguard the country's energy security*"... and ..."*We will accelerate the construction of strategic land corridors for importing oil and gas. We will make progress in building oil and gas storage facilities and strengthen capacity for oil and gas storage and peak shaving.*" Some more details on China's energy strategy are presented further below. With respect to food security in Chapter 18: *"We will actively pursue agricultural co-operation and development overseas, establish large-scale offshore centres for farm product production, processing, storage, and transportation, and cultivate internationally competitive multinational agricultural companies"*. These motivations for food and energy security and regional development in the BRI intersect with each other and it will be important to ensure they are mutually beneficial.

More balanced regional development

The western provinces of China, including the Xinjiang Uygur autonomous region of Xinjiang, and Gansu, Tibet, and Qinghai are very poor and a source of tensions with various ethnic groups. One aim of the BRI is to promote growth in China's west and the north-eastern provinces in order to reduce economic inequality. In President Xi's speech to the opening of the 19th Party Congress, he stresses: *"We will devote more energy to speeding up the development of old revolutionary base areas, areas with large ethnic minority populations, border areas, and poor areas. We will strengthen measures to reach a new stage in the large-scale development of the western region; deepen reform to accelerate the revitalization of old industrial bases in the northeast and other parts of the country; help the central region rise by tapping into local strengths; and support the eastern region in taking the lead in pursuing optimal development through innovation...We will create networks of cities and towns based on city clusters, enabling the coordinated development of cities of different sizes and small towns, and speed up work on granting permanent urban residency to people who move from rural to urban areas."* (Xi, J., 2017b, pages 28 and 29)

Figure 2.4. ROE minus COK: Private non-financial companies versus SOEs, 2002-2017

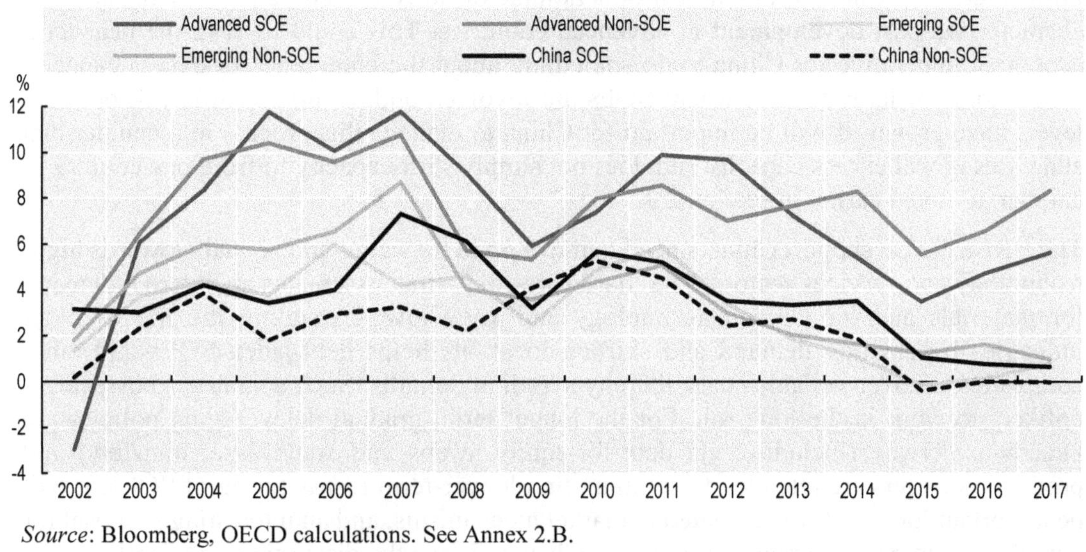

Source: Bloomberg, OECD calculations. See Annex 2.B.

StatLink http://dx.doi.org/10.1787/888933786363

Improving efficiency

Reforms have supported an impressive growth in China over several decades. China's unfinished transition to introduce and consolidate market mechanisms and institutions, has been associated in the past with problems of capital misallocation in some industries, as shown by the downward pressure on the return on equity (ROE) versus the cost of capital (COK) across a range of firms and industries. Dealing with past poorly-oriented investments and encouraging less-competitive firm exits is a part of this process, including where state support has maintained inefficient state firms (particularly those which depend on borrowing to survive, a point also noted by the IMF).[16] This transition process is normal for emerging economies looking to improve efficiency. In Figure 2.4, the ROE minus the COK has fallen for emerging economies, including China. This trend appears to have accelerated both in 2015 and has not yet reversed in 2016 and 2017.[17]

In his speech to the 19th Party Congress, President Xi puts these issues at the centre of China's development strategy: "*We should pursue supply-side structural reform as our main task, and work hard for better quality, higher efficiency, and more robust drivers of economic growth through reform. We need to raise total factor productivity and accelerate the building of an industrial system that promotes coordinated development of the real economy with technological innovation, modern finance, and human resources. We should endeavour to develop an economy with more effective market mechanisms, dynamic micro-entities, and sound macro-regulation. This will steadily strengthen the innovation capacity and competitiveness of China's economy.*" (Xi, J., 2017b, page 26)

Firm exits from industries and/or bankruptcies are the intended consequences of competitive processes when more efficient firms outperform the less efficient. When this competitive process does not function well, more efficient firms can be driven out of the market over time. These issues are difficult to deal with in countries where SOEs play an important role, since the role of market discipline can be reduced in these circumstances—an issue which is taken up in detail in Chapter 3. A part of the transition process for dealing with these issues for China and its neighbours is implementing the BRI. The BRI aims to create new markets, facilitate trade as well as investment, including with a shift of production capacity to where there is ready demand (arising, for example, from new infrastructure investment) or where production factors are cheaper—a process that has also characterised past development in advanced countries. This could fit with the near-term economic imperative for China to do something about the emergence of excess capacity across some of its industries where SOEs are involved and, as noted earlier, where debt levels have grown. It will be important for China to manage this process in a manner that addresses global excess capacity and does not simply shift capacity to from one country to another, as noted earlier in section 2.3.

The BRI will also support China's need to move up in the value-added chain towards high-technology and services sectors. The 'hardware-first' strategy creates an external demand for materials and for China's technology and knowhow. Extending the life of older industries by creating demand and shifting locations helps debt-laden SOEs and other companies to cover variable costs, thereby avoiding defaults. Such a strategy, however, is unlikely to work in the long run. For the longer term, gradual deleveraging policies are already underway (including via debt-for-equity swaps and some asset transfers) and production targets are intended to set in motion longer-term restructuring of SOEs. It will be important for targets to be related to market mechanisms, and an interesting proposal for how this could be encouraged is set out in Chapter 3 (see the discussion on "Santiago-like principles" in section 3.2). At the same time, the BRI lays longer-run economic foundations for economic growth based on connectivity and trade in the region (see Xi, J., 2017b and Johnson, 2016). All countries can benefit from this process if it is carried through with the openness and inclusiveness principles espoused by President Xi.

China is a large economy which is itself in transition. Speeding up its development with level playing field considerations in mind while also remaining consistent with the motivations stated above would be beneficial to trade, global growth and prosperity within the region. These objectives for broad sustainable growth sit very well with those of the OECD, with whom China could benefit with even greater engagement to help speed the transition process. This issue is taken up in Chapter 3.

Figure 2.5. Chinese outward investment in the construction sector, cumulative notional amount expressed in USD million, 2005-2018

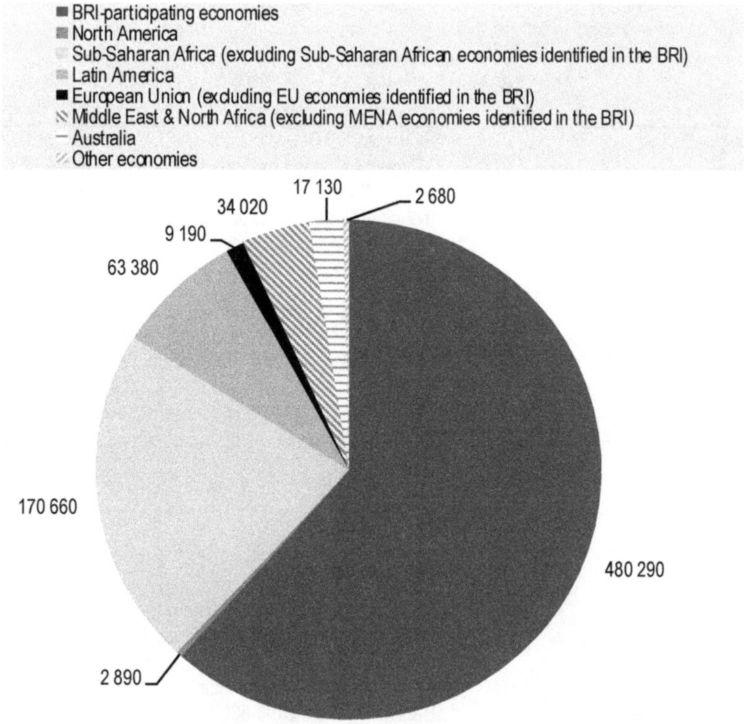

Note: 2018 data are to end-June.

Source: American Enterprise Institute (AEI), China Global Investment Tracker Database. It includes all investments of USD 100 million or greater. Ministry of Commerce, Republic of China (MoFCOM) data totals are around 10% higher for the same period due to the inclusion of small investments.

StatLink http://dx.doi.org/10.1787/888933786382

2.5. Size of investment for construction in the Belt and Road Initiative

Figure 2.5 shows China's global construction projects (mainly infrastructure) in millions of dollars from 2005 to 2017. The cumulative total is USD 480.3 billion for the BRI-participating economies, some 59% of the global total of USD 814.3 billion. The next most popular destination for Chinese construction is sub-Saharan Africa (USD 170.7 billion), then Latin America (USD 63.4 billion) and the Middle East and North Africa (MENA) countries not in the BRI at USD 34.0 billion. Chinese construction projects are smaller in OECD countries, with Australia being the most significant at around USD 17.1 billion (six times that of the United States and Canada together).

Relocation of low-technology industries abroad

Following general global patterns to shift low-technology abroad, the iron, steel and cement industries are being moved to provinces in the west of China and to the BRI-participating economies. The Premier of China, Li Keqiang, explicitly highlighted this objective in his remarks to the 17th ASEAN conference: *"After years of development, China now has a strong capacity in infrastructure development and Chinese equipment is of high quality. We encourage competitive Chinese producers of iron and steel, cement and plate glass, etc. to shift their operation to ASEAN countries to meet the local need of infrastructure development through investment, leasing and loan lending so as to achieve mutual benefit"* (Li Keqiang, 2014).

Table 2.4. Belt and Road Initiative financing

Institution (excluding Ministry of Finance and Ministry Commerce Aid, etc.)	Features	Estimated exposure (USD°billion)	Project examples
China Development Bank (notably the world's largest development finance institution)	Non-concessional loans and credit lines Concessionary loans Overseas investment support Can be tied to exports in most cases Imposes limits to sovereign borrowers (such as the IMF) Controls concentration of loans Government capital injections and access to PBoC pledged Supplementary lending programme keeps funding very cheap	110	By the end of December 2015, CDB had supported 400-plus projects in 37 countries along the Belt and Road Initiative, with banks totalling USD 110 billion. The projects covered energy resource co-operation, technical facility construction and other fields. These include foreign governments, foreign companies and Chinese corporations. An example is the 40-year concessionary loan to Indonesia, with no guarantee, for 75% of the USD 5.29 billion Jakarta Bandung high-speed railway. There is a 10-year grace period. 60% is denominated in US dollars at a low 2% interest rate. 40% is denominated in Renminbi at a 3.4% interest rate. The concessions that allowed it to win were mainly the absence of guarantees by Indonesia and local content agreements.
China Exim Bank	Preferential export credits (tied to exports) Export buyer's credit (tied to exports) Export seller's credit (tied to exports) Concessional loans (at least 50% are tied to exports) Non-concession loans and credit lines (can be tied) Overseas investment support (can be tied) Debt ceillings for each country Government capital injections and access to the PBoC pledged Supplementary lending programme keeps funding very cheap	80	By the end of 2015, EXIM Bank had supported 1000-plus projects in 49 countries along the Belt and Road Initiative, with loan balances exceeding CNY 520 billion (i.e. USD 80 billion). The projects include roads, railways, electricity, ports, communications and other fields. For example, EXIM Bank provided a USD 800 million low-interest rate loan to Malaysia to build the 22.5 kilometre second Penang bridge, the longest cross-sea bridge in Southeast Asia. Contribution to the USD 7 billion Lao People's Democratic Republic railway (5% GDP), provided at a low 3% interest rate. Exim Bank lends to foreign governments, foreign companies and Chinese corporations.
Agricultural Development Bank of China	Overseas investment support (can be tied to exports)		Supporting Silk Road Fund and for Chinese companies.
Industrial and Commercial Bank of China	Non-concessionary loans	159	212 BRI-related projects to a total of USD°67.4 billion to date. Potential projects expected to bring this to USD°159 billion.
Bank of China	Non-concessionary loans	100	Expected to have BRI-related project loans totalling USD°100 billion by the end of 2017.
Silk Road Fund	All BRI-related projects (ultimate full capitalisation shown)	40	The Silk Road Fund mainly invests in infrastructure projects in the energy sector. Their ongoing projects include the Karot Hydropower Project on the Jhelum River of Pakistan, the UAE Egypt Power Plant Project co-invested and developed by Chinese investors including the China Gezhouba (Group) Corporation. The Pakistan Karot Hydropower Project signed in April 2015 is a prioritised energy project in the "China-Pakistan Economic Corridor". It will be developed by the South Asia Company

Institution (excluding Ministry of Finance and Ministry Commerce Aid, etc.)	Features	Estimated exposure (USD billion)	Project examples
			under the China Three Gorges Corporation and financed by the Silk Road Fund. The syndicate formed by the Silk Road Fund, the Export-Import Bank of China, the Chinese Development Bank and the International Finance Corporation has provided a USD 200 million loan to the project.
China Construction Bank	Contributing to BRI related projects	10	MofCom states that it has provided USD 10 billion.
New Development Bank (NDB)	To play a larger role in BRI projects	1.261	NDB provides loans to its member countries in the infrastructure sector. It announced the first batch of loan projects in April 2016, providing total loans of USD 811 million to renewable energy projects in Brazil, China, South Africa and India to support the member countries' 2370 Mega Watt generating capacity of renewable energy. In July 2016, NDB resolved to provide USD 100 million in loans to small-scale energy projects in Karelia, Russia. In November 2016, NDB approved a USD 350 million loan in regions along the Belt and Road Initiative area.
China Export and Credit Insurance Corporation		570.56	By December 2015, SINOSURE had underwritten USD 570.56 billion for China's export, investment and contracting projects in the countries along the Belt and Road Initiative area, with USD 1.855 billion paid out as indemnities. In July 2015, SINOSURE signed a co-operation agreement on the Belt and Road Initiative with the Industrial and Commercial Bank of China, focusing on supporting projects in regions along the Belt and Road Initiative area.
Asia Infrastructure Investment Bank (AIIB)	Not BRI-related projects (China 36% voting)	2.33	By December 2016, AIIB had approved nine infrastructure projects involving a total investment of USD 1.73 billion. The nine projects are all located in the countries along the Belt and Road Initiative area, namely Tajikistan, Bangladesh, Pakistan, Indonesia, Myanmar, Oman and Azerbaijan. The projects mainly focus on energy, transportation and slum upgrading. The latest approved project is the Trans-Anatolian Natural Gas Pipeline Project (TANAP) in Azerbaijan, which as part of the Southern Gas Corridor of the European Union, will transport natural gas in the Caspian Sea to Europe via Turkey. The project requires a total investment of USD 8.6 billion, of which AIIB is contributing USD 600 million, the World Bank USD 800 million, and the remaining will be provided by other international financial institutions and commercial loans.

Note: It is difficult to dig deeper in the Chinese data to ascertain how much of the loans are to Chinese companies and how much are to foreign obligers.
Source: Chinese Academy, et al., (2017); Reuters (2017); US-China ESRC (2017); Silk Road Fund, www.silkroadfund.com.cn/enweb/23775/23767/index.html; and MOFCOM, http://caiec.mofcom.gov.cn/article/g/201709/20170902639797.shtml.

StatLink http://dx.doi.org/10.1787/888933786534

This has some benefit for China of reducing air pollution in Beijing to the extent that these industries move further away—though what it does for the global situation will depend on the policies that accompany this restructuring process to other locations. China's new environmental "polluter pays" regulations have reduced profits in cement industries within China, giving them a market incentive to move out along the Silk Road (see Kley, 2016; Chun, 2015). Once more, however, it should be underlined that it is the global "adding up" that matters for capacity utilisation and environmental issues as opposed to outcomes in any specific country.

The policy to move old iron and steel capacity out along the Belt and Road is associated with China (within the metals industry) moving up into cleaner, higher-tech, steel products and metal trading. According to the Global Times (2014), Hebei Province is moving capacity for 5.2 million tons of steel, 5 million tons of cement and 3 million units of glass abroad in 2017, and 20 million tons of steel, 30 million tons of cement and 10 million units of glass by 2023. Meanwhile, the Hebei Iron and Steel Group (HBIS) bought the controlling 51% interest in the Swiss-based steel trading firm Duferco reported to underline the shift to production abroad and trading the metal globally.[18]

By improving connectivity via infrastructure, the Initiative also has the potential to lay the foundation for a platform for trade and investment with China at its centre.

2.6. The financing of connectivity projects within the BRI

The main sources of funding for the bulk of these BRI-participating projects are the Chinese development banks, the USD 40 billion Silk Road Fund, and two of the large state-owned commercial banks. The main funding vehicles are set out in Table 2.4, along with examples of key projects.

Finance for the infrastructure goals of the BRI is already well underway.

- The China Development Bank has supported 400 projects in 37 economies worth USD 110 billion and is tracking more potential projects.[19]
- The Industrial and Commercial Bank of China (ICBC) is involved in 212 projects worth USD 67 billion, and is expected to arrive at around USD 159 billion.
- The Bank of China is pledging USD 100 billion for the period 2016-2018.
- China Exim Bank supported 1 000 projects in 49 economies worth USD 80 billion.
- The China Construction Bank also supports BRI projects.
- The Silk Road Fund, with pledged capital of USD 40 billion, is smaller in comparison, but works with other institutions in consortiums.[20]
- The New Development Bank has small investments thus far but is expected to play a larger global role in the future.
- The Asian Infrastructure Investment Bank (AIIB) is small in comparison to the above, at USD 2.3 billion of loans, and is in any case not formally a part of the BRI. Nevertheless, China contributed around half of the AIIB subscribed capital (voting rights), and all of the initial projects have been along the Belt and Road.

The president of the World Bank, an institution which is able to tap resources from all economies in the world, recently stated it had ongoing projects worth USD 86.8 billion in the (then) 65 BRI-participating economies (Kim, 2017). This compares with USD 420 billion already invested by China in BRI construction, with much more on the way.

Figure 2.6. Credit rating score by BRI-participating economy versus construction project investment

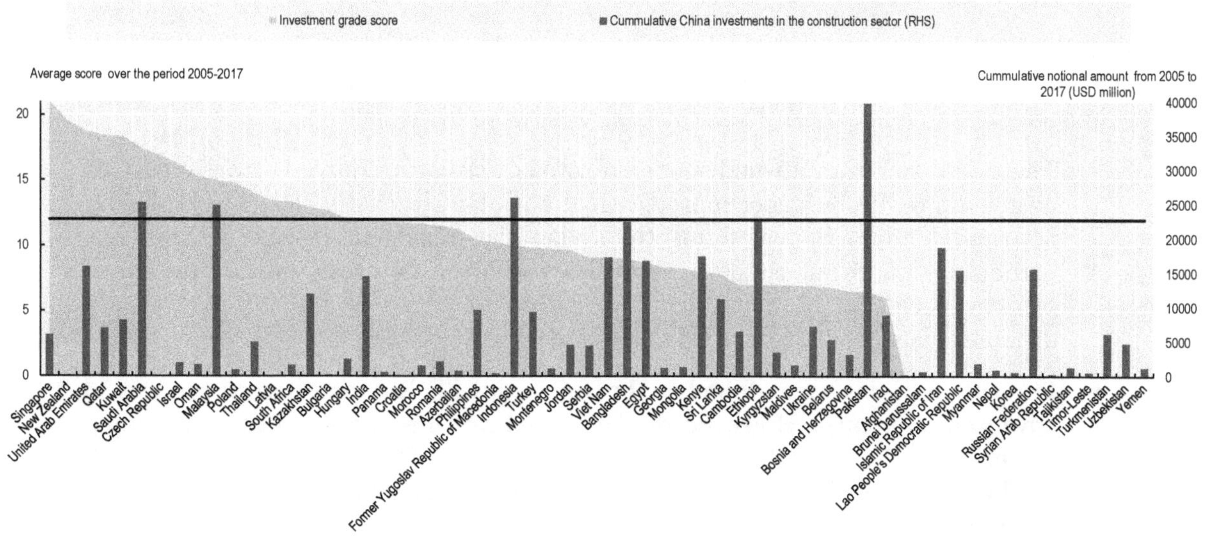

Source: S&P, Fitch, Moody's. AAA and Aaa are given a score of 21; AA+ and Aa1 are given a score of 20, and so on, down to 1 for D and C at the junk end. Investment grade ends at BBB-/Baa3 at a score of 12.

StatLink http://dx.doi.org/10.1787/888933786401

Potential debt issues to watch out for

Figure 2.6 shows the sovereign credit ratings calculated by scoring the ratings from Moody's and S&P/Fitch (the grey area) and the investment by China in construction projects for each economy. There are 17 economies with investment grade at or above BBB- with a score of at or above 12). There are 29 economies rated below investment grade and 14 with no rating at all (economies to the right of Iraq in the graph). Investment in construction infrastructure projects in these latter economies constitutes well over half of the cumulative totals since 2005: i.e. USD 253.8 billion compared to a total cumulative investment of USD 420 billion since 2005. It remains to be seen how viable these projects in below-investment-grade economies will prove to be.

Chapter 1 discusses in detail some of the problems building up in China's financial system. These present two issues for the BRI:

- China is beginning to restrict the expansion of credit and reduce levels of indebtedness in its domestic economy, while also still having strong needs for investment in poorer regions. This is likely to mean it will run into constraints on its ability to fund more of the huge needs of BRI-participating economies. Other large economies and multilateral institutions will need to become involved to meet the size of the gaps illustrated in section 2.2.
- It will be important not to waste resources by financing non-economic projects. One of the great lessons of the past is that funding to finance excessive investment that does not pay an adequate return will ultimately result in problem loans for the lenders.

Ansar et al. (2016) examine the benefit/cost ratios of Chinese investments (within China) using detailed project data. They report results on 95 transport infrastructure projects (road and rail) built in China between 1984 and 2008 and compare these to 806 transport projects built in advanced economies. Data on 24 variables are collected for each investment, including cost variables, time aspects (decision, implementation and completion), competitiveness of the procurement process, proportion of foreign exchange costs, and benefits (such as freight usage). Their findings were as follows:

- There is a tendency to underestimate project costs in China—actual costs, on average, are 30.6% higher than the final business case estimates (i.e. excluding preparation time) in real terms (removing the effects of inflation). This was particularly so in rail projects. Preliminary evidence suggests (since the size of projects could not be controlled for) that these overruns are not significantly different, statistically, compared to a rich democracies sample.
- Projects in China were found to be finished with less time overruns than in advanced economies. However, they also find that this is associated with trading off quality, safety, social equity and the environment. These are outcomes that will need to be changed in order for China to meet its stated environmental objectives for the BRI.
- With respect to benefits in traffic performance, the study finds evidence of poor resource allocation. The majority of routes have poor traffic volumes, while some have the opposite problem of extreme congestion.

The benefit/cost ratios were less than 1.0 on average, reflecting cost overruns and benefit shortfalls. The authors also compare the cost data with macroeconomic variables, and find cost overruns at the time of the study were equivalent to approximately one-third of China's debt. There is no suggestion that these findings will translate to the BRI investments. Nevertheless, they raise an issue about how best to improve efficiency and avoid any related excess indebtedness.[21]

2.7. High-technology corporate investments, China's technology and troubled assets

The strategy *Made in China 2025* aims to encourage Chinese technology, standards, equipment and engineering knowhow, which can also be adopted within the BRI in competition with advanced economies trying to do the same thing: i.e. to win business and lock-in future projects through sound benefit/cost outcomes. *Made in China 2025* also fits naturally with the strategy to move lower technology activities towards the Belt and Road, much as western countries have done in the post-war period.

Table 2.5. Selected targets for *Made in China 2025*

Selected higher value added indicators	2015	2020	2025
Manufacturing labour productivity (% change over 2015)	-	6.5	5.5
Manufacturing value added rate (% increase over 2015)	-	2	4
Penetration of broad band internet (% number of households)	50	70	82
Use of digital design in R&D (% number of firms)	58	72	84
Change in CO2 emissions versus 2015 (%)	-	-22	-40

Source: State Council of the People's Republic of China (2015).

StatLink http://dx.doi.org/10.1787/888933786553

Figure 2.7. Chinese investment in foreign companies, cumulative notional amount expressed in USD million, 2005-2018

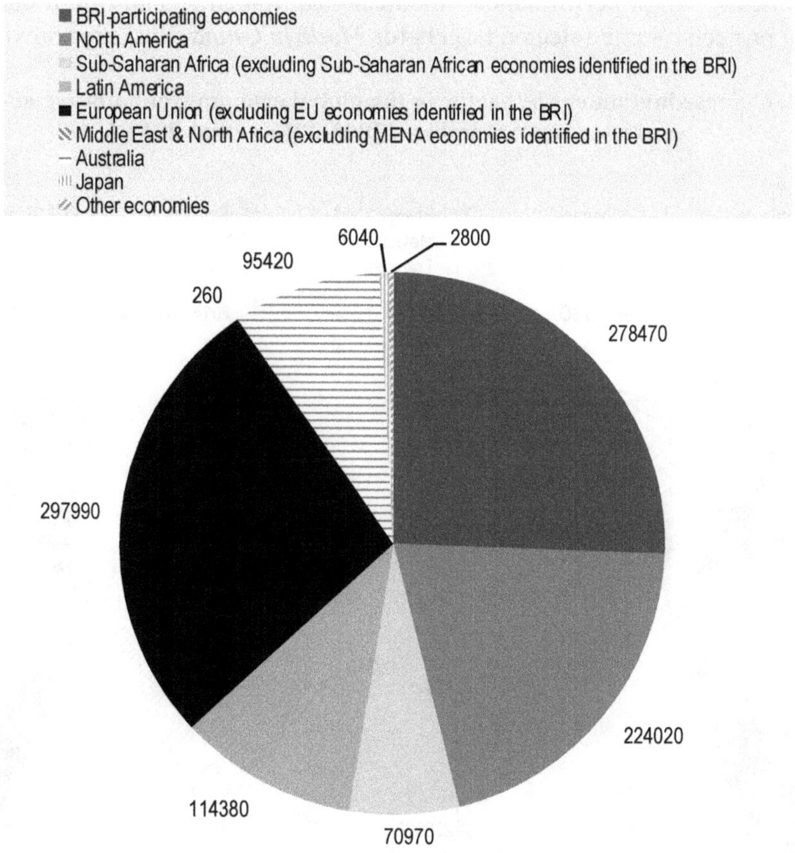

Note: 2018 data are to end-June.

Source: American Enterprise Institute (AEI), China Global Investment Tracker Database. It includes all investments of USD 100 million or greater. Ministry of Commerce, Republic of China (MoFCOM) data totals are around 10% higher for the same period due to the inclusion of small USD investments.

StatLink http://dx.doi.org/10.1787/888933786420

Figure 2.7 shows China's investment in established foreign companies, which help in goals such as upgrading industry through technology transfer. These investments sum to a total much larger than for construction projects (see Figure 2.6). Here the BRI-participating economies together amount to only USD 278.5 billion, or around 26% of the total of USD 1090.3 billion. The United States, Canada and Europe, at USD 522.0 billion, together account for 48% of the total. Australia alone, at USD 95.4 billion, accounts for 9% of the total, mainly in energy, mining and agricultural companies related to China's resource, energy and food security goals.

To move up in the value added chain to 2025 and beyond, requires China to shift away from energy, heavy industry (iron, steel, non-ferrous metals, basic machinery, and traditional automobiles) and construction, towards more sophisticated industries. This is a specific objective of the 13th Five-Year Plan, which supports the *Made in China 2025* initiative and the *Internet Plus* strategy (see State Council of the People's Republic of China, 2015 and SESEC, 2015). The breakthrough industries for 2025 include: next generation IT; high-end digital control machine tools and robots; aerospace; oceanographic engineering equipment and high-technology shipping; advanced rail transportation; energy efficient and new-energy automobiles; electrical power equipment with a focus on renewables; agricultural machinery; high-performance structural metals and materials; bio-pharmaceuticals; high-performance medical equipment; and high-end equipment innovation projects. Some selected targets for *Made in China 2025* are shown in Table 2.5.

Figure 2.8. Chinese investment by sector in the global economy, cumulative notional amount expressed in USD million, 2005-2013 versus 2014-2018

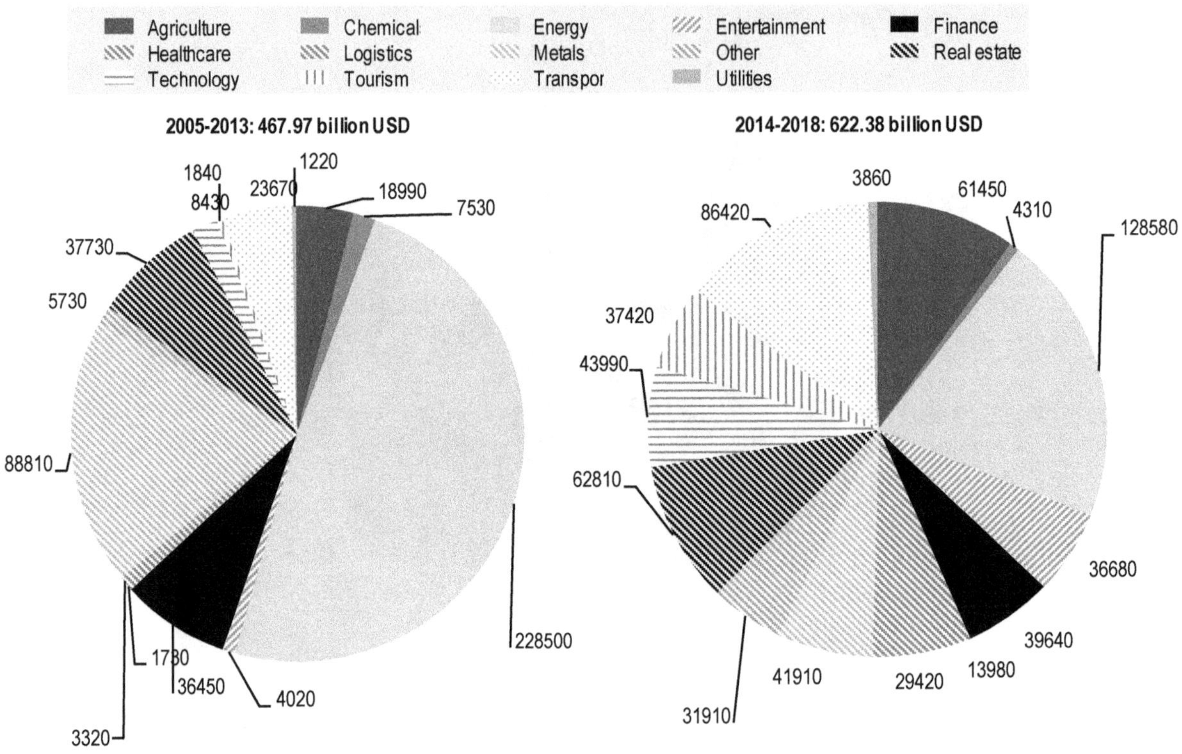

Note: 2018 data are to end-June.

Source: American Enterprise Institute (AEI), China Global Investment Tracker Database. It includes all investments of USD 100 million or greater. Ministry of Commerce, Republic of China (MoFCOM) data totals are around 10% higher for the same period due to the inclusion of small investments.

StatLink http://dx.doi.org/10.1787/888933786439

The composition of outward corporate investment has changed in recent years in line with China's changing economic priorities. Figure 2.8 shows the USD 1 090.4 billion foreign company investments broken down into the main industrial sectors and two sub-periods: 2005-2013, and the shorter, more recent 2014-2017 period. Prior to 2014, half of the USD 468 billion was in the energy sector and USD 88.8 billion was in metals (together around 68% of the total). Real Estate at USD 38.3 billion and Finance at USD 37.7 billion (mainly due to considerable investments in advanced-economy banks around 2008) were the third and fourth most important investments in the earlier nine-year period. In the period 2015-2018 the amount of investment is larger than in the preceding nine years, and its composition has shifted away from energy, metals and finance, towards a much more diversified set of industries. The main beneficiaries of the switch are: agriculture (seeds, agro-chemicals and processing); technology (especially robotics, medical, cloud computing, imaging and telecommunications), transport (mainly aviation, shipping, and rail); tourism; real estate; and the "other" category (including consumer goods and textiles).

While China had followed other emerging economies with a "copy and improve" approach in earlier years, this has since been replaced in large part by policies to accelerate indigenous innovation and large scale investment in human resources through training professionals overseas, and the (relatively new) programmes attracting foreign professionals, scientists, and researchers to work in China.

Table 2.6. Examples of recent Chinese acquisitions and high-technology construct-and-operate projects

Sector	Year	Investor	Party Acquired	Notional amount (USD billion)	Percent of ownership
Agriculture	2017	China Reform Holdings and Chem China	Syngenta / Swiss / Agro-Chemicals / Seeds	41.2	95
	2013	Shuanghui	Smithfield Foods / United States / Pork / Packaging	7.2	100
	2012	Bright Foods	Weetabix / UK	1.94	60
Technology	2016	HNA	IngramMicro Tech / United States / Computers / Cloud	6	100
	2014	Lenovo	Motorola Mobility / United States / Mobile Telephony	2.91	100
	2015	Hua Capital and CITIC	Omnivision Technologies / United States / Digital Imaging	1.9	100
	2016	Midea	Kuka / Germany / Robotics	5.1	95
Metals	2014	Minmetals, Suzhou Guoxin, and CITIC	Glencore / Peru / Copper	6.99	63 / 22 / 15
	2014	Hebei Iron and Steel	Duferco / Switzerland / Metal Trading	0.4	51
Transport	2015	Chem China	Pirelli / Italy	7.86	52
	2017	HNA	CIT Group / United States / Aviation	10.38	100
	2015	HNA	Avolon / Ireland / Aviation	5.17	100
Entertainment	2016	Tencent	Supercall / Finland / Video Games	8.6	84
	2016	Shanghai Giant-Led Consortium	Playtika / Israel / Social Games	4.4	100
Energy	2012	CNOOC	Nexen / Canada / Oil Sands / Shale Gas	15.1	100
	2015	China General Nuclear	Edra / Malaysia / Clean Energy	5.96	100
	2015	Three Gorges	Pakistan Karot Hydropower	2	100

Source: American Enterprise Institute (AEI), Investment Tracker, all investments of USD 100 million or greater. MoFCOM data totals are around 10% higher for the same period due to the inclusion of small investments.

StatLink http://dx.doi.org/10.1787/888933786572

Indigenous innovation is pursued by promoting "global champions"; giving favourable access to capital for acquisitions in technology; by investing in joint ventures and/or buying companies in advanced economies; encouraging joint ventures; giving preferential treatment for high technology imports (while protecting local innovation); helping facilitation of lower technology and spare capacity transfer to BRI-participating economies (see People's Republic of China, 2016); and promoting Chinese technology standards within the BRI-participating economies to help open up markets for China's products (see also, Cheung et al., 2016).

Table 2.6 drills down to a few examples of firm-specific acquisitions, illustrating the wide range of areas covered by some of the deals in recent years: high-tech agriculture (agro-chemicals, seeds, packaging), cloud computing, aviation, mobile telephony, digital imaging, robotics, base metals, video and social games, shale gas, oil sands, hydro power, and clean energy.

Promoting Chinese technical standards and services

The sheer scale of Chinese activity abroad puts it in a very strong position to establish its technical standards as "global defaults" in a number of fields. This is a strategy that many countries before China have also pursued for business reasons. One example includes ultra-high voltage (UHV) power lines, where China's indigenous technology programme has put it in a global leadership position. Scale is important, and the State Grid Corporation of China is establishing UHV standards throughout China and is in a solid position to allow Chinese companies operating within and outside of China to include national preferences in international UHV standards (see Paulson Institute, 2015).

Other examples of potential to promote Chinese standards and services can be found in aspects of the Digital Belt and Road. This is an attempt to harness 'big data' to tackle and solve some of the sustainable development challenges facing the planet. Smart buildings, smart electricity grids, and smart transport logistics would, if successful, help to reduce greenhouse gas emissions and water needs in BRI-participating economies.[22] Co-operation in respect to common standards for telecommunications, infrastructure for the 'internet of things' and e-commerce provides significant opportunities for Chinese multinationals. Examples include rolling out optical fibre built in China and Russia, the Beidou satellite program which is a competitor to GPS (currently being trialled in Pakistan), and the e-commerce push in the BRI-participating economies by Alibaba and JD.com, which may allow less developed economies to jump some of the need for more supermarket chains and shopping malls (see Brown, 2017).

China Telecom Corporation, China Mobile and China Unicom are investing and working with equipment providers like Huawei and ZTE in the 5G area where the race is on to push for standards that suit network objectives (see, for example, Forbes, 2018). 5G will be a key driver of the internet of things, autonomous vehicle operations, drones, smart cities and other major trends. The standards for each generation are set by those with the required intellectual property rights and network market share. China (unlike for previous generations of mobile telephony) is vying with the United States, Korea and Europe for 5G leadership status. 5G has two key aspects: millimetre wave band (that above 24 gigahertz); and Massive-Multiple-In-Multiple-Out (MMIMO), whereby hundreds of antennas and receivers can operate from one base station instead of the current few. China is well placed in trialing 5G and Huawei is now the largest producer of mobile phone equipment in the world.

Promoting Chinese energy solution technologies

The BRI requires energy, and there is little doubt that China is leading the world in many energy technology areas, notably: ultra-high voltage lines (discussed above), solar power cells where it controls 60% of production; advanced wind power; hydroelectric developments; and batteries, where it is expected to dwarf companies like Tesla by 2020, and particularly as it becomes dominant in cobalt mining where it controls around 62% of world production (see Buckley et al., 2017). For the BRI, power grid transmission technology is a key element, linking up multiple sources of energy (coal, gas, hydro, wind and solar) across the region.

Table 2.7. China energy development projects in 2017

Entity	Notional amount (USD billion)	Projects 2017	Country
China Three Gorges	6	Karot Hydro (USD 2 billion) / two Hydro Corporations / 3 Solar Projects	Pakistan
China Genzhouba / China Power	5.8	3GW Mambilla Hydro Development	Nigeria
CK Infrastructure (consortium)	5.3	Acquisitions of Ista Energy Solutions (Meters/Management)	Germany
Shanghai Electric (with ACWA Power)	3.9	Construct 700 Mega Watt CSP Solar in Dubai	United Arab Emirates
China Energy Investment Corporation	3.5	75% Stake in 4 Greek Wind Farms	Greece
SCIG / CXIG / QYEC	3	1 Giga Watt Hydro Project Developments	Nepal
State Power Investment Corporation	2.4	Sao Simao Hydroelectric Project	Brazil
China Genzhouba Group	1.8	Suki Kinari 870 Mega Watt Hydro Project	Pakistan
China Three Gorges	1.6	West Seti Hydro 750 Mega Watt Hydro Project Development	Nepal
State Grid Corporation	1.5	Matiari to Lahore Power Transmission Line	Pakistan
State Grid Corporation	1.5	Matiari (Port Qasim) to Falsalabad Transmission Line	Pakistan
SANY Group	1.5	Wind Energy Developements in Punjab	Pakistan
China Three Gorges / Hubel Energy	1.4	Purchase of 456 Mega Watt Chagila Hydro project	Peru
Pacific Hydro (SPIC)	1.3	Houghton Solar Farm in Queensland Australia	Australia
Power China	1	EPC for 500 Mega Watt AWA Pumped Hydro and Storage Project	Philippines
State Grid Corporation	1	2nd Phase of Egypt Transmission Development	Egypt
Shanghai Electric	1	Takeover of Rio Grande Do Sul Transmission project	Brazil
CIC Capital	0.5-1.0	10-20% of Equis Energy (Solar/Wind)	Singapore
Total, 38% Year-on-Year Growth	44.3		

Note: CK (Chueng Kong) Infrastructure is based in Hong Kong (China) and is the world's largest infrastructure company. ACWA Power is a huge developer, investor, operator and co-owner all over the BRI-participating economies. SCIG is Sichuan Communications Investment Group, a logistics company. CXIG is Chengdu Xincheng Investment Group. QYEC is Qing Yuan Engineering Consulting Company. SPIC is State Power Investment Corporation. CIC is China Investment Corporation, a sovereign wealth fund.

Source: Buckley *et al.* (2017), Company reports, OECD.

StatLink http://dx.doi.org/10.1787/888933786591

Thus, for example, the Karot Hydropower Co. special purpose vehicle (operating in the China-Pakistan economic corridor) is putting together a large-scale hydro project in Pakistan on a build-own-operate-transfer basis. The project, estimated to cost USD 2 billion, is being developed by the China Three Gorges South Asia Investment Limited, which is an investment arm of China Three Gorges Corporation (CTG) in South Asia (a wholly state-owned enterprise). China Machine Engineering Co. is a part of the project. This 720-MW high technology project will be built by 2020. The company has received a 35-year concession to run the station (including the five-year build phase). State Grid is playing a large role in developing power transmission in the BRI (USD 4 billion in projects in Table 2.7 for 2017) and is planning an ambitious, transcontinental, "super-grid" that would link China, Japan, Mongolia, Russia and Korea.

Building these projects and linking them up requires more than construction. The table also shows that China is buying into smart metering companies and energy management skills and high-technology energy companies in advanced economies.

Figure 2.9. Troubled assets related to past BRI/SOE corporate investments, cumulative notional amount expressed USD million over the period 2005-2018

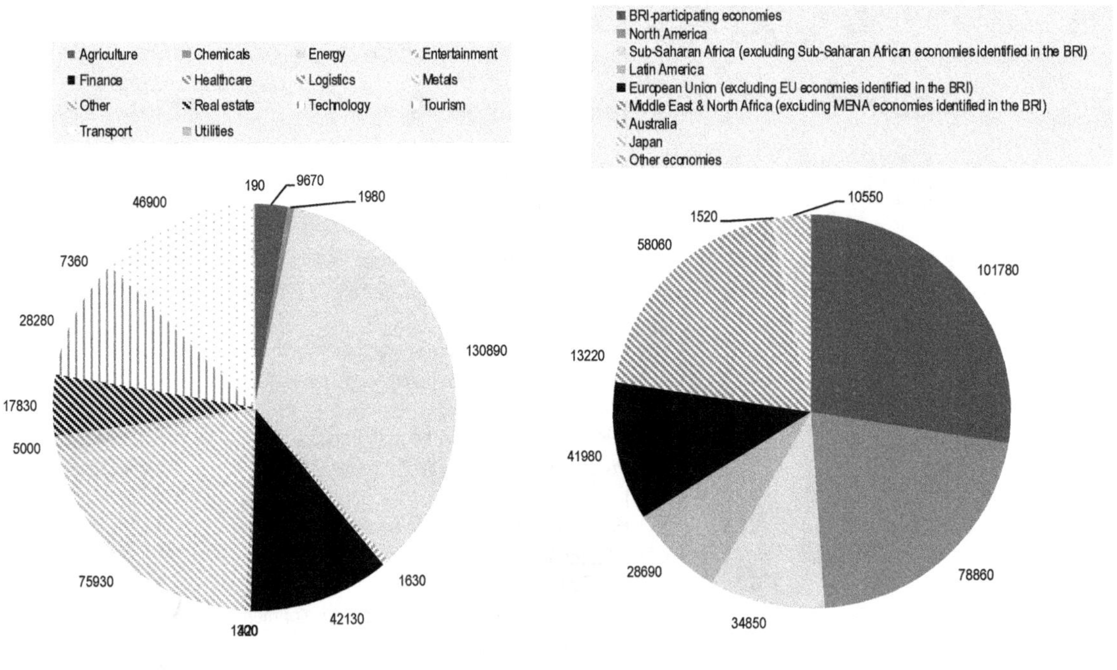

Note: 2018 data are to end-June.
Source: American Enterprise Institute (AEI), China Global Investment Tracker Database. All investments of USD 100 million or greater are included. Ministry of Commerce, Republic of China (MoFCOM) data totals are around 10% higher for the same period due to the inclusion of small investments.

StatLink http://dx.doi.org/10.1787/888933786458

Potential investment issues to watch out for

BRI investment projects have to be debt funded, often in difficult business environments, and financial difficulties can result. The risks that come with the BRI are already becoming apparent. Figure 2.9 shows the cumulative value of assets described as "troubled" since 2005, where: the collateral value of the investment is below its liabilities; where loans are not performing (due to benefit/cost outcome discussed above); where the deal has been cancelled for delays in reviews or political opposition, and so on. Troubled programmes are estimated to be associated with around USD 369.5 billion worth of transactions globally. The largest problem area concerns the BRI with USD 101.8 billion of troubled assets.

The BRI includes economies in less stable parts of the world, where deals get into trouble because of political violence, war, sanctions (e.g. those against Iran) and excessive dependence on single commodities such as oil and gas which are subject to price volatility.

For example, in Iran alone Chinese SOEs are associated with USD 25 billion of troubled energy projects (CNOOC, CNPC and Sinohydro). There are USD 12 billion of troubled real estate and rail construction projects in Libya, USD 4.6 billion energy projects in Pakistan and USD 3.8 billion of oil projects in Syria. The next most problematic regions for Chinese SOEs are North America and Australia.

In the left-hand panel of Figure 2.9, the main sectors where troubled assets are found globally are energy, metals, transport, finance and technology. Some of the issues that might help China reduce risk in this area are taken up in Chapter 3.

2.8. The BRI as a platform for promoting trade

Figure 2.10. Chinese exports to BRI-participating economies versus OECD countries, 1993-2017

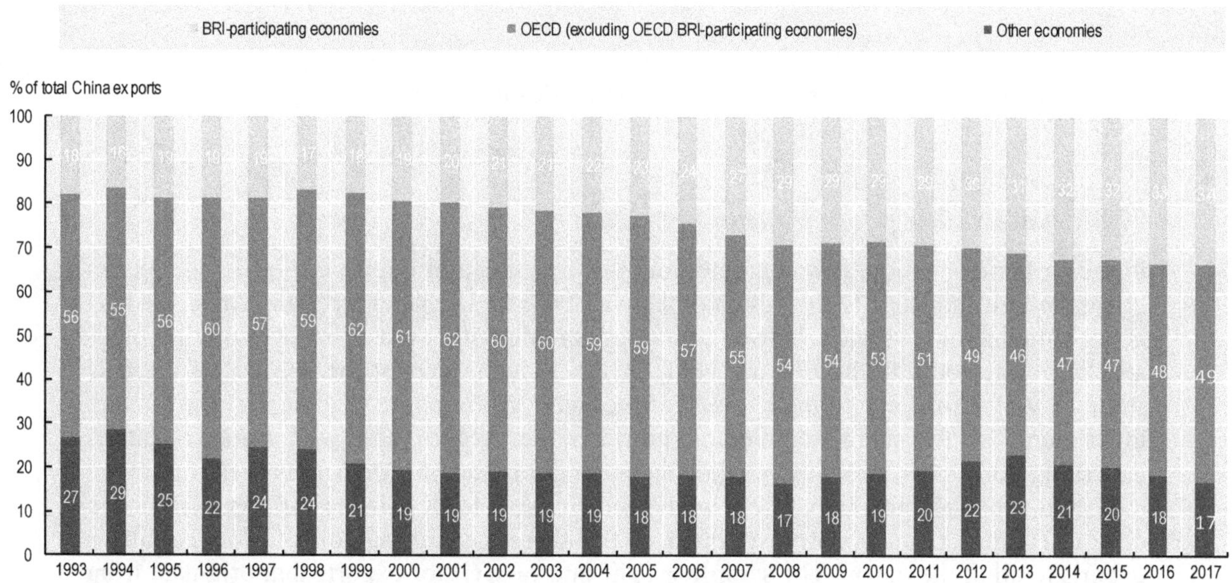

Source: IMF Direction of Trade Statistic Database, OECD calculations.

StatLink http://dx.doi.org/10.1787/888933786477

Figure 2.10 shows the share of Chinese exports going to BRI-participating economies, OECD countries and the group of all other economies. In 2000, exports to the OECD as a share of Chinese exports were around 61% while, for the BRI-participating economies, it was 19%. Subsequently, the trend in the share of BRI-participating economies has been continually upwards, reaching 34% in 2016, while that for the OECD declined gradually to around 49%.[23] This suggests that further progress in the region could have significant benefits for BRI-participating countries.

The main destination BRI-participating economies (as a share of Chinese exports) are shown in Figure 2.11. Consistent with gravity theories of trade, the larger shares are associated with larger, closer and/or richer economies in the group.

Figure 2.11. Percentage of Chinese exports to selected BRI-participating economies, 1993-2017

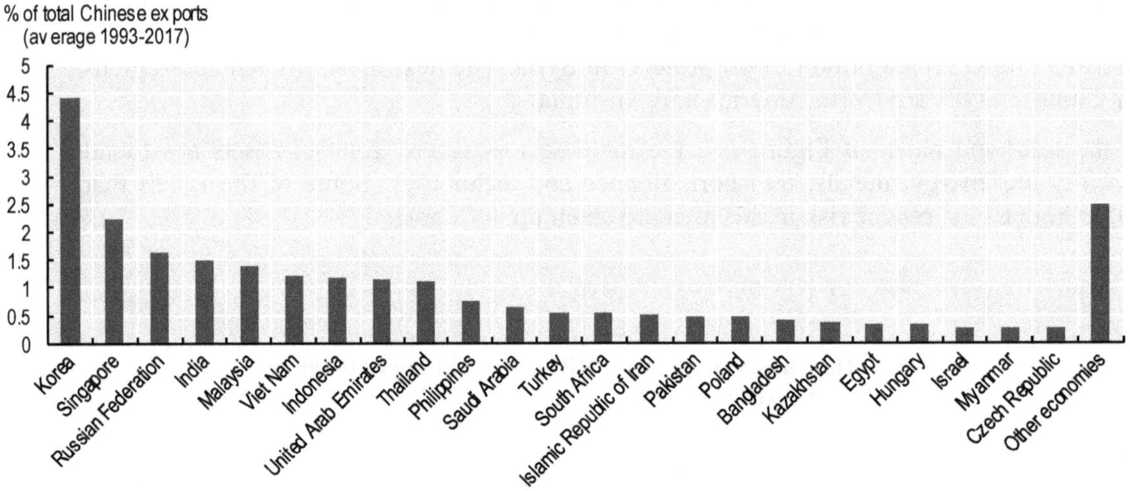

Source: IMF Direction of Trade Statistics Database, OECD calculations.

StatLink http://dx.doi.org/10.1787/888933786496

Trade blocs and regional trade agreements

In the earlier discussion, it was pointed out that creating and improving free trade blocks along the Belt and Road is an explicit objective of the BRI. It is important to stress the BRI is not a trading bloc as such. However, it does contain within it a number of trading blocs and these interact with the EU and NAFTA blocs. Some part of the success of the BRI strategy will ultimately turn on the 'connectivity' dividends of China's infrastructure investment for facilitating commerce between these blocs and with other countries generally. Some very preliminary evidence is set out based on a *gravity model* of bilateral trade and explained in Annex 2.A. The dependent variable (X_{ijt}) is the exports from origin country i to destination country j at time t, so that there is a large sample of every country's exports to all of the others. The sample is split into two: (i) for exports that originate from countries that are linked to the BRI (to each bilateral pair of every other country in the sample), and (ii) for where the bilateral export origin is from an OECD country (to each bilateral pair of every other country).

It uses a full complement of variables, including: relative size (the *similarity* index based on GDP); bilateral exchange rates; relative factor endowments; presence of a common language; investment openness (infrastructure investment builds connectivity and investing in distribution and joint ventures helps exports); physical distance between the trade partners; presence of common borders; presence of political instability; and whether the partner was a former colony. The gravity model works well, though a few variables are not well-supported by the data (mainly in the case of BRI export origin economies). The reason for developing this model is to explore where linkages are strongest and weakest and where the most advantages might be obtained via connectivity improvements. There are two types of influences tested simultaneously:

- One set of dummy variables (RTA_I and RTA_O in Annex 2.A) allow precisely for each bilateral pair to be a member of the same bloc, or one is a member and the other is not. These variables deal with trade creation and diversion for insiders versus outsiders. Presumably if two countries belong to the same bloc then more trade should be created (a positive coefficient is expected) (see Ekanayake et al., 2010). If one country belongs to a regional trade agreement and the other does not, trade might be diverted between the two, offsetting the gains from trade creation, so the expected sign on the coefficient is negative.
- Having allowed for trade creation and diversion, the regional dummy variables for explicit trading blocs (like NAFTA, ASEAN+1, and the Bangkok Agreement) should be interpreted as the extra-bloc exports and imports effect. The idea is that being a member of a group might create synergies in supply chains and income effects that are positive for exports and imports versus non-members.

The trading blocs considered are:

- The Association of Southeast Asian Nations (ASEAN) and China Free Trade Area (ASEAN+1): Brunei-Darussalam, Cambodia, Indonesia, Lao People's Democratic Republic, Malaysia, Myanmar, Philippines, Singapore, Thailand, Viet Nam and China.
- The Bangkok Agreement (BA): Bangladesh, China, Lao People's Democratic Republic, India, Korea, and Sri Lanka.
- The Economic Co-operation Organisation (ECO): Afghanistan, Azerbaijan, Iran, Kazakhstan, Kyrgyz Republic, Pakistan, Tajikistan, Turkey, Turkmenistan, and Uzbekistan.
- The South Asian Association of Regional Co-operation (SAARC): Bangladesh, India, Pakistan, Maldives, Nepal and Sri Lanka.
- The European Union (EU): 28 members of the union.
- The North American Free Trade Association (NAFTA): the United States, Canada and Mexico.

The results suggest that trade creation is definitely present for OECD-origin countries and less so in BRI-origin countries. The results for trade diversion suggest that it is not generally present in the data. That is, being a member of a bloc while a bilateral partner is not in that bloc, has no discernible impact on exports and imports between the two, a finding consistent with others using more recent trade data.[24] The finding for trade creation is not surprising if we take into account that infrastructure connectivity is currently weak in the Belt and Road. This underlines the importance of improving connectivity in the BRI. The whole point of the BRI is to reduce this source of weakness via infrastructure investment which, if successful, will improve connectivity over time. The results here are suggestive of significant dividends deriving from an improvement in connectivity.

Having allowed for member trade creation (with little diversion for non-members) does the existence of a trade bloc create extra-bloc benefits? The theory here is that the bloc creates income effects and interconnections that benefit all other countries outside of the bloc. If there are additional benefits from the bloc, then the sign should be positive. The results for these tests are as follows:

- For groupings where China is a member (ASEAN+1 and the BA), the regional membership is positive and statistically significant. That is, it benefits non-members, whether they are OECD countries or BRI-participating economies.
- For the ECO bloc, the results are opposite between the OECD-origin countries and BRI-origin economies. OECD-origin countries benefit in a statistically significant way, while the effect for BRI-participating economies is clearly negative.
- For SAARC-origin countries the relationship is negative and highly significant for OECD-origin countries and neutral with respect to the BRI.
- The extra-bloc effects of NAFTA are good for all countries regardless of origin (and especially so for the BRI-origin economy's exports).

In summary, the most important results are that both China and the United States are very important partners to have in free trade zones. While free trade zones that do not involve these countries are less positive, the important point to note is that China's BRI is precisely focused on changing this via connectivity investment. These results are suggestive only, but it appears that connectivity is stronger in some parts of the world than others, and it makes a lot of sense to invest in infrastructure where it is lacking to strengthen trade linkages for these countries.

As mentioned in Chapter 1, the 19th Party Congress endorsed greater openness and more use of the CNY in international transactions. The BRI provides a good opportunity to further the internationalisation of the CNY, and in this respect the People's Bank of China has announced a number of currency reforms specifically targeted at facilitating the Initiative. These relate to permitting cross-border settlement in CNY resulting from: enterprises investing and exporting; Chinese workers receiving salaries and making social security and family payments; and foreign investors in the BRI being able to receive dividends and related payments.[25]

2.9. Concluding comments

China has driven strong growth at home and has shown itself prepared to put money into projects on a large-scale basis to develop infrastructure trade and other aspects of connectivity in the BRI. The BRI is affecting the global trade, investment and finance landscape in significant ways:

1. **Investment**: From China's perspective, the strategy to develop markets for its products via hardware connectivity in the BRI, while investing in technology transfer to move quickly up the value-added chain, fits in with the need to alleviate industrial excess capacity at home in the short term, and in the longer run to create a global platform that will facilitate trade and investment with the countries involved in the Initiative, with China playing a central role. Like China, many BRI-participating economies see benefits in a strong role for the state and commercial relationships in line with the Bandung principles.[26]

   An important part of the hardware-first strategy is connectivity in energy supplies and electricity grids along the Belt and Road. There are multiple sources of energy across the

BRI, and how best to link these up and price them is also an important issue. China has leadership in ultra-high voltage lines. China is also well advanced in 5G broadband that is expected to play an important role in the use of big data and in the development of smart grids and cities, remote transport and other projects. Nevertheless, other countries also have a large role to play in these areas and openness in procurement practices may be useful for achieving the lowest-cost outcomes, as may a general strengthening of the investment environment (Ang et al., 2017).

2. **Trade**: Some very preliminary evidence was presented in this chapter on trade, distinguishing trade creation effects within a trade bloc from extra-bloc effects for other countries resulting from any positive flow-on income and other effects. Trade creation is greater in regions where connectivity is likely to be less problematic, and extra-bloc effects on exports and imports for BRI-participating economies are strong when they originate from trade blocs where either China or the United States are members. This underlines the need for investment that promotes greater connectivity and China's role in the BRI is especially important given the gravity effects of its economy.
3. **Finance**: China alone cannot fund all of the infrastructure needs of developing Asia; these needs are very large and China faces its own financial constraints at home (see Chapter 1). This means that there is a need for more effort by OECD countries to engage with those of the BRI and vice versa. The future of all economies is improved when well-being rises around the world. This requires a sound investment environment to attract the capital required and to ensure that host countries get the best value for money.
4. **Co-operation**: the OECD is in a sound position to help countries to improve their investment environments. As living standards rise, history teaches that the role of markets becomes more important in allocation decisions. Property rights, competition, level playing fields, and sound governance based on voice and accountability have helped to manage the transition. This is likely to become necessary in BRI-participating economies too, and moving in this direction will encourage more funding from advanced economies and multilateral lending institutions. The OECD has a number of regional initiatives under way that are proving fruitful. The Central Asia Competitiveness Initiative (which is part of the OECD Eurasia Competitiveness Programme) aims to help countries to enhance productivity by supporting entrepreneurship, private sector development, inclusiveness and the building of suitable knowledge-based economies. The OECD South-East Asia Regional programme also works to achieve similar goals. Countries work with OECD Committees covering a number of areas such as corporate governance, foreign direct investment, competition, bribery and corruption, pensions, the environment, social policies and taxation. Some of these issues are taken up in Chapter 3.

Notes

[1] This is the term used by President Xi in his Belt and Road speech.

[2] Leading Groups are coordinating bodies that address important policy areas. Often led by members of the Politburo or State Councils, they help to ensure strategic coordination from Beijing.

[3] This figure is the most often quoted from an adding up of projects already invested and foreshadowed for the next 10 years, using their own staff and expert consultants—see www.pwc.com/gx/en/growth-markets-center/assets/pdf/china-new-silk-route.pdf. In this study, the

figure seems in the right ballpark, based on actual investment from the start of the BRI and multiple references to a large number of foreshadowed projects.

[4] See: www.cikd.org/cikd/English_Version/E_AboutUS_CIKD.aspx?leafid=1324&chnid=374&acid=1.

[5] The goal is: "Keeping in mind both the domestic and international situations, China will implement the comprehensive strategy of building a moderately prosperous society in all respects, deepening reform, advancing the law-based governance of China, and strengthening Party self-conduct, seeking coordinated development in the economic, political, cultural, social and ecological fields as well as Party building under the guidance of the development concept featuring innovative, coordinated, green, open and shared development" (Chinese Government, 2016, page 7). The relevant departments of the Chinese government have also issued the following documents: Building the Belt and Road: Concept, Practice and China's Contribution, Vision and Actions on Promoting Energy Cooperation on the Belt and Road, Vision and Actions on Jointly Promoting Agricultural Cooperation on the Belt and Road, Guidance on Promoting Green Belt and Road and Vision for Maritime Cooperation on the Belt and Road Initiative. The Green Belt and Road can be traced back to 2012, when China's green credit guidelines were published. A full list of official documents can be found at: eng.yidaiyilu.gov.cn/info/iList.jsp?cat_id=10059.

[6] The United States has expressed concern in this area on a number of occasions. See The White House (2018) and references therein.

[7] The GI Hub estimate of USD 94 trillion is cumulative until 2040, making 50% of this number comparable to a 2030 estimate of around USD 28 trillion for Asia's infrastructure needs.

[8] Older estimates by Bhattacharyay (2010) quantify annual infrastructure investment needs for developing Asia at 6.52% of its GDP (USD 776 billion) for the period between 2010 and 2020.

[9] When excluding China from these calculations, the investment gap rises to 5% of projected GDP for the remaining economies (ADB, 2017).

[10] It is also worth noting that maintenance and rehabilitation investments account for a larger share of projected investment needs than actual new investments (ADB, 2017).

[11] See http://english.gov.cn/archive/publications/2015/03/30/content_281475080249035.htm.

[12] See Johnson (2016) and Paal (2013). Paal analyses the Peripheral Diplomacy Week Conference of October 2013, which saw the end to Deng's *'hide your strength and bide your time'* approach. See also Cai (2017) for the economic aspects of BRI objectives.

[13] From Chapter 2, section 2, of the 13th Five Year Plan.

[14] See, for example, Patil (2015). India lies between two countries with which it has fought wars in the last 60 years and mistrusts the strategic objectives of the BRI. It has repeatedly asked that the BRI project be designed with India's participation as an equal partner.

[15] See, for example, www.mining.com/chinese-companies-build-700-coal-plants-outside-china/ where it is reported that the environmental group Urgewald has documented that China will build 700 new coal fired power plants inside and outside China.

[16] See IMF (2017). According to the IMF, the Chinese government defines 'zombie companies' as "firms that incur three years of losses, cannot meet environmental and technological standards, do not align with national industrial policies, and rely heavily on government or bank support to survive." The IMF also focuses on over-capacity sectors and suggests measures to deal with this are not ambitious, and the debt in overcapacity sectors has not fallen (see IMF, 2017, pp 23-27). See also Girma et al. (2008) for a subsidies study. Problems with exit issues are well known and recent attempts to improve them are reported in www.ft.com/content/35fa6886-fcc9-11e6-96f8-3700c5664d30.

[17] The non-SOE sector measure, as defined, sits just under that of the SOE sector in China. SOEs may still be underperforming given their subsidisation and subsequent lower cost of debts. Globally,

the steel and shipbuilding industries are a useful illustration of these issues, where internal OECD reports have shown they are still dominated by state firms globally and that closures in state enterprises proceed at a much slower rate than private firms in these industries around the world, even though they are less profitable.

[18] See www.reuters.com/article/duferco-ma-hebei-ir-st/china-steel-company-takes-controlling-stake-in-swiss-trader-duferco-idUSL6N0T83BM20141118; www.chinadaily.com.cn/business/2014-11/19/content_18938457.htm; and www.metalbulletin.com/Article/3312695/Delong-enters-joint-venture-for-600000-tpy-flat-steel-mill-in-Thailand.html.

[19] It is said to be tracking some 900 projects in 60 economies to a total of USD 890 billion, as was cited in the 21st Century Business Herald, 20 May 2015.

[20] And the government has pledged even more funds, see www.reuters.com/article/us-china-silkroad-africa/china-pledges-124-billion-for-new-silk-road-as-champion-of-globalization-idUSKBN18A02I.

[21] One issue here concerns bidding for BRI contracts. This often tends to occur outside of the WTO General Procurement Agreement and 'rules of the game' common in OECD countries.

[22] See, for example, www.xinhuanet.com/english/2017-12/04/c_136797807.htm.

[23] It is worth recalling that China is now the largest merchandise exporter in the world with a share of over 14%.

[24] Structural change in world trade where global value chain interactions at all points in the supply chain have become more important in recent data so that, regardless of source, the effect may trump treaty effects. Thus, Ekanayake et al., (2010) find evidence of trade diversion in a gravity model for sample periods 1980-2009, 1980-1989, 1990-1999, but not for the recent period closest to our own 2000-2009.

[25] See: www.pbc.gov.cn/english/130721/3459067/index.html.

[26] In response to retreating colonial powers, at the 1955 Bandung Conference principles consistent with the non-aligned movement were enunciated: self-determination, mutual respect for sovereignty, non-aggression, non-interference in internal affairs and equality.

References

ADB (2017), *Meeting Asia's Infrastructure Needs*, Asian Development Bank, www.adb.org/sites/default/files/publication/227496/special-report-infrastructure.pdf.

Allison, G. (2015), *The Thucydides Trap*, The Atlantic, September. www.theatlantic.com/international/archive/2015/09/united-states-china-war-thucydides-trap/406756/.

Ang, G., D. Röttgers and P. Burli (2017), "The empirics of enabling investment and innovation in renewable energy", OECD Environment Working Papers, No. 123, OECD Publishing, Paris. http://dx.doi.org/10.1787/67d221b8-en.

Ansar, A., B. Flyvbjerg, A. Budzier and D. Lunn (2016), *Does infrastructure investment lead to economic growth or economic fragility? Evidence from China*, Oxford Review of Economic Policy, Volume 32, Number 3.

Bhattacharya, B. 2010. "Estimating Demand for Infrastructure in Energy, Transport, Telecommunications, Water and Sanitation in Asia and the Pacific: 2010-2020". ADBI Working Paper 248. Tokyo: Asian Development Bank Institute. www.adbi.org/working-paper/2010/09/09/4062.infrastructure.demand.asia.pacific/.

Bhattacharya, A., et al. (2016), *Delivering on Sustainable Infrastructure for Better Development and Better Climate*, Brookings Institution, Washington DC, www.brookings.edu/wp-content/uploads/2016/12/global_122316_delivering-on-sustainable-infrastructure.pdf

Buckley, T., S. Nicholas, and M. Brown (2017), *China 2017 Review: World's Second-Biggest Economy Continues to Drive Global Trends in Energy Investment*, Institute for Energy Economics and Financial Analysis.

Brown, R. (2017), *Beijing's Silk Road Goes Digital*, Council on Foreign Relations, June, www.cfr.org/blog/beijings-silk-road-goes-digital.

Cai, P. (2017), *Understanding China's Belt and Road Initiative*, Lowy Institute, Sydney. www.lowyinstitute.org/publications/understanding-belt-and-road-initiative#_ednref1.

Chinese Academy of International Trade and Economic Co-operation, Ministry of Commerce and United Nations Development Program China (2017), *Supporting the Belt and Road Regions to Achieve the 2030 Agenda for Sustainable Development*, May.

Christopher K. Johnson (2016), *President Xi Jinping's 'Belt and Road' Initiative: A Practical Assessment of the Chinese Communist Party's Roadmap for China's Global Resurgence*, Center for Strategic and International Studies, March. https://csis-prod.s3.amazonaws.com/s3fspublic/publication/160328_Johnson_PresidentXiJinping_Web.pdf.

Cheung, T. M., T. Mahnken, D. Seligsohn, K Pollpeter, E. Anderson, F. Yang (2016), *Planning for Innovation: Understanding China's Plans for Technological, Energy, Industrial and Defence Development*, University of California, Institute on Global Conflict and Co-operation. Report prepared for the US-China Economic and Security Review Commission. www.uscc.gov/sites/default/files/Research/Planning%20for%20Innovation-Understanding%20China%27s%20Plans%20for%20Tech%20Energy%20Industrial%20and%20Defense%20Development072816.pdf

Chinese Government (2016), China's National Plan on Implementation of the 2030 Agenda for Sustainable Development, www.fmprc.gov.cn/web/ziliao_674904/zt_674979/dnzt_674981/qtzt/2030kcxfzyc_686343/P020170414689023442403.pdf.

Chun, Z. (2015), *China's cement industry could crack as tougher environmental laws bite*, www.chinadialogue.net/article/show/single/en/8277-China-s-cement-industry-could-crack-as-tougher-environmental-laws-bite.

Davies, K. (2013), *China Investment Policy: An Update*, OECD Working Papers on International Investment, 2013/01, OECD Publishing, Paris, http://dx.doi.org/10.1787/5k469l1hmvbt-en.

Easterly, W. (2003), "IMF, and World Bank Structural Adjustment Programs and Poverty", in Dooley and Frenkel (eds) *Managing Currency Crises in Emerging Markets*.

Ekanayake, E.M. and A. Mukherjee (2010), "Trade Blocs and the Gravity Model: A Study of Economic Integration among Asian Developing Countries", Journal of Economic Integration 25(4), December.

European Parliament (2017), *EU framework for FDI Screening.*

Forbes Magazine (2018), "The U.S., China And Others Race To Develop 5G Mobile Networks", April, www.forbes.com/sites/stratfor/2018/04/03/the-u-s-china-and-others-race-to-develop-5g-mobile-networks/#36f473a55875.

Fukuyama, Francis, (1989), *The End of History*, National Interest, Summer.

Gaukrodger, D. (2010), "Foreign State Immunity and Foreign Government Controlled Investors", OECD Working Papers on International Investment, 2010/02, OECD Publishing, Paris, http://dx.doi.org/10.1787/5km91p0ksqs7-en.

Global Times (2014), *Hebei looks to relocate its largest and most polluting industries abroad*, 22 December. www.globaltimes.cn/content/898086.shtml

GI Hub (2017), *Global Infrastructure Outlook*, Global Infrastructure Hub, https://outlook.gihub.org/.

Girma, S., Y. Gong, H. Gorg and Z. Yu (2008), "Can Production Subsidies Explain China's Export Performance? Evidence from Firm Level Data", Kiel Institute for the World Economy, Working Paper number 1442.

IMF (2017), *Peoples Republic of China: Selected Issues*, International Monetary Fund, Washington DC, July, www.imf.org/en/Publications/CR/Issues/2017/08/15/People-s-Republic-of-China-Selected-Issues-45171.

Kennedy, S. (2010), *The Myth of the Chinese Consensus*, Journal of Contemporary China.

Kennedy, S. (2015), *Made in China 2025*, Critical Questions, Center for Strategic and International Studies, 1 June, www.csis.org/analysis/made-china-2025.

Kennedy, S. and Johnson, C.K. (2016), "Perfecting China Inc.", Center for Strategic and International Studies, May. https://csis-prod.s3.amazonaws.com/s3fs-public/publication/160521_Kennedy_PerfectingChinaInc_Web.pdf.

Kim, J.Y. (2017), Remarks of World Bank Group President Jim Yong Kim at the Belt and Road Forum for International Co-operation – Opening Plenary Session, May. Available at: www.worldbank.org/en/news/speech/2017/05/14/remarks-of-world-bank-group-president-jim-yong-kim.

Kley, D. van der (2016), "China Shifts Polluting Cement to Tajikistan", chinadialogue, 8 August 2016, available at: www.chinadialogue.net/article/show/single/en/9174-China-shifts-polluting-cement-to-Tajikistan.

Levesque, G. and M. Stokes (2016), *Blurred Lines: Military-Civil Fusion and the Going Out of China's Defence Industry*, Pointe Bello, December.

Li Keqiang (2014), Remarks by H.E. Li Keqiang Premier of the State Council of the People's Republic of China At the 17th ASEAN-China Summit, www.fmprc.gov.cn/mfa_eng/wjdt_665385/zyjh_665391/t1212266.shtml.

Lowy Institute, (2017), *China, America and the Thucydides Trap: An Interview with Graham Allison*, www.lowyinstitute.org/the-interpreter/china-america-and-thucydides-interview-graham-allison.

McKinsey (2016), Bridging Global Infrastructure Gaps, www.mckinsey.com/industries/capital-projects-and-infrastructure/our-insights/bridging-global-infrastructure-gaps.

Miyamoto, K. and Y. Wu (forthcoming, 2018), *Enhancing Connectivity through Transport Infrastructure: The Role of Official Development Finance and Private Investment*, OECD, Paris.

Ministry of Ecology and Environment (2017), *The Belt and Road Ecological and Environmental Cooperation Plan*, http://english.sepa.gov.cn/Resources/Policies/policies/Frameworkp1/201706/t20170628_416869.shtml.

NCE (2014), *Infrastructure Investment Needs of a Low-carbon Scenario*, New Climate Economy, https://newclimateeconomy.report/workingpapers/wp-content/uploads/sites/5/2016/04/Infrastructure-investment-needs-of-a-low-carbon-scenario.pdf.

OECD (2018), Trade in Counterfeit Goods and Free Trade Zones, Evidence from Recent Trends, Paris, http://dx.doi.org/10.1787/9789264289550-en.

OECD (2017a), Investing in Climate, Investing in Growth, OECD Publishing, Paris, http://dx.doi.org/10.1787/9789264273528-en.

OECD (2017b) Investing in Climate Investing in Growth, Technical note on estimating infrastructure investment needs, www.oecd.org/environment/cc/g20-climate/Technical-note-estimates-of-infrastructure-investment-needs.pdf.

OECD (2017c), Steel Market Developments Q4 2017, Paris, www.oecd.org/sti/ind/steel-market-developments-Q42017.pdf.

OECD (2016), OECD Code of Liberalisation of Capital Movements, www.oecd.org/investment/codes.htm.

OECD (2015), OECD Guidelines on Corporate Governance of State-Owned Enterprises. www.oecd.org/corporate/guidelines-corporate-governance-soes.htm.

OECD (2011), OECD Guidelines for Multinational Enterprises, http://mneguidelines.oecd.org/guidelines/.

Office of the Leading Group for the BRI (2017), Building the Belt and Road: Concept, Practice and China's Contribution, May, https://eng.yidaiyilu.gov.cn/wcm.files/upload/CMSydylyw/201705/201705110537027.pdf.

Paal, D. (2013), "Contradictions in China's Foreign Policy", Carnegie Endowment for International Peace, 13 December 2013, http://carnegieendowment.org/2013/12/13/contradictions-in-china-s-foreign-policy-pub-53913 - comments.

Patil, S. (2015), "OBOR and India's Security Concerns", Gateway House, May. www.gatewayhouse.in/security-implications-of-chinas-transnational-corridors/.

Paulson Institute (2015), "Power Play: China's Ultra-High Voltage Technology and Global Standards", *Paulson Papers on Standards*, April, www.paulsoninstitute.org/wp-content/uploads/2015/04/PPS_UHV_English.pdf.

People's Republic of China (2016), 13th Five-Year Plan on National Economic and Social Development, March 17. Translation. http://en.ndrc.gov.cn/newsrelease/201612/P020161207645765233498.pdf.

People's Republic of China (2015), "Chronology of China's Belt and Road Initiative," March 28, 2015. http://english.gov.cn/news/top_news/2015/04/20/content_281475092566326.htm.

Qi, Jin (2016), "Speech at Belt and Road Summit", Hong Kong, China, 18 May.

Reuters, (2017), *Behind China's Silk Road Vision: Cheap Funds, Heavy Debt, Growing Risk,* 15 May, www.reuters.com/article/us-china-silkroad-finance-idUSKCN18B0YS.

Rodrik, D. (2006), *Goodbye Washington Consensus, Hello Washington Confusion? A Review of the World Bank's Economic Growth in the 1990s: Learning from a Decade of Reform*, Journal of Economic Literature, vol. XLIV, December.

Rosier, K. (2015), *China's Great Legal Firewall: Extraterritoriality of Chinese Firms in the United States*, U.S.-China Economic and Security Review Commission, May.

State Council of the People's Republic of China (2015), *Made in China 2025*, 8 May (English translation), www.cittadellascienza.it/cina/wp-content/uploads/2017/02/IoT-ONE-Made-in-China-2025.pdf.

SESEC (2015), *China Internet Plus Strategy*, SESEC Newsletter Issue 6, Annex 2. http://sesec.eu/app/uploads/2015/06/2015_05_SESECIII_Newsletter_April_2015_Annex02_China_Internet; plus_Strat....pdf.

The Straits Times (2016), *Thailand Rebuffs Railway Deal with China*, 5 May. www.straitstimes.com/asia/se-asia/thailand-rebuffs-railway-deal-with-china.

UK Government (2017), *National Security and Infrastructure Investment Review*, Green Paper, October. www.gov.uk/government/uploads/system/uploads/attachment_data/file/652505/2017_10_16_NSII_Green_Paper_final.pdf.

US-China Economic and Security Review Commission (2015), *Annual Report to Congress*, November.

US-China Economic and Security Review Commission (2017), *Hearing on Chinese Investment in the United States: Impacts and Issues for Policymakers*, January.

White House Office of Trade and Manufacturing Policy (2018), How China's Economic Aggression Threatens the United States and the World, www.whitehouse.gov/wp-content/uploads/2018/06/FINAL-China-Technology-Report-6.18.18-PDF.pdf.

Williams R.D. (2017), *CFIUS Reform and U.S. Government Concerns over Chinese Investment: A Primer*, Lawfare, November 13. www.lawfareblog.com/cfius-reform-and-us-government-concerns-over-chinese-investment-primer.

Williamson, J. (2004), *A Short History of the Washington Consensus*, Paper commissioned by Fundación CIDOB for a conference "From the Washington Consensus towards a new Global Governance", Barcelona, 24–25 September.

World Bank (2005), *Economic Growth in the 1990s: Learning from a Decade of Reform*, Washington DC.

Xi, J. (2017a), *Work Together to Build the Silk Road Economic Belt and The 21st Century Maritime Silk Road*, Opening speech, The Belt and Road Forum for International Cooperation, May.

Xi, J. (2017b), *Secure a Decisive Victory in Building a Moderately Prosperous Society in all Respects and Strive for the Great Success of Socialism with Chinese Characteristics for a New Era*, Delivered at the 19th National Congress of the Communist Party of China, 18 October.

Zhang, Wei-wei (2006), *The Allure of the Chinese Model*, New York Times, 1 November 2006.

Zhaou, S. (2010), *The China Model: Can it Replace the Western Model of Modernisation*, Journal of Contemporary China, vol. 19, issue 65.

Annex 2.A. Trade Gravity Model

The econometric analysis uses a Poisson model proposed by Santos Silva and Teneyro (2006). Santos Silva and Teneyro (2006) showed that a linear estimation of the log-linearised gravity equation is valid only with a specific assumption on the distribution of the residuals. This specific assumption does not necessarily hold in practice. In particular, estimates can be biased in the presence of heteroskedasticity. In addition, the Poisson model makes it possible to take into account cases where the dependent variable is equal to zero. For these reasons, the following model[1] is estimated in this paper using a Poisson pseudo-maximum likelihood (PPML) estimator:

$$X_{ijt} = \beta_0 + \beta_1 RTA\_I + \beta_2 RTA\_O + \beta_3 ASEAN_j + \beta_4 BA_j + \beta_5 ECO_j + \beta_6 SAARC_j + \beta_7 NAFTA_j + \beta_8 EU_j + \sum_{k=1}^{K} \beta_k Z_{j,t-1} + \sum_{g=1}^{G} \beta_g Z_{ij,t-1} + u_{it} + v_{jt} + \varepsilon_{ijt}$$

Time-varying origin country (u_{it}) and destination country (v_{jt}) dummies are included in the model. Such time-varying fixed effects capture influences such as the stringency of regulation, policy settings that can change over time (e.g. taxation) and of other country-specific developments (e.g. exchange rate changes, local financial market developments). The standard errors are clustered by country-pair because there can be a high persistence of the level of exports within each country pair over time.

The dependent variable (X_{ijt}) is the exports from origin country i to destination country j at time t. The bilateral export data are from the OECD Bilateral Trade in Goods Database. Data for GDP in millions of US dollars are taken from the International Monetary Fund's (IMF) World Economic Outlook. Data for trade openness indicator are taken from the Chinn-Ito website (http://web.pdx.edu/~ito/Chinn-Ito_website.htm). The political instability variable is taken from the World Bank's Worldwide Governance Indicators database (www.govindicators.org). The exchange rate data are from the IMF database. Data on distance, colonial past, common language, contiguity are taken from the CEPII GeoDist database (http://www.cepii.fr). The sample is based on an unbalanced panel dataset of annual data on 52 origin economies and 141 destination economies over the period 1997 to 2014.

The dummy RTA_I measures the degree of trade-creation effects of the regional trade agreement between members, while the dummy RTA_O captures the degree of trade-diverting effects between members and non-members, compared to "normal" bilateral trade flows.

The relative factor endowment variable (RFE) is defined as the absolute value of the difference between natural logarithm of per capita GDPs between country i and country j. The choice of this variable as an explanatory variable is based on the standard comparative advantage explanation of trade. This variable aims to capture technology differences between countries in explaining trade patterns. Though this variable is generally measured as the absolute value of the difference between natural logarithm of capital-labour ratio, due to the unavailability of that data, per capita GDP is used in place of capital-labour ratios. Thus, relative factor endowment is defined as:

$$RFE_{ijt} = |lnPGDP_{it} - lnPGDP_{jt}|$$

The similarity index (SIM) is defined as:

$$SIM_{ijt} = ln\left[1 - \left(\frac{GDP_{it}}{GDP_{it} + GDP_{jt}}\right)^2 - \left(\frac{GDP_{jt}}{GDP_{it} + GDP_{jt}}\right)^2\right]$$

Similarity with respect to GDP per capita implies increased similarity in size of country-specific product diversity in the differentiated goods sector and that leads to an increased trade volume.

The natural logarithm of Chinn-Ito financial openness indicator of country (FIOP) is an indicator of capital account openness in the destination country. The index was initially introduced in Chinn and Ito (2006). It is the natural logarithm of normalised Chinn-Ito index. Investment openness influences trade (export linked investment in distribution, infrastructure connectivity, etc.).

The World Bank political instability (PI) indicator of destination country j measures perceptions of the likelihood of political instability and/or politically-motivated violence, including terrorism. The indicator has a spread of -2.5 (high political instability) to 2.5 (low political instability). It is rescaled to facilitate the interpretation of the results by deducting it from 2.5 so that a higher number represents higher political instability.

Note

1. This model has benefited greatly from discussions with the OECD Trade Directorate.

Annex Table 2.A.1. Gravity model for trade, and the effect of free trade zones

Mnemonic	Variable definition	BRI origin countries	OECD origin countries
RBER	Natural logarithm of real bilateral exchange rate	0.197***	0.245***
		(6.04)	(13.21)
FIOP	Natural logarithm of Chinn-Ito financial openess indicator of country j	2.097***	2.339***
		(5.62)	(12.82)
SIM	Similarity index between country i and country j	-0.01	0.0590*
		(-0.18)	(1.95)
RFE	Relative factor endowment between country i and country j	0.02	0.034
		(0.52)	(0.79)
DIST	Natural logarithm of distance between country i and country j	-0.938***	-0.823***
		(-16.33)	(-19.22)
BORDER	Dummy variable equals 1 if countries i and j share a contiguous border and zero otherwise	0.212*	0.313***
		(1.95)	(4.45)
LANG	Dummy variable equals 1 if countries i and j share a common language	0.191	0.194**
		(1.58)	(2.37)
COLONY	Dummy variable equals 1 if country j is a former colony of country i or if the two countries share a common colonial linkage and zero otherwise	0.057	-0.042
		(0.26)	(-0.43)
PI	World Bank political instability indicator of country j	0.136	0.146**
		(1.10)	(2.00)
RTA_I	Dummy variable equals 1 if countries i and j belong to the same regional trade agreement and zero otherwise	-0.235	0.383**
		(-1.57)	(2.28)
RTA_O	Dummy variable equals 1 if country i belong to a regional trade agreement and country j does not, or vice versa and zero otherwise	-0.156	0.05
		(-1.35)	(0.43)
ASEAN	Dummy variable equals 1 if country j is a member of the Association of Southeast Asian Nations and zero otherwise	3.678***	3.069***
		(12.79)	(10.86)
BA	Dummy variable equals 1 if country j is a member of the Bangkok Agreement and zero otherwise	1.126***	2.545***
		(3.67)	(10.25)
ECO	Dummy variable equals 1 if country j is a member of the Economic Co-operation Organization and zero otherwise	-1.040***	1.537***
		(-2.69)	(5.89)
SAARC	Dummy variable equals 1 if country j is a member of the South Asia Association for Regional Cooperation and zero otherwise	-0.265	-2.177***
		(-0.67)	(-8.90)
NAFTA	Dummy variable equals 1 if country j is a member of the NAFTA trade agreement and zero otherwise	5.095***	3.242***
		(14.04)	(10.33)
EU	Dummy variable equals 1 if country j is a member of the European Union and zero otherwise	1.523***	0.461
		(3.76)	(1.40)
C	Constant	7.175***	10.75***
		(6.78)	(21.51)
	Observations	49529	77983

Note: *, ** and *** indicate statistical significance at the 10%, 5% and 1% levels, respectively. Standard errors adjusted for country-pair clusters are in parentheses.

StatLink http://dx.doi.org/10.1787/888933786610

Annex 2.B. List of economies by group

Two groups of economies are defined following the IMF country group classification: advanced economies and emerging and developing economies.

Advanced economies

Australia, Austria, Belgium, Canada, Cyprus, Czech Republic, Denmark, Estonia, Finland, France, Germany, Greece, Hong Kong (China), Iceland, Ireland, Israel, Italy, Japan, Korea, Latvia, Lithuania, Luxembourg, Macau, China, Malta, Netherlands, New Zealand, Norway, Portugal, Puerto Rico, San Marino, Singapore, Slovak Republic, Slovenia, Spain, Sweden, Switzerland, Chinese Taipei.

Emerging and developing economies

Afghanistan, Albania, Algeria, Angola, Antigua and Barbuda, Argentina, Armenia, Azerbaijan, Bahamas , Bahrain, Bangladesh, Barbados, Belarus, Belize, Benin, Bhutan, Plurinational State of Bolivia, Bosnia and Herzegovina, Botswana, Brazil, Brunei Darussalam, Bulgaria, Burkina Faso, Burundi, Cabo Verde, Cambodia, Cameroon, Central African Republic, Chad, Chile, People's Republic of China, Colombia, Comoros, Democratic Republic of the Congo, Republic of the Congo , Costa Rica, Côte d'Ivoire, Croatia, Djibouti, Dominica, Dominican Republic, Ecuador, Egypt, El Salvador, Equatorial Guinea, Eritrea, Ethiopia, Fiji, Gabon, Gambia, Georgia, Ghana, Grenada, Guatemala, Guinea, Guinea-Bissau, Guyana, Haiti, Honduras, Hungary, India, Indonesia, Islamic Republic of Iran, Iraq, Jamaica, Jordan, Kazakhstan, Kenya, Kiribati, Kosovo, Kuwait, Kyrgyzstan, Lao People's Democratic Republic, Lebanon, Lesotho, Liberia, Libya, Former Yugoslav Republic of Macedonia, Madagascar, Malawi, Malaysia, Maldives, Mali, Marshall Islands, Mauritania, Mauritius, Mexico, Federated States of Micronesia, Republic of Moldova, Mongolia, Montenegro, Morocco, Mozambique, Myanmar, Namibia, Nauru, Nepal, Nicaragua, Niger, Nigeria, Oman, Pakistan, Palau, Panama, Papua New Guinea, Paraguay, Peru, Philippines, Poland, Qatar, Romania, Russian Federation, Rwanda, Samoa, Sao Tome and Principe, Saudi Arabia, Senegal, Serbia, Seychelles, Sierra Leone, Solomon Islands, Somalia, South Africa, South Sudan, Sri Lanka, Saint Kitts and Nevis, Saint Lucia, Saint Vincent and the Grenadines, Sudan, Suriname, Swaziland, Syrian Arab Republic, Tajikistan, United Republic of Tanzania, Thailand, Timor-Leste, Togo, Tonga, Trinidad and Tobago, Tunisia, Turkey, Turkmenistan, Tuvalu, Uganda, Ukraine, United Arab Emirates, Uruguay, Uzbekistan, Vanuatu, Bolivarian Republic of Venezuela, Viet Nam, Yemen.

Chapter 3.

Reaping the full benefits of large infrastructure projects

This chapter focuses on ways to help economies linked to the Belt and Road Initiative (BRI) to maximise the longer-term benefits of infrastructure projects as recipient countries and to ensure an open and transparent environment for international investment. This means ensuring a level playing field for investors from both emerging and advanced economies. Asia's longer-term infrastructure needs will require much more investment than any one country can ultimately provide (USD 26 trillion to 2030, according to the Asian Development Bank) so efficient and cost effective solutions are essential. Host countries are likely to benefit most, with positive spill-over effects resulting for other economies when the process is based on level playing field considerations.

Five broad areas that could benefit from the implementation of, and wider adherence to, international standards for promoting a level playing field have been identified: the role of SOEs, given their growing presence in the international market; competition and the integrity of processes in procurement; mitigating corruption risk and ensuring responsible business conduct; incorporating environmental impact assessments in projects; and ensuring openness to international investment. In all areas, OECD standards provide useful guidance for both infrastructure-recipient economies and supplying economies.

The statistical data for Israel are supplied by and under the responsibility of the relevant Israeli authorities. The use of such data by the OECD is without prejudice to the status of the Golan Heights, East Jerusalem and Israeli settlements in the West Bank under the terms of international law.

3.1. Introduction

Globalisation involves the opening up of markets for trade and investment. Its history includes the early World Trade Organisation (WTO) rounds, the formation of the European Union and the creation of the North American Free Trade Agreement (NAFTA). International trade and investment need considerable infrastructure: ports, road, rail, air, and ancillary services. Most recently, the Belt and Road Initiative (BRI) is perhaps one of the most ambitious global transformations in its potential scope. It is not a formal treaty arrangement as such, nor is it based on any international organisation. Rather, it is a series of bilateral co-operation agreements promoted by China, which opens the possibility of contracts for infrastructure building and broader strategic, cultural and educational co-operation.[1]

As noted in Chapter 2, the Asian Development Bank (ADB) estimates that developing Asia will require USD 26 trillion in infrastructure investment between 2017 and 2030 to maintain current growth rates and adapt to climate change (ADB, 2017). Meeting these needs in the coming decades will require diversified and efficient project selection and funding. For the BRI, there is a strong need to dismantle trade and investment barriers by building roads, rail, ports, sea transportation facilities, electricity grids and telecommunication networks across six land-based economic corridors and a maritime corridor. Such connectivity is important to further develop supply chains, helping to improve well-being, reduce poverty and raise living standards around the world. No single country can provide the funding required for this initiative because the sums are huge and all financial systems have leverage limits if debt sustainability is to be achieved. Global infrastructure needs extend well beyond the BRI to all corners of the globe, including Latin America, Australasia and sub-Saharan Africa. Estimates for global infrastructure needs lay within the range of USD 50-100 trillion (Table 2.1). Wherever the investment occurs, it is always important to respect sustainable growth motivations that encompass many aspects: not only connectivity investment but also procurement principles, anti-bid rigging, anticorruption practices, corporate governance, responsible business conduct and a commitment to openness in trade and investment.

This need for a broader approach fits very well with OECD guiding principles and instruments, and also opens avenues for potential support through engaging the use of these OECD tools. They may help to inform some of the specific decisions that are going to be taken in the years to come and from which all countries involved in the push for connectivity infrastructure and sustainability goals can benefit.

This chapter focuses on four broad areas particularly relevant to infrastructure projects, and where applying internationally agreed standards and using tools that inform decision making may prove conducive to cost-effective solutions and fairness to all stakeholders in both developing and advanced economies, while also taking into account social and environmental impacts:

1. The **role of state-owned enterprises (SOEs)**. Closeness to government raises three broad types of concerns:
    a. *The level playing field:* Closeness to government can involve mixing economic and non-economic objectives and SOEs governed this way can be the beneficiaries of subsidies and other advantages (or disadvantages) that create an uneven playing field in achieving their goals. This can result in resource misallocation, including excessive debt levels, if full life-cycle costs and benefits of projects do not derive from transparent and competitive processes.

   b. *National security concerns* can emerge where SOEs are involved. Examples include: the loss of strategically sensitive technology – a concern not limited to, but sometimes aggravated by, state ownership of the acquiring company; and strategic infrastructure assets falling under the control of other sovereign governments.

   c. *Possible gaps in legal accountability for SOEs* in their operations abroad relating to potential claims of foreign state immunity.

   Section 3.2 focuses on issues related to the role of SOEs and presents some illustrations of these.

2. **Open competition in procurement.** Infrastructure is very costly up front, and benefits are uncertain and accrue over a long period of time. Projects therefore need to be open to international competition on a level playing field to ensure host countries achieve the lowest cost and highest quality facilities, not distorted by undue influence of governments. These issues are discussed in section 3.3.

3. **Anti-corruption, responsible business conduct and the environment.** The cost of infrastructure investment also needs to take into account the heavy cost of bribery and corruption and the social and environmental impacts of projects undertaken.

   a. *Bribery and corruption* is often associated with SOEs and not least in the area of large scale infrastructure projects. This can influence contracts that are awarded, making the playing field less even, and corruption always wastes societies' resources (see OECD, 2017a).

   b. *Responsible business conduct (RBC)* is required in order for projects to be carried out with the least disruption to local communities and the environment. The absence of RBC risks unforeseen costs in mitigation, labour disputes, delays and cancellations.

   c. *Environmental impact assessments* (EIAs) are also a cornerstone of sustainable development and complement the RBC requirements of multinational companies working to build facilities and infrastructure consistent with long-term development plans that meet environmental goals.

   Domestic policies and international co-operation for managing corruption risks, and implementing RBC and environment strategies are discussed in section 3.4.

4. **The need for openness to international investment.** The longer-term goal of building connectivity in developing economies is to boost trade and investment so that well-being and living standards can rise. Excessive restrictions on inflows and outflows of investment reduce these potential benefits by increasing costs, limiting technological choices, and working against the very connectivity that infrastructure strategies are supposed to build. Such inefficiencies can be reduced over the longer run by promoting transparent rules and liberalising cross-border investment, if infrastructure investment is to fully deliver the desired benefits. These issues are taken up in section 3.5.

   Finally, section 3.6 offers concluding remarks.

3.2. State-owned enterprises and corporate governance

SOE governance and the level playing field

SOEs play an important role in the world economy, particularly in natural monopoly sectors such as utilities. This role has been growing due to the rapid growth of emerging economies.[2] Table 3.1 shows where the Fortune 500 world's largest companies are headquartered. While Chinese companies feature prominently, this must be seen in the context of China's rapid growth and its centrally-planned economic structure starting point. Whereas 9 out of 10 Fortune 500 companies were state-owned in 2000, this has declined to 75 out of 109 in 2017, or 69%, as growth has been combined with economic reforms over the intervening period.

Table 3.1. Location of the headquarters of the Fortune 500 world's largest companies: Changes 2000-2017

	2000	2017	Change
United States	179	132	-47
China	10	109	99
Japan	107	51	-56
France	37	29	-8
Germany	37	29	-8
United Kingdom	38	24	-14
Korea	12	15	3
Netherlands	10	14	4
Switzerland	11	14	3
Canada	12	11	-1
Other economies	47	72	25
of which SOEs	27	102	75
of which Chinese SOEs	9	75	66

Source: Ernst and Young (2017).

StatLink http://dx.doi.org/10.1787/888933786743

At a general level, an uneven playing field can emerge as the simple result of state support for SOEs. This can include: export tax rebates (which can be considerable since the early stages of infrastructure projects boost construction material exports); below-market interest rate loans from state-controlled financial institutions; and preferential treatment in procurement. This can apply to the activity of SOEs anywhere in the world. Geopolitical, cultural and other non-economic objectives may also play an important role. Government-to-government and SOE-to-SOE negotiations therefore become a factor in concluding transactions.

Table 3.2 provides an indication of state ownership based on stock-market listed SOEs for selected economies. It shows that SOE operations tend to be concentrated in the public utilities sector (energy; telecommunication; public transportation).

Table 3.2. State ownership of listed companies in selected economies

Country	State's share of equity market capitalisation	Percentage of SOEs found in the public utilities sector[1]
India	20%	65%
Indonesia	16%	61%
Korea	13%	54%
Malaysia	33%	47%
Singapore	10%	47%
Thailand	10%	65%
Viet Nam	14%	35%
Turkey	9%	50%
Poland	9%	23%

1. In OECD countries, the share is calculated on the basis of all SOEs, whether listed or not.
Source: OECD (2017b) and OECD (2017c). The data are based on Factset, and authors' calculations.

StatLink http://dx.doi.org/10.1787/888933786762

China, the United Arab Emirates, Russia, Indonesia, Malaysia, Saudi Arabia, India, Brazil, Norway and Thailand are the ten countries with the highest SOE-shares of GDP. OECD (2013) finds that sectors with a high SOE presence also tend to be intensely traded (including raw materials, merchandise and services). With respect to foreign subsidiaries, the report finds that larger advanced country privately-owned companies are most prevalent in activities abroad (particularly the United States), and that subsidiaries with SOE parents tend to be less active in this sense. Where companies do have SOE parents, however, the study finds that non-OECD economies tend to be relatively more internationally active. OECD (2013) concludes *inter alia*: "*This suggests that there is a potential for economic distortions in world markets if the SOEs operating in these sectors benefit from unfair advantages granted to them by governments. The large state presence and international orientation of SOEs in some non-OECD countries highlight the need for enhanced dialogue on cross-border effects of state ownership going beyond the OECD membership*". These observations suggest scope for greater engagement with the OECD corporate governance guidelines to ensure maintenance of a level playing field among state-owned and privately-owned companies operating on a commercial basis.

If SOEs are properly separated from other public sector functions, held to high standards of governance and accountability and operate on a "level playing field" with private competitors, this should not give rise to concerns. The OECD Guidelines on Corporate Governance of State-Owned Enterprises (see Box 3.1) provide detailed guidance on how this can be obtained in practice. Conversely, if good practices of ownership and governance are not implemented, commercial relationships between SOEs may effectively become state "contracts" with low levels of transparency and accountability.

Transparency and accountability in the SOE sector will also help reduce the risk of countries becoming compromised by corruption (see below), or other non-transparent practices. Most recent OECD research shows heightened risks among SOEs operating with significant non-commercial objectives in sectors with high economic rents and, not least, in public utilities where large public procurement contracts predominate.[3] Adequate internal control and risk management at SOE and state levels, consistent with the OECD Guidelines on Corporate Governance of SOEs, will help to manage the risks that could arise in the corporate value chains of SOEs involved with the BRI and in other parts of the world.

These issues are important, both because of level playing field considerations with respect to private companies, and because host countries entering into contracts with SOEs face very real economic constraints. If resource misallocation results from the influence of non-economic objectives, leading to excessively costly projects that are not justified by economic benefits, then the host's ability to repay debt may be reduced, leading to further sets of economic and social problems. A recent study finds that eight developing economies associated with BRI projects may have run up excessive debts (see Hurley et al., 2018).

Box 3.1. OECD standards for corporate governance

The OECD has, thus far, developed two standards to help governments and enterprises improve corporate governance, with a view to enhancing companies' access to finance and ensuring a level playing field in the marketplace. Implementation of these standards is underpinned by OECD Council Recommendations.

- The G20/OECD Principles of Corporate Governance (OECD, 2015a) provide policy makers with the key legal, regulatory and institutional building blocks that help companies' access to capital markets and reassure investors that their rights are protected. They provide recommendations in a number of critical areas, such as the rights of shareholders, the functioning of the investment intermediation, stock market practices, the role of stakeholders, corporate disclosure, and the responsibilities of the board of directors. They also address the quality of supervision and enforcement. The Principles were last revised in 2015 and are one of the Financial Stability Board's twelve key standards for sound financial systems.
- The OECD Guidelines on Corporate Governance of State-Owned Enterprises (OECD, 2015b) advise public authorities on how to effectively manage their responsibilities as company owners, making SOEs more efficient and transparent. They provide concrete guidance on how to ensure that SOEs do not have any undue competitive advantages when they operate in markets, and establish good practices for financial and non-financial disclosure by SOEs and their owners. From their inception in 2005, the Guidelines have served as an international benchmark for the corporatisation and commercialisation of SOEs. Increasingly, they have also come to serve as a reference for international trade and investment regulators for assessing internationally active SOEs. The Guidelines were last revised in 2015.

Implementation of the relevant OECD standards for corporate governance shown in Box 3.1 would help to reduce concerns about unfair practices in the global economy in general and within the BRI in particular.

National security concerns

Since the 2000s, a growing number of countries have introduced or tightened the screening and review of foreign investment projects to mitigate risks to national security.

Box 3.2. Security concerns related to infrastructure investment

Concern about strategic infrastructure being controlled by foreign governments is hardly new, and a number of OECD countries are evolving policies to evaluate and deal with the issues. A useful survey of practices can be found in Wehrlé et al., (2016). Transport infrastructure and energy grids have been of some concern in this respect when government-linked entities attempt to buy or obtain contracts to run such facilities. Issues can also arise when government entities are involved in building new facilities. The problem seems to arise when transactions result in excessive debt levels that cannot be serviced. This is sometimes resolved through the handing of strategic assets to foreign governments (essentially as debt-for-equity swaps). This may occur: (i) after construction, when financing terms prove to have been too costly and revenue less than anticipated (creditor countries can accept equity in the assets to reduce the debt, resulting in the de facto transfer of strategic infrastructure to other countries); or (ii) at the start of negotiations, when essential projects are not affordable by the host country and costs can be reduced by granting large equity positions to the investor.

An example of the former is the USD 1.1 billion BRI project for Port Hambantota in Sri Lanka that has substantial strategic importance of both a commercial and non-commercial nature.[1] The project loan was based on a non-concessional 6.3% interest rate applied to an excessive level of debt. This resulted in a foreign government taking a 70% equity stake and 6000 hectares of land around the port in order for Sri Lanka to avoid defaulting.[2] An example of the latter arrangement is the 70% equity stake in the port of Kyauk Pyu (Myanmar) and nearby Madae Island, essential for twin gas and crude oil pipelines through to Yunnan Province in China, which allows a short-cut for shipping (to avoid the congested Malacca Straits and the South China Sea).

Concern about such issues has resulted in a number of countries denying or cancelling projects.[3] As with advanced countries, these tensions could be avoided by all SOEs adopting Santiago Principles-like arrangements which might address concerns about the role of the state and national security.

1. From William and Mary, AidData: http://china.aiddata.org/projects/33256
2. This has been followed up with the government granting tax concessions for China to develop other projects around the port. See Schultz (2017).
3. Examples include Pakistan's Diamar-Bhasha USD14bn dam project in 2017. The too harsh financial conditions attached to the loan are considered to be the main reason for the subsequent cancellation of the project (see Dasgupta, 2017). Nepal cancelled the USD2.5bn Guda Gandaki hydro dam project for similar reasons (see Bagchil, 2017).

A recent OECD study shows that over a third of the 58 advanced and emerging economies that participate in the OECD-hosted Freedom of Investment policy dialogue now operate such mechanisms (see Wehrlé, et al., 2016, and Box 3.2). The growing presence of foreign SOEs in the international marketplace explains this trend to a large extent. In several of these economies, investment proposals involving SOEs are subject to greater scrutiny.

Santiago Principles-like arrangements

Concerns about international investment by SOEs could be significantly attenuated if investors would agree to abide by specific standards of transparency and good governance. This approach was successfully implemented a decade ago, when similar concerns arose from high profile investors participating in the International Forum of Sovereign Wealth Funds (IFSWFs). The "Santiago Principles", a set of Generally Accepted Principles and Practices adopted in 2008 by the International Working Group of Sovereign Wealth Funds (IWG),[4] commit SWFs to transparent governance that helps to avoid countries using national security arguments as a cover for protectionism against foreign SWFs.

A decade later, the upsurge of SOEs in global investment has triggered similar concerns, especially as many SOEs are less transparent than private firms (OECD, 2015b). However, the imposition of outright or unqualified restrictions on SOE investments in recipient countries benefits neither host nor home countries, as opportunities for mutually beneficial international investment are forgone.

To alleviate these legitimate concerns in host countries and reap the benefits of investment, SOEs would need to commit to respect good practices for governance, disclosure, accountability and transparency (OECD, 2015b). These principles are part of the OECD Guidelines on Corporate Governance of SOEs and include specific provisions on the legal and regulatory framework for SOEs, as well as for their practices, that promote a level playing field and fair competition in the marketplace when SOEs engage in economic activities.

Translated to an international market context, these provisions could address concerns that investment regulators may have. The last element required to emulate the "Santiago Principles" would be to secure a commitment by SOEs to abide by these standards.

Reciprocally, recipient economies should commit themselves not to use national security as a cover for protectionism and follow the principle of non-discrimination, transparency/ predictability, regulatory proportionality and accountability to guide their investment policies relating to national security, as recommended by OECD Guidelines for Recipient Country Investment Policies Relating to National Security, which were adopted in parallel with the Santiago Principles.[5]

Possible gaps in legal accountability for SOEs abroad

Concerns about uneven playing fields and national security reviews for SOEs, discussed above, are also affected by the broader legal environment for SOEs, private companies and governments. OECD-hosted investment policy dialogue, which regularly gathers government representatives of OECD countries, the G20 and others, has seen concerns raised about whether the doctrine of foreign state immunity may create gaps in the legal accountability of certain SOEs which are active as investors abroad (Gaukrodger, 2010). Among other issues, these gaps may be relevant to competitive neutrality between SOEs and other companies.

Resolving possible gaps in the legal accountability of SOEs abroad would improve trust with respect to their investments, particularly if coupled with attention to other recommendations, such as implementation of the OECD Guidelines on Corporate Governance of SOEs.

Two particular areas of concern have been identified:

- whether foreign state immunity as applied to SOEs may make it difficult for private parties to pursue legitimate claims against them; and
- whether the doctrine creates regulatory enforcement gaps for host countries.

Foreign state immunity and private party claims

Under the doctrine of foreign state immunity, a sovereign state is not subject to the full force of rules applicable in another state. National courts are barred from adjudicating or enforcing certain claims or judgments against foreign states. At one time, states enjoyed "absolute" immunity: all proceedings against foreign states were barred unless the foreign state consented. With the greater involvement of governments in commercial activities, many jurisdictions began to apply a "restrictive" theory of immunity, at least in cases brought by private parties. Under the restrictive approach, courts continue to recognise immunity for "sovereign" acts, but deny immunity for "commercial" acts. The commercial exception helps protect business partners that engage in commercial transactions with foreign states and foreign state entities.

The restrictive approach is reflected in case law, national statutes and international conventions, although with significant variations. The United Nations Convention on the Jurisdictional Immunities of States and their Property, adopted by the United Nations General Assembly in 2004 (the UN Immunity Convention), incorporates a restrictive approach and was negotiated over many years by many countries. However, it has not entered into force.

The restrictive approach is not universally recognised. China, in particular, has taken a clear position in favour of absolute immunity in a recent high-profile case in Hong Kong, China. China has signed, but not ratified, the UN Immunity Convention.

China's affirmation of absolute immunity is noteworthy for BRI projects and other Chinese investments abroad. For some aspects, the foreign state's views on absolute, as opposed to restrictive, immunity may not be of great practical importance. State immunity is governed in the first instance by the law where the court is situated (the forum state, which may often be the host state). When it is well-established in the forum state that restrictive immunity applies, it is likely that the foreign state's views on immunity will not affect the court's approach. Depending on the circumstances, however, the foreign state's views on immunity could be an important factor in the overall political climate of a case in the host state, the scope of co-operation with regard to the gathering of evidence, or the attitude of host state regulators. In addition to rules in the host state and the home state of the foreign entity, the rules on immunity in third states where assets may be available for enforcement of judgments or awards against the entity can also be relevant. Advance clarification of the rules can be valuable.

With regard to SOEs, two general legal issues can be noted:

- whether SOEs, as entities, fall within the domain of the "foreign state" for purposes of foreign state immunity; and
- if, in some situations, an SOE entity can be considered to be part of a broad conception of the "foreign state", whether its actions are commercial or sovereign. This is generally only relevant if restrictive immunity applies.

International conventions and different national legal systems vary in their definition of what constitutes a "foreign state". OECD-hosted investment policy discussions in the late 2000s took into account two broad approaches to the relationship between SOEs and the foreign state.[6] Under the European Convention on State Immunity (ECSI), and in the United Kingdom and most civil law jurisdictions, it appears that such entities have generally been considered to fall outside the domain of the foreign state providing they operate independently from the state.[7] The ECSI uses separate legal personality and the capacity to sue and be sued as factors to determine whether an entity or company operates independently of the state.[8] In general, separate entities are not entitled to immunity from adjudication or execution. Such entities are immune only if they carry out acts in the exercise of sovereign authority.

In contrast to the ECSI-type approach, the US Foreign Sovereign Immunities Act (FSIA) defines the overall foreign state more broadly. It includes certain majority state-owned companies under its definition of "agencies and instrumentalities" of the foreign state. Less information was available for many other jurisdictions. The UN Immunity Convention has been described as somewhat ambivalent on the issue of SOEs (see Fox, 2005).

Some Chinese SOEs have claimed immunity in recent cases. Some cases and declarations have suggested application of a "control" test for separateness of Chinese state entities from the state for immunity purposes and that the legal form of the entity is important.[9] Control is a flexible concept and may be subject to more interpretation than the ECSI criteria. The notion of state control has been narrowly interpreted by China in some recent contexts, suggesting a view that SOEs generally would not be considered to be part of the state when they operate abroad.[10] At the same time, recent statements and actions to ensure that the Communist Party of China (CPC) maintains control over Chinese SOEs, and possible variations in SOE governance over the course of projects, may need to be considered in this context.[11]

Possible regulatory gaps in host countries

The second broad concern raised in OECD-hosted investment policy discussions is the possible impact of the doctrine of foreign state immunity on host country regulation of SOEs. While there is extensive commentary and many cases addressing foreign state immunity in the context of private lawsuits, little attention has been paid to the issue of its impact on regulation. It has been suggested in OECD-hosted discussions of state immunity that regulation may best be analysed in functional terms on a sliding scale depending on a number of factors which would affect the strength of the case for applying a restrictive theory of immunity (or otherwise limiting, or excluding, immunity). Key factors could include the applicable definition of the foreign state and type of foreign state entity at issue, the nature of regulatory remedies to be applied (e.g. whether they are compensatory or punitive in nature) and the public or private nature of the enforcement agency. Where a regulated entity is from a state that applies absolute immunity, the definition of the "foreign state" and whether the entity in question might be covered, could be critically important issues for the political context for regulation (Gordon and Gaukrodger, 2012).

Another factor meriting consideration is whether relevant entities, or their owners or affiliates, have a track record of making relatively aggressive assertions of immunity. Depending on applicable law, even an assertion of immunity can delay cases and increase costs for private parties and regulators.

Policy recommendations

In light of these developments and considerations, the OECD suggests that governments and companies interested in attracting investment from foreign SOEs, or which are considering transactions with foreign SOEs, should examine and clarify the applicable law on immunities in advance in order to ensure that immunity will not raise unexpected issues in the event of disputes.[12] Waivers of state immunity are widely used to ensure that other entities, that could conceivably assert a claim for state immunity at a later date, waive any claims to immunity in advance when transactions are being negotiated. Where there is a shared view about the rules in advance, waivers can document it for the duration of projects. Waivers are particularly important if there are areas of legal uncertainty in relevant international or national law on immunity. Waivers may need to address both immunity from jurisdiction (barring a state's courts from judging the actions of another state) and immunity from execution (barring a state from taking coercive measures against another state's assets for the purpose of enforcing a judgement). In addition to the content of waivers, their legal basis and form can be important. In some contexts, it has been suggested that some waivers must be in treaties, rather than contracts, to be effective.[13]

Increased international co-operation in articulating approaches to similar regulatory issues and in seeking common approaches would provide many benefits. It could assist in providing a clear and predictable framework for foreign investment by SOEs and regulatory action affecting them, reducing the likelihood of costly and politically sensitive investment disputes.

3.3. Open competition in procurement

As indicated earlier, the massive presence of SOEs and the closeness of regulatory regimes for foreign investment favour the role of government-to-government deal making. While this may speed up agreements and get the job done on time, it may not necessarily be at the lowest cost.

This has resulted in some lack of diversity. According to the *Reconnecting Asia Database,* 89% of projects financed by Chinese banks go to Chinese companies, 7.6% to local companies (which are usually a part of a joint venture with a Chinese firm) and 3.4% goes to foreign companies (defined as neither Chinese nor local). Many projects also receive joint funding by Chinese banks and Multilateral Development Banks (MDBs), such as the World Bank or the ADB, though the scale of the latter is smaller. In comparison to Chinese banks, 29% of MDB funding goes to Chinese companies, 40.8% to local firms and 30.2% to foreign firms.

Foreign construction and logistics firms may not always be aware of project opportunities. Projects documented in the database involving Chinese banks show no evidence of early stage announcements (open calls for tender). The risk for recipient economies is that the lack of diversity and openness in bidding, where present, may not lead to the lowest cost and stakeholder friendly outcomes for host economies. Costs might be higher, and the oft-given reason for awarding a contract being based on speed of execution can be at the expense of local communities and the environment (see below).[14]

Competition in bidding

Open, transparent and competitive procurement processes help to avoid undesirable outcomes. It will be recalled from Chapter 2 that an Oxford academic study (Ansar et al., 2016), using detailed project data, found that Chinese transport construction companies tend: to under-estimate costs (30.6% average overruns); to finish on time, but at the expense of quality and the environment; and that evidence of misallocation is present (under-usage of road and rail in the majority of cases and congestion in others). This kind of outcome is not confined only to Chinese SOEs. The study found that these findings were not statistically different to a sample of company projects from a 'rich democracy' sample. Similar findings have been found for India (see Singh, 2010), where in a sample of 894 projects 40% experienced serious cost overruns and 82% had completion delays. Referring to November 2017 data, the Times of India reports that of 1 289 projects, 359 face cost overruns and time delays.[15] That is, these issues concern all countries. To achieve better benefit/cost outcomes over the long-term requires a realistic picture of the upfront and full life-cycle costs. Examples of recent transactions in Box 3.3 illustrate why processes need to be improved.

Box 3.3. Illustrations of procurement issues from BRI projects

Belgrade-Budapest high speed rail link

China's first rail line project in Europe was with Hungary and Serbia, consisting of a USD 2.89 billion, 350 kilometre Belgrade-Budapest high-speed railway by the China Railway International Corporation, with financing from China's Export-Import Bank. This project has been delayed after questions arose as to whether an open procurement process should have been used under the terms of the EU's procurement laws (see European Commission, 2017; and Qiong, 2017).

Bandra-Worli sealink (India)

This project was to link Worli and central Mumbai to Bandra and the western suburbs with a cable-stay bridge. Compared to its original cost estimate of Rs 300 crore (around USD 3 billion), the final cost proved to be Rs 1600 crore (around USD 16 billion). The project was completed 5 years after its original scheduled opening (Singh, 2010).

Matiari-to-Lahore high voltage transmission line

Pakistan is very short of power and the USD 1.7 billion project to build the transmission line from the coal power station being built on the coast (Matiari) to industry in Lahore was awarded to State Grid with funding from the China Development Bank and Exim Bank, despite initial discussions with large advanced country firms (General Electric and Siemens). This was in the form of a government-to-government contract with no formal open procurement process. It is reported that this was in spite of a significantly lower estimate for the convertor stations (the most significant part of the cost) by an advanced country company, and that the telling factor was timeliness (see Jorgic, 2017). To fully prepare and execute the project was estimated by the advanced country firm to be 48 months, versus a 27-month estimate from State Grid. Withholding tax concessions were offered but only to the Chinese firm.

To achieve the most beneficial outcomes for all countries, bids need to be based on open processes and a level playing field for all competent suppliers of construction and related services.[16] Instruments that provide a useful starting point to improve transparency and openness in procurement processes are discussed in Box 3.4.

Where these instruments do not apply there is a risk that trade distortions, of the type envisaged at the time of their agreement, will unfold. Since the agreements appear to have proved effective at preventing trade distortions based on export credits between signatories, it would appear sensible to look at ways to renew efforts towards building participation in these or similar agreements, either multilaterally or incrementally (for example, through bilateral trade agreements).

As economies participating in BRI projects become more open and continue the reform process, OECD tools on detailed competition policy will become increasingly relevant. These tools include the OECD Competition Toolkit (OECD, 2017e), and the framework that the OECD has developed to counter bid rigging (OECD, 2009b).

Box 3.4. Instruments to improve transparency and openness in procurement processes

1. The OECD Recommendation of the Council on Public Procurement is the overarching OECD guiding principle on public procurement that promotes its strategic and holistic use. It is a reference for modernising procurement systems and can be applied across all levels of government and SOEs. It addresses the entire procurement cycle while integrating public procurement with other elements of strategic governance, such as budgeting, financial management and additional forms of services delivery. The 2015 Recommendation builds upon the foundational principles of the 2008 OECD Recommendation on Enhancing Integrity in Public Procurement, expanding them to reflect the critical role governance of public procurement must play in achieving efficiency and advancing public policy objectives. www.oecd.org/gov/public-procurement/recommendation.

   In order to support implementation of the Recommendation, the Public Procurement Toolbox was also developed and made available online. In addition to exploring each of the 12 principles of the Recommendation, the Toolbox provides policy tools, country examples and indicators to measure a country's public procurement system.

2. The OECD Arrangement on Officially Supported Export Credits (the Arrangement), sets out the most generous export credit terms and conditions that may be supported by its participants. It places limitations on the terms and conditions of officially supported export credits (e.g. minimum interest rates, risk fees and maximum repayment terms) and the provision of tied aid. Originally agreed in 1978, the Arrangement is a "gentleman's agreement", i.e. soft law. Current participants to the Arrangement are: Australia, Canada, the European Union, Japan, Korea, New Zealand, Norway, Switzerland and the United States. www.oecd.org/tad/xcred/arrangement.htm.

   The Arrangement, which is routinely updated, includes procedures for prior notification, consultation, information exchange and review for export credit offers that are exceptions to or derogations of the rules, as well as tied aid offers. The main purpose of the Arrangement is to provide a framework for the orderly use of officially supported export credits. In practice, this means removing the scope for governments to undercut one another by providing ever more attractive financial terms in support of exporters that compete for overseas sales. Prior to these rules, many governments provided financial subsidies in favour of their national exports, thereby creating trade distortions. Thus, the intention of the Arrangement was to provide a level playing field where firms competed on the basis of price and quality of the exported goods and not on the quality of the financial support that was provided by their government.

3. The WTO General Procurement Agreement (the GPA) aims to open government procurement markets mutually among its parties, with a view to achieving greater liberalisation and expansion of, and improving the framework for, the conduct of international trade. The GPA therefore establishes rules requiring that open, fair

and transparent conditions of competition be ensured in procurements by covered entities purchasing listed goods, services and construction services of a value exceeding specified threshold values.
www.wto.org/english/tratop_e/gproc_e/gp_gpa_e.htm.

This agreement is plurilateral within the framework of the WTO, meaning that not all WTO members are parties to the GPA. At present, the GPA has 19 parties comprising 47 WTO members.[1] Another 31 WTO members participate in the GPA Committee as observers. Out of these, ten members (including China) are in the process of acceding to the Agreement.[2]

1. The 19 are: Armenia, Canada, EU (including its members), Hong Kong (China), Iceland, Israel, Japan, Korea, Lichtenstein, Moldova, Montenegro, Aruba, New Zealand, Norway, Singapore, Switzerland (updating), Chinese Taipei, Ukraine, and the United States.
2. The ten are: Albania; Australia; China; Georgia; Jordan; Kyrgyzstan; Oman; Russian Federation; Tajikistan; the Former Yugoslav Republic of Macedonia.

3.4. Fighting corruption and promoting responsible business conduct

Infrastructure projects often involve enormous sums of money and can be lucrative so bidding between companies for these contracts is highly competitive. One means of winning contracts, whilst still offering competitive quotes, can be to accompany the proposal with a bribe. These cost considerations also create an incentive to minimise the financial aspects associated with social and environmental cost mitigation. This section looks at each issue and proposes options.

Fighting bribery and corruption

Bribery is still widespread in many economies and is a very corrosive crime. It erodes the integrity of economic and political institutions, weakens market competition and undermines the trust of citizens. Through its work on the OECD Convention on Combating Bribery of Foreign Public Officials in International Business Transactions (the OECD Anti-Bribery Convention), the OECD spearheads the fight against the supply-side of bribery – that is, against givers of bribes to foreign public officials in international business transactions.

This issue is very relevant to public procurement (and particularly in utilities and infrastructure), which is at the heart of efforts to close infrastructure gaps. The *OECD Foreign Bribery Report* documents around 57% of bribes were paid to obtain public procurement contracts (OECD, 2014b, p.27). With regard to the infrastructure sector, the OECD's G20 contribution on corruption and growth suggests a reason for this: "*One of the characteristics that make this sector especially prone to corruption is the frequent monopoly situation, in which those who control the entities receive large rents. Additionally, due to the need for constant government intervention in this sector, there are many opportunities for misuse of authority and demand for bribes*" (OECD, 2015e, p.9).

As part of this work, the OECD keeps track of cases of international bribery that have ended with sanctions for individuals or companies that engaged in bribery. The OECD data show that public officials of 39 out of 72 economies that participate in the BRI were the bribe recipients in 226 of the 270 bribery schemes that the Working Group on Bribery (WGB) database contains. These cases are merely the tip of the iceberg because they omit cases that were never detected, prosecuted and sanctioned and only cover cases where the briber was subject to the jurisdiction of a member to the WGB. Nevertheless, they shed light on these economies' experiences with bribery of their public officials. Indeed, the cases highlight the importance of two key features of bribery: the relative predominance of SOEs as a source of heightened corruption risks, and the cross-border nature of bribery. **First, countries with a relative predominance of SOEs are more vulnerable**, because these firms tend to be both involved in high-risk sectors and sometimes have weak governance frameworks. The WGB database shows that officials from SOEs are major recipients of bribes – executives of SOEs and other associated parties were, by far, the most common bribe recipients, accounting for 86 of the 184 bribery cases for which information is available on who was bribed (see Figure 3.1).

Furthermore, SOE cases were heavily concentrated in the energy sector (accounting for 51 cases) and telecommunications (10 cases). These are known to be high-risk sectors for bribery. The largest sanction ever imposed for foreign bribery in the OECD cases was for a USD 331 million bribe paid to a close relative of the then-president of a country participating in the BRI. This relative was also a public official who used her influence over telecommunications regulation to help the company effect market entry. As noted in Box 3.1, the OECD Guidelines on Corporate Governance of SOEs can help economies deal with the significant bribery risks associated with their SOEs, while also achieving the non-commercial objectives that they might have for their SOEs in high-risk sectors, such as telecommunications.

Second, all economies that want to fight corruption need to engage in international co-operation – they cannot wage this fight on their own. Many of the 226 bribes in the sample were part of bribery schemes straddling large numbers of countries. These are schemes run by multinational companies, including some which are state-owned, that are well versed in managing global legal risks using intermediaries, offshore jurisdictions and complex corporate groups. By way of illustration, the top-three bribing companies in the BRI sample – measured in terms of the number of jurisdictions they bribed in – were:

- An automobile manufacturer that paid bribes in a total of 20 countries, including in 16 that participate in the BRI; the bribe scheme also involved Chinese, German and Russian subsidiaries, as well as US and Latvian bank accounts held by shell companies.
- An engineering and electronics firm that bribed in 20 countries, 10 of which were linked with the BRI. The cash for these bribes was funnelled through numerous off-the-books entities, including several slush funds held in the name of US shell companies.
- An engineering and manufacturing company that bribed in 14 countries, 10 of which were linked with BRI projects. The scheme also involved intermediaries in Monaco, Portugal, Panama, Singapore, Thailand, and the United Kingdom.

In this list, the economies participating in BRI projects are not necessarily over-represented in terms of their numbers and economic weight—all countries face these issues. The point is that these bribe schemes are international in scope. Detection, investigation and sanctioning of bribery of their public officials poses challenges that extend well beyond their own jurisdictions. The global nature of the crime of bribery requires a global response from the law enforcement community.

Faced with these challenges, law enforcement agencies in all economies need to be as sophisticated and international as the businesses that seek to bribe. They need to keep up with recent law enforcement developments (e.g. case information processing technology) and to collaborate with other law enforcement agencies. They also need to focus on domestic legal frameworks, including legislation and courts.

The WGB provides a platform in which law enforcement officials can share information and experiences and forge social ties that can help expedite the more formal processes of mutual legal assistance. G20 member economies that have not yet joined the Convention should consider doing so, as encouraged by the G20 Anti-Corruption Working Group.

Figure 3.1. SOE officials as recipients in sanctioned bribery transactions

(Out of 226 sanctioned bribery transactions, where bribe recipients were in economies participating in the BRI)

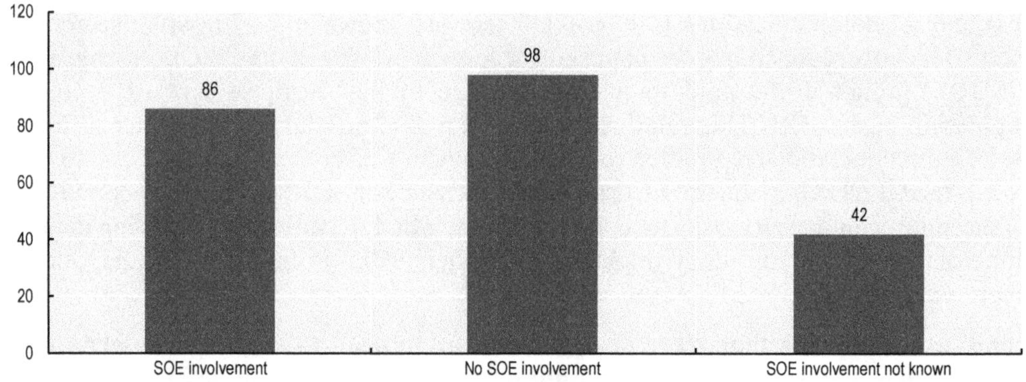

Source: Calculations from the OECD Working Group on Bribery case database.

StatLink http://dx.doi.org/10.1787/888933786629

It is also worth noting that foreign direct investment (FDI) is affected by bribery and corruption, which is relevant for all developing economies trying to attract investment from OECD countries. An OECD empirical study shows that, once countries have adhered to the OECD Anti-Bribery Convention, their companies invest less in corrupt geographies and more in countries with sound property rights and accountability (see Blundell-Wignall and Roulet, 2016). More corrupt countries therefore forego the benefits of more investment (and hence better potential for productivity growth) from Parties to the Convention and notably OECD countries that are amongst the largest international investors.

Third, bribery is not the only corruption risk in infrastructure projects. Policy capture, embezzlement, abuse of functions, and trading in influence are common examples of corrupt acts, although the exact legal definitions of these vary across countries. Corruption allegations concerning government-financed infrastructure projects are common. Indeed, the extent of public officials' discretion over the investment decision, the large sums of money involved, and the multiple stages and stakeholders implicated, contributes to making them more vulnerable to undue influence.

Promoting responsible business conduct

While infrastructure investments are generally intended to provide improvements to societies, in terms of access to energy, transport and connectivity, in certain cases they can also bring large-scale negative impacts. RBC is critical to ensuring sustainable development and avoiding serious social and environmental harms.

The OECD Guidelines for Multinational Enterprises (OECD Guidelines) provide the leading international guidance on RBC (OECD, 2011). The OECD Guidelines are supplemented by due diligence guidance which targets specific sectors.[17]

Evidence from cases arising in connection with the OECD Guidelines shows that ensuring an adequate framework for investment and promoting and enabling RBC is important for developed and developing economies alike. The OECD Guidelines reflect the expectation that businesses will undertake risk-based due diligence on issues such as human rights, employment and industrial relations, environment,[18] and other areas to avoid and address any negative impacts of their operations, including in their supply chain and business relationships.[19] Each Adherent to the OECD Guidelines establishes a National Contact Point (NCP).[20] NCPs are mandated to promote the recommendations of the OECD Guidelines and to resolve issues in the event that an enterprise does not observe them, thereby acting as a grievance mechanism. All OECD countries and, as of 2018, 18 out of the 72 economies participating in the BRI (of which five are not OECD countries) adhere to this important international standard on RBC.[21]

Figure 3.2. Host countries of cases filed with NCPs for the OECD Guidelines for Multinational Enterprises

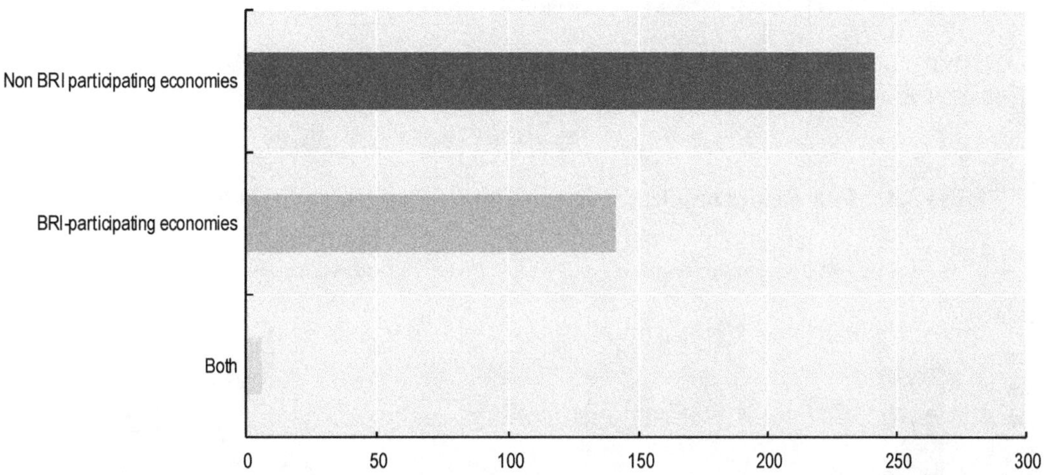

Note: The database contains information about complaints relating to the activities of MNEs headquartered in countries adhering to the OECD Guidelines. It does not reflect information about the operations of MNEs headquartered in countries that have not adhered to the OECD Guidelines in other non-adhering countries. The database does, however, give an indication of the nature of the RBC problems that can be encountered in BRI-participating countries.
Source: OECD Guidelines for Multinational Enterprises Database for Specific Instances, http://mneguidelines.oecd.org/database/.

StatLink http://dx.doi.org/10.1787/888933786648

To date, complaints filed with the NCPs ("specific instances") have involved issues arising in 42 of the economies participating in the BRI.[22] Out of 389 complaints filed with NCPs,[23] 148 concern issues arising in these economies (38% of all complaints filed). Six (2%) of these 389 complaints involve issues arising in both BRI-participating and other economies (as issues filed with NCPs may arise in multiple countries and territories). Issues reported to NCPs represent only those that are linked to the operations, products or services of multinational enterprises operating in or from one of the 48 Adherents to the OECD Guidelines. As such, they represent only a small proportion of possible RBC-related impacts in the global economy.

The leading themes raised in complaints filed with NCPs involving issues arising in economies participating in the BRI have been: employment and industrial relations (referenced in 59% of these complaints (88 complaints)); human rights (referenced in 37% of these complaints (55 cases)); and the environment (referenced in 15% of all cases (23 complaints)). These rates are above those for complaints filed involving issues arising in other economies in relation to human rights issues and employment and industrial relations.

Figure 3.3. Key issues raised in cases with OECD NCPs, 2000-2017

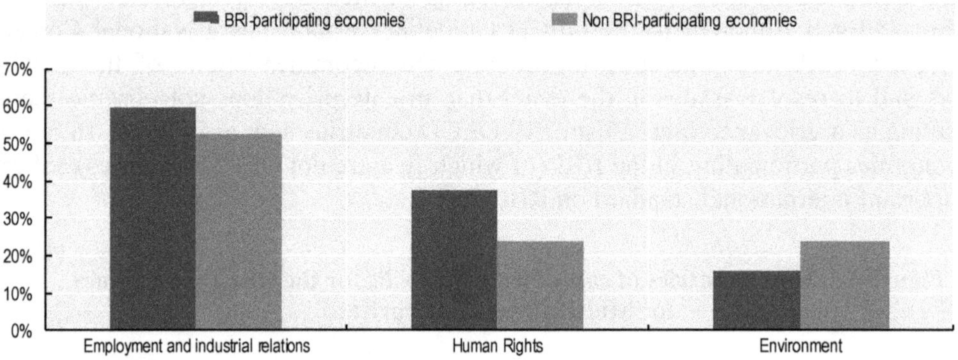

Source: OECD Guidelines for Multinational Enterprises Database for Specific Instances, http://mneguidelines.oecd.org/database/.

StatLink http://dx.doi.org/10.1787/888933786667

Figure 3.4. Main sectors implicated in complaints filed with OECD NCPs, 2000-2017

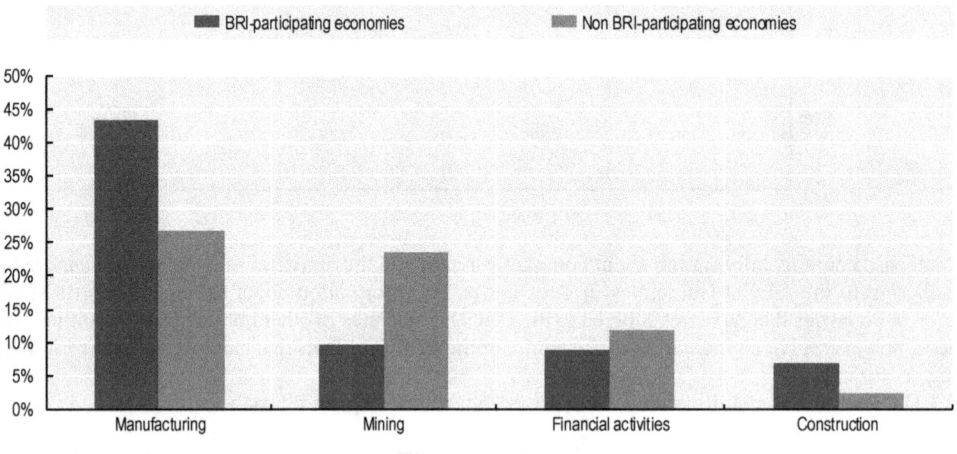

Source: OECD Guidelines for Multinational Enterprises Database for Specific Instances, http://mneguidelines.oecd.org/database/.

StatLink http://dx.doi.org/10.1787/888933786686

The main sectors implicated in complaints involving issues arising in economies that participate in the BRI are: manufacturing (64 complaints, or 43% of the total); mining and quarrying (14 complaints, or 9% of the total); financial and insurance activities (13 complaints, or 9% of the total); and construction (10 complaints, or 7% of the total). Among cases filed involving issues arising in other economies, these rates are significantly lower for manufacturing (27%) and construction (2%), the sectors most directly concerned with physical infrastructure building (Figure 3.4).

Box 3.5. Promoting responsible business conduct in Southeast Asia: Findings from the *OECD Investment Policy Review of Southeast Asia*

Southeast Asia has been one of the most successful emerging regions, in terms of export-led development, in part through foreign direct investment (FDI). The Association of Southeast Asian Nations (ASEAN) economies have already recognised the importance of RBC in certain policy areas. This is true both at the regional level, as seen by the inclusion of RBC expectations in various ASEAN Blueprints, and at the national level, even if specific government actions vary widely across the region. A promising trend has been the inclusion of RBC provisions in a recent wave of investment strategies and laws, as well as the elaboration of comprehensive national action plans related to RBC. Such initiatives can bring about improved outcomes from investment, in terms of broader value creation and sustainable development, and also help to position the region as a reliable location for production and safe sourcing by helping to reduce the reputational risks faced by investors.

Nevertheless, more can be done to support and encourage responsible businesses and quality investment. Several objectives envisioned for the integrated ASEAN Economic Community will depend in large part on improving the business environment beyond investment liberalisation.

To further promote and enable RBC, ASEAN could develop a regional action plan in the context of integration in global supply chains to set out an expectation for investors and ASEAN businesses to adopt RBC principles and standards consistent with international standards, such as those contained in the OECD Guidelines for Multinational Enterprises. Elements of RBC could also be included in investment incentives schemes.

Both national governments and the ASEAN Secretariat could clearly communicate RBC expectations to investors, including as part of investment promotion efforts on the "Invest in ASEAN" website and in supplier databases and matchmaking events. At the same time, policy dialogue among ASEAN members could be strengthened with a view to position ASEAN as a responsible investment region.

The processes related to environmental and social impact assessments could be harmonised, clarified and strengthened, while encouraging early participation by affected stakeholders. Governments in the region could also promote National Action Plans on Responsible Business Conduct in order to mainstream RBC across government agencies and as a way to prioritise and advance reforms needed to ensure an adequate legal framework that protects the public interest and underpins RBC.

The 2018 *OECD Investment Policy Review of Southeast Asia* builds on national reviews of seven countries in Southeast Asia and looks at common challenges across the region and at the interplay between regional initiatives and national reforms.

Source: OECD (2018a).

Issues raised in complaints filed with NCPs show some of the significant social and environmental risks that can arise in the context of infrastructure projects. For example, in 2017, the Swiss NCP considered a specific instance related to human rights violations of migrant workers in the construction of facilities for the 2022 FIFA World Cup in Qatar. The Swiss NCP accepted and mediated the instance, which led to an agreement between the parties in a number of areas, including development of processes for monitoring labour conditions, establishment of an on-the-ground oversight body, and mechanisms to address workers' complaints and labour conditions.

Ensuring that government decisions on infrastructure investment meet high integrity and governance standards, including adequate stakeholder engagement, can go a long way for the success of these projects. For example, secure and well-defined land rights are a critical component of avoiding conflicts. Without a credible mechanism for meaningful, effective and good-faith consultation with land rights holders, in particular indigenous peoples or local communities, (e.g. clear and transparent criteria on resettlement, compensation, and tendering and lease/concession contract terms), projects can be at a significant risk (OECD, 2015). Such cases have come up in the context of the BRI (see Box 3.3).

One way to ensure greater uptake of RBC practices is co-operation between economies linked with the BRI and adherents to the OECD Guidelines in promoting RBC practices in infrastructure investment. The OECD has been working with Southeast Asian partners on creating an enabling framework for investment and RBC (Box 3.5). In addition, co-operation with China on the implementation of RBC standards in overseas investment can help raise awareness of the economic and social benefits of engaging in RBC practices. Large capital-exporting partners in the BRI that have not yet adhered to the OECD Guidelines are encouraged to enhance the social and environmental benefits of their infrastructure projects by adhering to this international standard for conducting business responsibly and establish an NCP to ensure their effective observance.

Promoting environmental impact assessment

While the OECD Guidelines expect companies to have sound environmental management systems, the OECD Recommendation on the Assessment of Projects with Significant Impact on the Environment (OECD, 1979) is for adhering governments to apply environmental assessment prior to implementing proposed projects for facilities and infrastructure. Assessment is a process of systematic prior analysis and evaluation of the environmental impacts of the proposed activity and the consideration of alternatives. It includes consultation with affected parties and the inclusion of the results of the assessment in the planning and authorisation process before any implementation of the activity. This OECD Recommendation also advocates the participation of the affected parties in order to find socially acceptable solutions.

The OECD Recommendation is currently being revised to include Strategic Environmental Assessment (SEA). SEA is implemented in various countries and regions (e.g. the European Union, which was first to mandate SEA in 2001, Canada, Korea and Chile). SEA aims to integrate environmental considerations into country and regional strategies that evaluate plans in terms of their linkages with both economic and social considerations with full transparency of the decision-making process.[24] The OECD is also using SEA in its development co-operation work, which is highly relevant for all developing countries (see OECD, 2006).

Mitigating corruption risks in public investment

The costs of fraud and corruption in public investment are not only economic, but also institutional and political, with serious implications for the legitimacy of the state apparatus and the ability of elected leaders and government institutions to function effectively. The OECD Integrity Framework for Public Investment helps governments and private sector actors to mitigate corruption risks in public investment by identifying corruption entry points over the entire public investment cycle. The framework identifies tools and mechanisms to promote integrity in public investment, including measures for promoting ethical standards, managing conflict of interest, strengthening monitoring and controls, and increasing transparency. The instrument can be applied at national and sub-national levels and across sectors, including transport, construction, extractive industries, and energy supply, taking into account the needs and characteristics of the specific investment at stake.

3.5. Towards greater openness to international investment

The longer-term goal of investing in infrastructure and building connectivity in the global economy is to boost trade and investment in order for living standards to rise sustainably over time. Excessive restrictions on inflows of FDI reduce these potential benefits by reducing choice and increasing costs. Reducing restrictions on capital flows over time is therefore important if these longer-run benefits are to be realised.

Barriers to foreign direct investment

Figure 3.5. OECD FDI Regulatory Restrictiveness Index, 2016

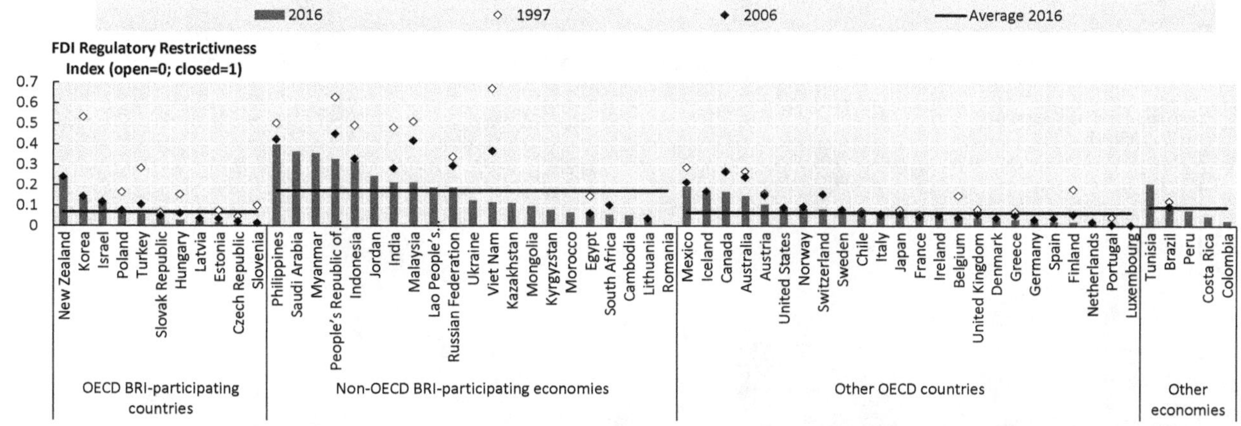

Note: The OECD FDI Regulatory Restrictiveness Index covers only statutory measures discriminating against foreign investors (e.g. foreign equity limits, screening & approval procedures, restriction on key foreign personnel, and other operational measures). Other important aspects of an investment climate (e.g. the implementation of regulations, the presence of state monopolies, the preferential treatment for export-oriented investors and the special economic zone (SEZ) regimes among other) are not considered. The FDI Index reflects regulatory restrictions as of December 2016. The FDI Index is available for only 36 of the 72 BRI-participating economies. Data are preliminary for the following countries: Albania, Bosnia and Herzegovina, Brunei Darussalam, Former Yugoslav Republic of Macedonia, Montenegro, Serbia, Singapore and Thailand. Please refer to Kalinova et al., (2010) for further information on the methodology.

Source: OECD FDI Regulatory Restrictiveness Index database, www.oecd.org/investment/fdiindex.htm.

StatLink http://dx.doi.org/10.1787/888933786705

OECD countries have limited restrictions on inward FDI. Emerging economies, while much less open, have been making their regulatory regimes less restrictive over time. The OECD's FDI regulatory restrictiveness index is shown in Figure 3.5. This index covers statutory measures discriminating against foreign investors (e.g. foreign equity limits, and screening and approval procedures), though it cannot take account of the extent to which these restrictions are enforced. In Figure 3.5, OECD and economies linked with the BRI are distinguished in a number of ways.

While FDI in manufacturing is generally allowed without restrictions, except when a horizontal measure applies across the board, many primary and service sectors remain partly off limits to foreign investors in emerging countries, holding back potential economy-wide productivity gains.[25] Some significant liberalisation has been achieved recently across several BRI-participating economies, mostly on a unilateral basis (where the bars for 2016 lie below the markers for earlier years). However, foreign investors still face relatively higher barriers to entry and discriminatory treatment than in OECD countries in various sectors, including agriculture, mining, construction, distribution, transport, media and business services.[26]

OECD countries participating in the BRI tend to have fewer restrictions than non-OECD participating economies. The average for the latter (the horizontal line) sits above that for the OECD groups. Restrictiveness is particularly strong in Asia. Restrictions on FDI cut off sources of investment and technology for host countries. The question arises, therefore, as to whether further trade and investment reforms in the BRI could see greater and more affordable benefits from infrastructure investments coming from diverse and more cost effective sources.

Figure 3.6. Index of restrictions on capital inflows by asset class, 2015

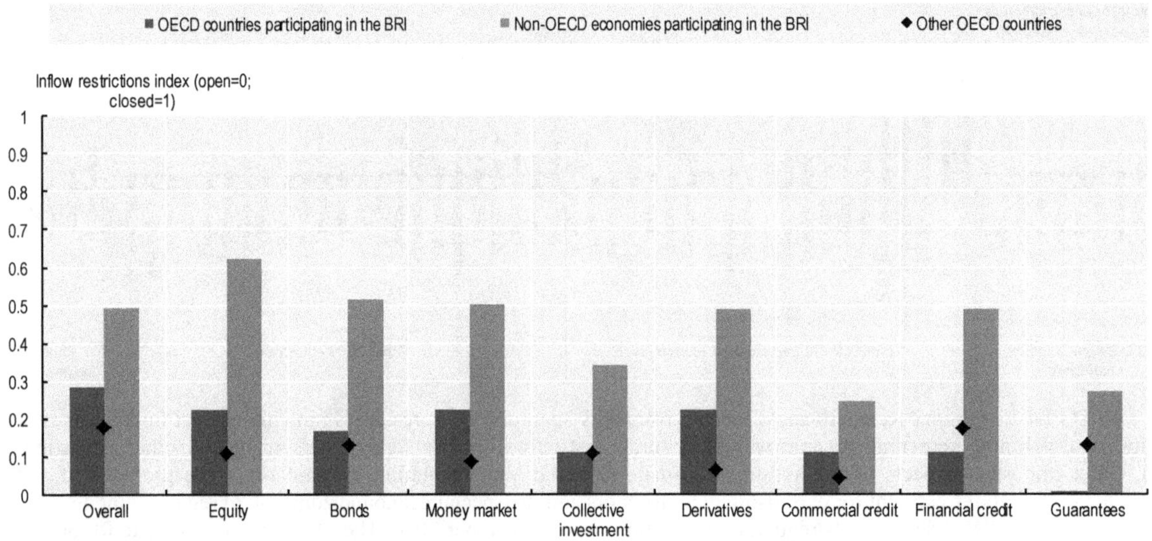

Note: OECD countries participating in the BRI: Czech Republic, Hungary, Israel, Korea, Latvia, New Zealand, Poland, Slovenia, Turkey. Non-OECD economies identified in the BRI: Bahrain, Bangladesh, Brunei Darussalam, Bulgaria, China, Egypt, Ethiopia, Georgia, India, Indonesia, Islamic Republic of Iran, Kazakhstan, Kenya, Kuwait, Kyrgyzstan, Lebanon, Malaysia, Republic of Moldova, Morocco, Myanmar, Oman, Pakistan, Panama, Philippines, Qatar, Romania, Russian Federation, Saudi Arabia, Singapore, South Africa, Sri Lanka, Thailand, Ukraine, United Arab Emirates, Uzbekistan, Viet Nam, Yemen. Other OECD countries: Australia, Austria, Belgium, Canada, Chile, Denmark, Finland, France, Germany, Greece, Iceland, Ireland, Italy, Japan, Mexico, Netherlands, Norway, Portugal, Spain, Sweden, Switzerland, United Kingdom, United States.
Source: Fernandez, Andrés, Michael Klein, Alessandro Rebucci, Martin Schindler, and Martin Uribe (2016), "Capital Control Measures: A New Dataset", IMF Economic Review, vol. 64, 548-574, www.columbia.edu/~mu2166/fkrsu/.

StatLink http://dx.doi.org/10.1787/888933786724

Figure 3.6 focuses on restrictions on financial flows and is based on the IMF's *Annual Report on Exchange Arrangements and Exchange Restrictions*. Like the OECD FDI measure, it consists of *de jure* legal restrictions and provides data on a wide range of asset classes and countries. OECD countries are bound to high standards of openness and transparency through the OECD Code of Liberalisation of Capital Movements (see Box 3.6) and so have lower restrictiveness on these financial flows, whether or not they participate in the BRI.

Vast investment from China in participants in the BRI (documented in Chapter 2) occurs despite the presence of strong barriers to investment in the region. This may be due to the presence of government-to-government transactions (including direct appointments to contracts not subject to restrictions).

Potential benefits of greater openness

Connectivity infrastructure plays a critical role in allowing countries to integrate better within geographical regions and to join up to other regions, thus increasing participation in the benefits. This is a key objective of the BRI. Its success would contribute to spreading development opportunities in many participating economies which inevitably will spill into other regions.

Chapter 2 uses a gravity model of bilateral trade relationships to test two types of benefits in trade that come about from regional trade blocs in the world economy:

- the **intra-bloc benefits** that accrue to bloc members; and
- the **extra-bloc benefits** that arise for non-members due to increased income and productivity, as scale economies improve and as supply chain connectivity increases.

The intra-bloc findings suggest that, while trading blocs generally "create" trade for members, this is most evident for the more open OECD exporting countries. The extra-bloc flow-on effects to other economies are strongest for blocs where China is a member (such as ASEAN+1, and the Bangkok Agreement), the European Union and, most of all, NAFTA.

These findings suggest that linkages between developing and advanced economies have the potential to enhance benefits through greater FDI openness, particularly given the central role that FDI plays in the development and organisation of global and regional value chains (OECD, WTO and UNCTAD, 2013).

To capture the full benefits of infrastructure connectivity, BRI economic corridors need to be viewed within a broader global trade and investment strategy for sustainable economic development. Expected multiplier and long-term effects of hard infrastructure investments do not accrue automatically, often proving lower than expected. In the long-run, the economic benefits of such investments are sustained by improved economic activity and services provided over the installed infrastructure. This requires complementary soft-infrastructure systems, such as: consistent border regulations and procedures; strong logistics services; and compatible behind-the-border regulations, including appropriately-open services sectors regulations.

The BRI foresees greater co-operation on a number of relevant policy areas in this respect, e.g. enhancing economic and trade co-operation and expanding production capacity and investment co-operation (see Government of China, 2017). To date, however, China's focus on infrastructure investments has overshadowed the importance of addressing such complementary policies.

An international framework for managing capital flows

A large part of the problem of not attracting more diversified funding for BRI projects is the bilateral nature of transactions between countries that are not a part of any framework of common globally-accepted rules of the game. The OECD Code of Liberalisation provides such a framework, and does not require countries to be members of the OECD in order to adhere. The Code is designed to make capital account management policies more transparent and to provide a framework for moving towards more openness in the longer run, while still allowing for different stages of economic development (Box 3.6). Adherence to the Code by China and other major investment players would be welcome, as encouraged by the G20, and would constitute an important step towards a more transparent global approach to capital flows, which will also benefit the BRI.

Box 3.6. The OECD Code of Liberalisation of Capital Movements

The OECD Code of Liberalisation of Capital Movements (OECD, 2016b) is an international agreement under which adherents commit to progressively liberalise capital flows. They may lodge reservations as regards operations they are not in a position to liberalise at the time of adherence, and at any time as regards short-term capital flow operations. In situations of serious balance of payment difficulties or economic and financial disturbance, adherents can also avail themselves of the derogation clauses of the Code for new restrictions on other operations.

The Code's system of notification and peer monitoring ensures transparency and mutual accountability in adherents' policies related to capital flows.

Countries have adhered to the Code in recognition of the fact that open capital accounts bring market disciplines that foster productivity, facilitate investment financing and provide opportunity to expand and diversify businesses abroad. By adhering to the Code, countries have agreed to abstain from a "beggar-thy-neighbour" approach to capital flow restrictions, as this can prompt countermeasures and lead to negative collective outcomes in the end.

Today, adherents to the Code have more open capital accounts than non-adherents. This divided situation contributes to imbalances and distortions in the global economy. The Code was opened in 2012 for adherence by non-OECD countries and those countries that are interested are encouraged to join. By doing so, non-OECD countries will build a reputation as responsible international players while enjoying the benefit of the protection provided by the Code against potential discrimination on the part of their peers.

3.6. Policy recommendations

This chapter focussed on four broad areas: the role of SOEs; competition and processes in procurement; bribery and other acts of corruption, responsible business conduct and the environment; and investment openness. In all four areas, a strong case can be made for developing a common set of transparency principles that are consistent with mutually-beneficial outcomes and which will help promote quality and sustainable infrastructure projects that work for all. More than this, OECD guidelines and standards all have associated toolboxes that help countries drill down to specifics. That is, to inform decision-making with analytical tools that countries are welcome to take advantage of when decisions are being made, whether or not they are members of the OECD.

To achieve this, the OECD recommends:

1. With respect to SOEs:
    a. **Improve the governance of SOEs engaged in cross-border activities.** Concern about subsidies and non-transparent processes which work to create an uneven playing field must be addressed. Governance of SOEs in their cross-border activities needs to be improved, based on global standards. OECD guidelines provide an effective framework to achieve this. They encourage arms-length relationships between SOE ownership and other functions exercised by the state.
    b. **Develop a Santiago-Principles-like set of arrangements.** Concerns reflected in the move towards tougher national security reviews, in cases where SOEs are involved, need to be addressed. Santiago-Principles-like arrangements have proved effective in resolving these problems where sovereign wealth fund investments were concerned.
    c. **Examine and clarify the applicable law on immunities in advance.** To reduce uncertainty about gaps in legal accountability for SOEs in their activities abroad (*inter alia* where the issue of foreign state immunity is concerned), governments and companies are encouraged to examine and clarify the applicable law on immunities in advance. Waivers of sovereign immunity should be included in the initial negotiations of contracts. In the longer term, a clear and predictable framework is needed for foreign investment by SOEs, including legal enforcement and regulatory action affecting them, which would reduce the likelihood of costly and politically-sensitive investment disputes.
2. Embrace clear principles on open competition in procurement based on OECD procurement recommendations, the OECD arrangement on export credits and the WTO general procurement agreement. These principles have proved effective in preventing trade distortions between signatories. Where gaps still exist, clear standards for procurement in infrastructure investment projects will need to be established. The same goes with respect to how relationships between developing economies and OECD investors will be conducted. There are also detailed tools for assessing competition frameworks within countries that also condition cross-border activities.[27]
3. Anti-bribery, responsible business conduct considerations in infrastructure project negotiations, and environmental impact. Corruption is most closely linked to SOEs, not least in large scale infrastructure projects where the bribery of public officials is commonplace. At the same time, unforeseen problems and costly disruptions to local communities and the environment have been a feature of projects in economies benefiting from infrastructure investment through the BRI once construction was underway. These issues need to be addressed in advance.
    a. **Adhere to the OECD Anti-Bribery Convention.** Countries that take the fight against corruption seriously are encouraged to address this by adherence to the OECD's Anti-Bribery Convention which comprises both principles and, most importantly, rigorous monitoring and peer-review processes. Using the OECD Integrity Framework for Public Investment is a useful adjunct to the Convention.
    b. **Establish a policy environment conducive to RBC.** Countries are encouraged to promote corporate due diligence in addressing social and environmental risks

associated with infrastructure and consider adhering to the OECD Guidelines for Multilateral Enterprises.

c. Governments themselves need to lead by example and integrate **environment impact assessments** in infrastructure projects they sponsor.

4. **Be open to the lowest-cost and best-technology investments.** Cost-effective solutions based on a diverse universe of investors, including from OECD countries, will be essential to meet infrastructure needs, to contain debt burdens for developing countries and to avoid handing equity to foreign governments that give them control of sensitive strategic assets. Countries are encouraged to adhere to the OECD Code of Liberalisation of Capital Movements. The Code fully recognises different levels of economic development and provides a sound framework for improving openness between OECD and developing economies to enhance investment and trade linkages.

5. **Take advantage of OECD co-operation initiatives in the region**. A considerable power imbalance often exists between large and/or more developed economies operating in less developed economies. Less developed economies may be ill-placed to negotiate contracts and develop policies that enable them to get the most out connectivity strategies and projects. OECD programmes such as "The Central Asia Competitiveness Initiative", the Eurasia Competitiveness Programme more generally and the Southeast Asia Regional programme all aim to help countries create a business climate to enhance productivity through entrepreneurship, private sector development, and the knowledge-based economy. These programmes draw on the expertise of OECD committees in all of the areas discussed in this chapter.

Notes

[1] As noted in Chapter 2, the initiative involves 72 economies, which include 12 OECD countries and five OECD Key Partners (see Box 2.1).

[2] Based on 2015-16 data, Norway is at the high end with 8.9% SOE employment versus total employment, France 3%, China 2.6% and Italy 2.2%.

[3] See OECD (2018b), which draws on a survey of 300+ SOEs on perceptions of corruption and integrity risks.

[4] The IWG consists of Australia, Azerbaijan, Bahrain, Botswana, Canada, Chile, China, Equatorial Guinea, Islamic Republic of Iran, Ireland, Korea, Kuwait, Libya, Mexico, New Zealand, Norway, Qatar, Russian Federation, Singapore, Timor-Leste, Trinidad and Tobago, the United Arab Emirates, and the United States. Permanent observers of the IWG are Oman, Saudi Arabia, Viet Nam, the OECD, and the World Bank (see the Santiago Principles, note 5, www.ifswf.org/sites/default/files/santiagoprinciples_0_0.pdf).

[5] See OECD (2009a) for the Recommendation. In 2008, the International Working Group of Sovereign Wealth Funds published the Generally Accepted Principles and Practices (GAPP), known as the 'Santiago Principles', see IWG (2008). The GAPP cross references the OECD Investment Committee report on sovereign wealth funds, OECD (2008).

[6] Such enterprises are addressed under national laws and treaties under various rubrics, including "separate entities" (United Kingdom), "agencies and instrumentalities" (United States) and "legal entities" (ECSI).

[7] See Gaukrodger (2010), page 15, and references and discussions therein.

[8] The ECSI (art. 27) distinguishes agencies of the state from its organs by excluding from the expression "Contracting State" any legal entity of a Contracting State which is distinct therefrom and is capable or suing and being sued. Such distinct entities are not part of the state even if they have been entrusted with public functions. Under Article 27(2), proceedings may be brought against such entities "in the same manner as a private person" except in respect of sovereign acts.

[9] See, for example, Cheng, T. and A. Lai (2011) addressing whether PRC state entities, including both "*Guoyou Qiye*" and "*Shiye Danwei*" type entities, "can plead, assert and enjoy state immunity under the auspices of the state of the PRC when sued in a foreign court", and whether they would be considered to be "under the control of the state and hence [could] be considered part of the state"; arguing that "*Guoyou Qiye*" entities would not benefit from state immunity abroad). The authors acted as counsel in both cases they discuss. Ms. Cheng was appointed Secretary for Justice in Hong Kong (China) on 6 January 2018.

[10] Id.; see also *TNB Fuel Services Sdn Bhd v. China National Coal Group Corp.*, [2017] HKCU 1439 (Hong Kong Court of First Instance 8 June 2017) (based in part on a submission by the PRC, narrow application of the possibly related concept of "Crown immunity" of PRC entities in Hong Kong (China) to reject a claim of immunity by a Chinese SOE).

[11] See, for example, Feng (2016), quoting a Xinhua report on statements by Xi Jinping at a meeting with Chinese SOEs that "Party leadership and building the role of the party are the root and soul for state-owned enterprises. ... The party's leadership in state-owned enterprises is a major political principle, and that principle must be insisted on." See also Hughes (2017), reporting on changes to articles of association by more than 30 SOEs to add references to the role of the CPC. See also Chen (2016), who states "senior management personnel of SOEs is controlled and managed by a special committee of the CPC. Hence, the CPC and the government not only control the appointment and dismissal of managers, but they also control much of the micro-level operation of companies.".

[12] See Gaukrodger (2010) which reports on work related to the OECD Freedom of Investment Roundtable, page 14.

[13] Waivers in the context of agreements to commercial arbitration and participation in dispute settlement raise specific issues that are not addressed here.

[14] For example, in Box 3.3 the timeliness factor is reported to have trumped the cost factor, in that one of the bidders from a developed economy had a lower estimate for the bulk of the project costs (the converter stations). Examples from India are also presented.

[15] https://timesofindia.indiatimes.com/business/india-business/359-infrastructure-projects-show-cost-overrun-of-rs-2-05-lakh-crore/articleshow/63156392.cms

[16] There is an interesting issue here about the best route to achieve lowest cost outcomes. On the one hand host countries might benefit from not requiring competitive neutrality. This may enable them to extract additional guarantees and special deals from one bidder versus another with only a few participants. However, it is not clear that special deals with local content requirements provide the most affordable outcomes. There are gains to be had if host countries and bidders play by the global rules that are set out in the OECD & WTO rules in an open transparent process at the global level.

[17] OECD Due Diligence Guidance for Responsible Supply Chains in the Garment and Footwear Sector; OECD Due Diligence Guidance for Meaningful Stakeholder Engagement in the Extractive Sector; OECD-FAO Guidance for Responsible Agricultural Supply Chains and OECD Due Diligence Guidance for Responsible Supply Chains of Minerals from Conflict-Affected and High-Risk Areas; and Responsible Business Conduct for Institutional Investors. https://mneguidelines.oecd.org/duediligence/.

[18] And see, for example, very early work in this area in OECD (2004).

[19] OECD co-operates with China in the area of RBC. Chinese government hosted a peer exchange on National Contact Points in 2015. In 2016, co-operation focused on implementation of the Chinese

Due Diligence Guidelines for Responsible Minerals Supply Chains, which were set out in 2015 on the basis of the OECD Due Diligence Guidance for Responsible Supply Chains of Minerals from Conflict-Affected and High-Risk Areas. For more information, see OECD (2017c).

[20] The Declaration and its Guidelines are open to adherence by non-OECD economies. There are currently 48 Adherents, which include 14 G20 members.

[21] Czech Republic, Egypt, Estonia, Hungary, Israel, Jordan, Kazakhstan, Korea, Latvia, Lithuania, Morocco, New Zealand, Poland, Romania, Slovakia, Slovenia, Turkey, Ukraine. Economies related to BRI projects are listed on China's official BRI Portal - https://eng.yidaiyilu.gov.cn/info/iList.jsp?site_id=CMSydylyw&cat_id=10076&cur_page=1. Adherents to the OECD Declaration and its Guidelines are listed at https://mneguidelines.oecd.org/about.htm.

[22] Bahrain, Bangladesh, China (People's Republic of), Czech Republic, Ethiopia, Georgia, Hungary, India, Indonesia, Iraq, Israel, Kazakhstan, Korea, Republic of (South), Lao People's Democratic Republic, Latvia, Malaysia, Maldives, Mongolia, Montenegro, Morocco, Myanmar, New Zealand, Pakistan, Palestinian Administered Areas, Philippines, Poland, Qatar, Romania, Russian Federation, Saudi Arabia, South Africa, Sri Lanka, Thailand, Turkey, Ukraine, United Arab Emirates, Uzbekistan, Yemen.

[23] The OECD specific instance database registers 389 complaints filed with NCPs since 2000, as of 10 March 2018. As some NCPs only report on complaints when they are concluded which means that the database does not yet reflect these ongoing cases, http://mneguidelines.oecd.org/database/.

[24] See for example: http://ec.europa.eu/environment/eia/sea-legalcontext.htm

[25] See, inter alia, Nordås and Kim (2013); Arnold, Javorcik and Mattoo (2011); Arnold et al. (2012); Fernandes and Paunov (2012); Duggan, Rahardja and Varela (2013).

[26] China announced in April 2018 the intention to relax FDI restrictions in a number of industries, including finance and transport equipment, while also committing to improve the investment climate and better enforce the protection of property rights, including intellectual ones. See "Highlights of Xi's keynote speech at Boao Forum", www.chinadaily.com.cn/a/201804/10/WS5acc15a6a3105cdcf6517259.html.

[27] Such as competitive neutrality with respect to SOEs, merger analysis, OECD work on bid rigging and competition assessments in procurement.

References

Ansar, A., B. Flyvbjerg, A. Budzier and D. Lunn (2016), "Does infrastructure investment lead to economic growth or economic fragility? Evidence from China", Oxford Review of Economic Policy, Volume 32, Number 3.

Arnold, J., B.S. Javorcik, M. Lipscomb, A. Mattoo (2012), Services Reform and Manufacturing Performance: Evidence from India, *World Bank Policy Research Working Paper No. 5948*, January.

Arnold, J., B.S. Javorcik, A. Mattoo (2011), Does Services Liberalization Benefit Manufacturing Firms? Evidence from the Czech Republic, *Journal of International Economics No. 85*, pp. 136-146.

Asian Development Bank (2017), *Meeting Asia's Infrastructure Needs*, February, www.adb.org/sites/default/files/publication/227496/special-report-infrastructure.pdf

Bagchil, I. (2017), "Nepal cancels Budi Gandaki hydropower project with Chinese company", Times of India, November 14.

Blundell-Wignall, A. and C. Roulet (2017), "Foreign direct investment, corruption and the OECD Anti-Bribery Convention", *OECD Working Papers on International Investment*, No. 2017/01, OECD Publishing, Paris, http://dx.doi.org/10.1787/9cb3690c-en.

Chen, R. (2016), "Evolution of Corporate Law in China: Mission Possible to Reform State-Owned Enterprises (SOEs)?" , in Chang, Y., W. Shen, & W. Wang (eds.), *Private Law in China and Taiwan: Legal and Economic Analyses*, Cambridge University Press.

Cheng, T. and A. Lai (2011), *Lessons learned from the FG Hemisphere vs DRC and Huatianlong Cases*, www.arbitration-icca.org/media/4/135233720 58325/media1132342764462706-lessons_learned_from_the_fg_hemisphere_vs_drc_and_huatianlong_case.pdf.

Dasgupta, S. (2017), "Pakistan, Nepal, Myanmar Back Away from Chinese Projects", Voice of America News Service, www.voanews.com/a/three-countries-withdraw-from-chinese-projects/4148094.html.

Duggan, V., S. Rahardja and G. Varela (2013), Service sector reform and manufacturing productivity: evidence from Indonesia, *World Bank Policy Research Paper No. 6349*, January.

European Parliament (2017), *EU framework for FDI Screening*, www.europarl.europa.eu/RegData/etudes/BRIE/2018/614667/EPRS_BRI%282018%29614667_EN.pdf

European Commission (2017), Reply by the EU Delegation to China on recent media reports related to the Belgrade Budapest railway project, 28 February, https://eeas.europa.eu/delegations/china/21594/reply-eu-delegation-china-recent-media-reports-related-belgrade-budapest-railway-project_en.

Ernst and Young (2017), *Tax News Update*, US Edition, https://taxnews.ey.com/news/2017-1810-the-changing-headquarters-landscape-for-fortune-global-500-companies

Feng, E. (2016), Xi Jinping Reminds China's State-owned Companies Who's the Boss, New York Times, 13 October.

Fernandes, A.M. and Paunov, C. (2011), Foreign direct investment in services and manufacturing productivity: Evidence for Chile, *Journal of Development Economics No 97*, pp. 305-321.

Fernández, A., M.W. Klein, A. Rebucci, M. Schindler and M. Uribe (2016), "Capital Control Measures: A New Dataset", *IMF Economic Review*, Vol. 64 (3): 548-574.

Fox, H. (2005), *In Defense of State Immunity: Why the UN: Convention on State Immunity is Important,* Cambridge University Press.

Gaukrodger, D. (2010), "Foreign State Immunity and Foreign Government Controlled Investors", OECD Working Papers on International Investment, 2010/02, OECD Publishing, Paris, http://dx.doi.org/10.1787/5km91p0ksqs7-en.

Gordon, K. and D. Gaukrodger (2012), Foreign government-controlled investors and recipient country investment policies: Overview of the work of the OECD, in Sauvant, K.P., L.E. Sachs and W.P.F. Schmit Jongbloed, Sovereign Investment: Concerns and Policy Reactions, Oxford.

Government of China (2017), *Building the Belt and Road: Concept, Practice and China's Contribution*, Office of the Leading Group for the Belt and Road Initiative, May.

Hurley, J., S. Morris and G. Portelance (2018), "Debt Implications of China's Belt and Road Initiative", Centre for Global Development, www.cgdev.org/sites/default/files/examining-debt-implications-belt-and-road-initiative-policy-perspective.pdf.

IADB (2017), Lessons from Four Decades of Infrastructure Project-Related Conflicts in Latin America and the Caribbean. https://publications.iadb.org/bitstream/handle/11319/8502/Four_decades_of_infrastructure_project-related_conflicts.pdf?sequence=4&isAllowed=y

Hughes, J. (2017), China's Communist Party writes itself into company law, Financial Times, 14 August, www.ft.com/content/a4b28218-80db-11e7-94e2-c5b903247afd.

International Working Group of Sovereign Wealth Funds (2008), Sovereign Wealth Funds: Generally Accepted Principles and Practices, October. www.ifswf.org/sites/default/files/santiagoprinciples_0_0.pdf

Jorgic, D. (2017), Ïn Pakistan, China Presses Built-in Advantage for Silk Road Contracts", www.reuters.com/article/us-china-silkroad-pakistan-insight/in-pakistan-china-presses-built-in-advantage-for-silk-road-contracts-idUSKBN19503Y

Kalinova et al. (2010), "OECD's FDI Restrictiveness Index: 2010 Update", *OECD Working Papers on International Investment, No. 2010/03*, OECD Publishing, Paris, https://doi.org/10.1787/5km91p02zj7g-en.

Nordås, H. and Y. Kim (2013), *The Role of Services for Competitiveness in Manufacturing*, OECD Trade Policy Papers, No. 148, OECD Publishing, Paris, http://dx.doi.org/10.1787/5k484xb7cx6b-en.

OECD (2018b), *State-Owned Enterprises and Corruption: What are the Risks and What can be Done?*, OECD Publishing, Paris, https://doi.org/10.1787/9789264303058-en.

OECD (2018a), *OECD Investment Policy Reviews: Southeast Asia,* www.oecd.org/investment/oecd-investment-policy-review-southeast-asia.htm.

OECD (2017), *OECD Business and Finance Outlook 2017*, OECD Publishing, Paris, https://doi.org/10.1787/9789264274891-en.

OECD (2017b), *OECD Equity Markets Review Asia 2017*, Paris, www.oecd.org/corporate/oecd-equity-markets-review-asia.htm.

OECD (2017c), *The Size and Sectoral Distribution of State-Owned Enterprises*, OECD Publishing, Paris, https://doi.org/10.1787/9789264280663-en.

OECD (2017d), *Annual Report on the OECD Guidelines for Multinational Enterprises 2016*, Paris. https://mneguidelines.oecd.org/annualreportsontheguidelines.htm.

OECD (2017e), *Competition Assessment Toolkit: Volume 3. Operational Manual,* www.oecd.org/competition/toolkit.

OECD (2016a), *OECD Due Diligence Guidance for Responsible Supply Chains of Minerals from Conflict-Affected and High-Risk Areas*, 3rd edition, Paris, https://mneguidelines.oecd.org/mining.htm.

OECD (2016b), *OECD Code of Liberalisation of Capital Movements*, www.oecd.org/investment/codes.htm.

OECD (2016c), *Integrity Framework for Public Infrastructure*, www.oecd.org/corruption/ethics/Integrity-Framework-For-Public-Infrastructure-Brochure.pdf

OECD (2015a), *G20/OECD Principles of Corporate Governance,* www.oecd.org/corporate/principles-corporate-governance.htm.

OECD (2015b), *OECD Guidelines on Corporate Governance of State-Owned Enterprises,* www.oecd.org/corporate/guidelines-corporate-governance-soes.htm.

OECD (2015c), *Policy Framework for Investment*, www.oecd.org/investment/pfi.htm.

OECD (2015d) *OECD Recommendation of the Council on Public Procurement,* www.oecd.org/gov/public-procurement/recommendation.

OECD (2015e), *Consequences of Corruption at the Sector Level and Implications for Economic Growth and Development*, OECD Publishing, Paris, http://dx.doi.org/10.1787/9789264230781-en.

OECD (2014a), *OECD Investment Policy Reviews: Myanmar,* http://dx.doi.org/10.1787/9789264206441-en

OECD (2014b), *OECD Foreign Bribery Report*, www.oecd.org/corruption/oecd-foreign-bribery-report-9789264226616-en.htm.

OECD (2013), "State-Owned Enterprises: Trade Effects and Policy Implications", OECD Trade Policy Paper No. 147, OECD Publishing, Paris, https://doi.org/10.1787/5k4869ckqk7l-en.

OECD (2011), *OECD Guidelines for Multinational Enterprises, 2011 Edition,* Paris, https://mneguidelines.oecd.org/guidelines/.

OECD (2009a), Guidelines for Recipient Country Policies Relating to National Security: Recommendation adopted by the OECD Council, www.oecd.org/investment/investment-policy/43384486.pdf

OECD (2009b), Guidelines for Fighting Bid Rigging in Public Procurement, www.oecd.org/competition/guidelinesforfightingbidrigginginpublicprocurement.htm.

OECD (2006), *Applying Strategic Environmental Assessment: Good Practice Guidance for Development Co-operation*, www.oecd.org/environment/environment-development/37353858.pdf.

OECD (2004), "Encouraging the Contribution of Business to the Environment", *Annual Report on the OECD Guidelines for Multinational Enterprises,* https://doi.org/10.1787/mne-2004-en.

OECD (1979), *Declaration on Anticipatory Environmental Policies*, https://legalinstruments.oecd.org/en/instruments/67.

OECD, WTO and UNCTAD (2013), "Implications of Global Value Chains for Trade, Investment, Development and Jobs", Background Note for the G20 Leaders Summit, Saint Petersburg, September.

OECD (2008), *Sovereign Wealth Funds and Recipient Country Policies*, Paris. www.oecd.org/investment/investment-policy/40408735.pdf.

Qiong, Yan (2017), "EU investigates China-funded rail project in Hungary and Serbia", CGTN, 21 Feb 2017, https://news.cgtn.com/news/3d676a4d35556a4d/share_p.html?t=1487672421298.

Schultz, K. (2017), "Sri Lanka, Struggling with its Debt, Hands a Major Port to China", 12 December, www.nytimes.com/2017/12/12/world/asia/sri-lanka-china-port.html?_r=0.

Singh, R. (2010), "Delays and Cost Overruns in Infrastructure Projects: Extent, Causes and Remedies", *Economic and Political Weekly*, vol. 45, No. 2, May.

UK Government (2017), *National Security and Infrastructure Investment Review*, Green Paper, October, www.gov.uk/government/uploads/system/uploads/attachment_data/file/652505/2017_10_16_NSII_Green_Paper_final.pdf

United States Congress (2017), *Foreign Investment Risk Review Modernization Act of 2017.* www.congress.gov/bill/115th-congress/house-bill/4311.

Wehrlé, F. and J. Pohl (2016), "Investment Policies Related to National Security: A Survey of Country Practices", OECD Working Papers on International Investment, No. 2016/02, OECD Publishing, Paris. http://dx.doi.org/10.1787/5jlwrrf038nx-en

Annex 3.A. List of economies by group

Two groups of economies are defined following the IMF country group classification: advanced economies and emerging and developing economies.

Advanced economies

Australia, Austria, Belgium, Canada, Cyprus, Czech Republic, Denmark, Estonia, Finland, France, Germany, Greece, Hong Kong (China), Iceland, Ireland, Israel, Italy, Japan, Korea, Latvia, Lithuania, Luxembourg, Macau, China, Malta, Netherlands, New Zealand, Norway, Portugal, Puerto Rico, San Marino, Singapore, Slovak Republic, Slovenia, Spain, Sweden, Switzerland, Chinese Taipei.

Emerging and developing economies

Afghanistan, Albania, Algeria, Angola, Antigua and Barbuda, Argentina, Armenia, Azerbaijan, Bahamas , Bahrain, Bangladesh, Barbados, Belarus, Belize, Benin, Bhutan, Plurinational State of Bolivia, Bosnia and Herzegovina, Botswana, Brazil, Brunei Darussalam, Bulgaria, Burkina Faso, Burundi, Cabo Verde, Cambodia, Cameroon, Central African Republic, Chad, Chile, People's Republic of China, Colombia, Comoros, Democratic Republic of the Congo, Republic of the Congo, Costa Rica, Côte d'Ivoire, Croatia, Djibouti, Dominica, Dominican Republic, Ecuador, Egypt, El Salvador, Equatorial Guinea, Eritrea, Ethiopia, Fiji, Gabon, Gambia, Georgia, Ghana, Grenada, Guatemala, Guinea, Guinea-Bissau, Guyana, Haiti, Honduras, Hungary, India, Indonesia, Islamic Republic of Iran, Iraq, Jamaica, Jordan, Kazakhstan, Kenya, Kiribati, Kosovo, Kuwait, Kyrgyzstan, Lao People's Democratic Republic, Lebanon, Lesotho, Liberia, Libya, Former Yugoslav Republic of Macedonia, Madagascar, Malawi, Malaysia, Maldives, Mali, Marshall Islands, Mauritania, Mauritius, Mexico, Federated States of Micronesia, Republic of Moldova, Mongolia, Montenegro, Morocco, Mozambique, Myanmar, Namibia, Nauru, Nepal, Nicaragua, Niger, Nigeria, Oman, Pakistan, Palau, Panama, Papua New Guinea, Paraguay, Peru, Philippines, Poland, Qatar, Romania, Russian Federation, Rwanda, Samoa, Sao Tome and Principe, Saudi Arabia, Senegal, Serbia, Seychelles, Sierra Leone, Solomon Islands, Somalia, South Africa, South Sudan, Sri Lanka, Saint Kitts and Nevis, Saint Lucia, Saint Vincent and the Grenadines, Sudan, Suriname, Swaziland, Syrian Arab Republic, Tajikistan, United Republic of Tanzania, Thailand, Timor-Leste, Togo, Tonga, Trinidad and Tobago, Tunisia, Turkey, Turkmenistan, Tuvalu, Uganda, Ukraine, United Arab Emirates, Uruguay, Uzbekistan, Vanuatu, Bolivarian Republic of Venezuela, Viet Nam, Yemen.

ORGANISATION FOR ECONOMIC CO-OPERATION AND DEVELOPMENT

The OECD is a unique forum where governments work together to address the economic, social and environmental challenges of globalisation. The OECD is also at the forefront of efforts to understand and to help governments respond to new developments and concerns, such as corporate governance, the information economy and the challenges of an ageing population. The Organisation provides a setting where governments can compare policy experiences, seek answers to common problems, identify good practice and work to co-ordinate domestic and international policies.

The OECD member countries are: Australia, Austria, Belgium, Canada, Chile, the Czech Republic, Denmark, Estonia, Finland, France, Germany, Greece, Hungary, Iceland, Ireland, Israel, Italy, Japan, Korea, Latvia, Lithuania, Luxembourg, Mexico, the Netherlands, New Zealand, Norway, Poland, Portugal, the Slovak Republic, Slovenia, Spain, Sweden, Switzerland, Turkey, the United Kingdom and the United States. The European Union takes part in the work of the OECD.

OECD Publishing disseminates widely the results of the Organisation's statistics gathering and research on economic, social and environmental issues, as well as the conventions, guidelines and standards agreed by its members.

OECD PUBLISHING, 2, rue André-Pascal, 75775 PARIS CEDEX 16
(21 2018 01 1 P) ISBN 978-92-64-29881-1 – 2018

www.ingramcontent.com/pod-product-compliance
Lightning Source LLC
Chambersburg PA
CBHW061219240926
51846CB00006B/1282